Tom Parker Bowles is a food writer with a weekly column in the *Mail on Sunday*'s *Live* magazine. He is also a contributing editor to *GQ.* He co-hosts *The Market Kitchen* on UK TV and is a regular contributor on Gordon Ramsay's *The F Word*. He is the author of *E is for Eating: An Alphabet of Greed* and *The Year of Eating Dangerously*.

Also by Tom Parker Bowles

E is for Eating
The Year of Eating Dangerously

TOM PARKER BOWLES

Full English

A JOURNEY THROUGH
THE BRITISH AND THEIR FOOD

EBURY
PRESS

1 3 5 7 9 10 8 6 4 2

Published in 2009 by Ebury Press, an imprint of Ebury Publishing
A Random House Group Company

The Random House Group Limited Reg. No. 954009

Addresses for companies within the Random House Group can be found
at www.randomhouse.co.uk

A CIP catalogue record for this book is available from the British Library

Penguin Random House is committed to a sustainable future for
our business, our readers and our planet. This book is made from
Forest Stewardship Council® certified paper.

Printed and bound in Great Britain by Clays Ltd, St Ives plc

Designed and set by seagulls.net

ISBN 9780091926687

To buy books by your favourite authors and register for offers visit
www.rbooks.co.uk

To Lola

Contents

List of Recipes

THE WEST
Pigeons in Cider with Apples

Brawn

Cheese Toast or English Rabbit

Apple and Rhubard Crumble

THE NORTH
Lancashire Hotpot

Potted Shrimps

Battered Tripe

Winnie's Eccles Cakes

THE MIDLANDS
Charles Campion's Chilli-Pickled Onions

Cyrus Todiwala's 'Country Captain Pie' with
Mutton and Spinach

Real Pork Scratchings

Balti Chicken and Mushroom

THE EAST

Stephen Harris's Angels on Horseback

Lincoln's Inn Cherries

Dressed Crab

Kentish Huffkins

LONDON

Roast Bone Marrow and Parsley Salad

Devilled Bones

Deep-Fried Whitebait

Steak, Kidney and Oyster Pudding

Eel Pie

FULL ENGLISH

Devilled Kidneys

Kedgeree

Fried Plaice with Shrimp Butter

Snipe on Toast

Prologue

The French, they say, live to eat. The English, on the other hand, eat to die.

Martin Amis, *Money* (1984)

In the eighteenth century English inns were so renowned for their good cheer as to have caused contemporary French travellers to lament that in no French province could their equals be found.

P. Morton Shand, *A Book of Food* (1927)

As pies go, this one sat somewhere between glum and downright suicidal. The crust was mean and purse lipped, and despite a good half-hour spent sweating in the oven it stubbornly refused to brown. Little wonder, being constructed from a dreary mélange of potatoes, margarine and baking powder. The filling, though, was more depressing still – a pound each of diced potatoes, carrots, swedes and cauliflower, boiled mercilessly until each soggy lump had oozed into one homogenous mess. Then baked, just to ensure that any last traces of texture were utterly obliterated. A few pinches of salt fought valiantly for life but stood little chance against this relentless vegetative assault. As for the spring onions, they disappeared into the sludge, never to be heard from again.

The name of this wretched concoction was Lord Woolton pie, named after the eponymous Minister of Food when it was introduced in May 1941. Two years into the Second World War, Woolton was a largely popular figure, cajoling the public into munching on meatless rissoles, mock hare soup and all manner of ersatz creations. The pie, although cheap and easy on the ration book, was hardly a high point of British cooking. And it trudged across the palate, watery and morose, little more than a primeval soup of root vegetables. The pastry added nothing, save a coating of cheap fat, slathered across the roof of one's mouth – joyless fodder for difficult times. My friend Bill, with whom I was cooking the damned thing, agreed. He took a bite, wrinkled his nose and set down his fork. 'I'm starting to feel the wartime drudgery already.'

The mock goose was marginally better, but only in the way that death by lethal injection is preferable to the electric chair. A few ounces of split red lentils are cooked to a mush, then seasoned with a touch of lemon juice (a modern embellishment), salt and pepper. A large onion is then 'sautéed' in water (those wartime recipe books were certainly inventive with their euphemisms), mixed with sage and breadcrumbs, stuffed between two cake-shaped portions of the lentils, and baked until dry and turgid. What it has to do with goose, I don't know, although it's certainly a fascinating study in different shades of beige. I suppose that the sage, onion and breadcrumbs are meant to ape a traditional stuffing, but without the pork (which was fiercely rationed), it sort of loses the will to live.

We had meant to move on to 'donkey' (or mealie) pudding, where all sorts of indecent things are done to leeks and oatmeal, and mock fish cakes, where bloater paste took the place of fresh fish. Or even mock clotted cream, a sorry coming together of margarine, sugar, dried milk powder and vanilla essence. Instead we had given up, sunk into an all-too-real gloom cast by these ersatz recipes. The experiment over, we binned the wretched results and wandered off down to the pub, for sausages, beer and salt-beef sandwiches.

The afternoon of cooking had started as a very loose sort of experiment. I was researching an article about rationing in Britain. I could just about remember those posters from school, 'Dig for Victory' and 'Food is a Munition of War', but they were little more than colourful splashes on the classroom wall, something to gaze at while some poor teacher grappled with the intricacies of the Schleswig Holstein Question. My favourite of all was 'Better Pot-Luck with Churchill today than humble pie under Hitler tomorrow. Don't waste food.' Leaving aside the Hun bashing, the advice now seems as pertinent as ever. In these financially challenged times, the papers are filled with eulogies to the cheaper cuts of meat, and parsimony, they say, is back in vogue. We do tend to assume, though, that in the past, every woman up and down the land was blessed with exquisite cooking skills, and a culinary knowledge to match.

It is obvious, even before the Second World War, that this was a little wide of the mark. 'A butcher with a sense of humour, whose shop was in a wealthy district, once said to me,' wrote Florence White in 1923, '"They all want cutlets or chops; an animal ain't made up only of chops, but they can't cook anything else. I wish they'd learn to cook the cheaper cuts." A woman greengrocer in a poor district said to me: "It's pitiful to think young married women – mere girls! – can't cook. They come to me and ask me to tell them. They don't even know how to cook a potato, and we can't sell them some vegetables because they don't know how to cook them."' This was like the scent of truffle to a snuffling pig, spurring me deeper still. Everything I had previously believed of English food, of its pre-war glories and pies for all, was suddenly challenged. My assumptions were shallow, my understanding strictly limited.

We emerged from those bleak war years with an understandable acceptance of the bland and uninspiring, and a reliance on foods of convenience, tinned, frozen or freeze dried. Good food was seen as a luxury and to abandon oneself to the pursuit of gastronomic pleasure was 'not the done thing'. 'Rationing lasted for approximately fifteen years,' writes Philippa Pullar in *Consuming Passions*. 'It had the effect of changing the British diet in a major way. It reduced the overall standard to a uniform level. Everyone, whether rich or poor, whether in town or country, was eating the same food.'

Many Victorians saw a love of food as synonymous with weak morals, natural indolence and suspect, continental ways. Victorian children were 'steeped in original sin', according to

Pullar, and were therefore never indulged or allowed to show pleasure in eating, in case it led to improper passion. Table-cloths, it's said, were there to cover exposed table legs, lest those wooden protuberances excite an ungodly stirring of the loins. Sensual enjoyment was seen as shameful in public (while in private, pornography reached a quivering crescendo of lascivious popularity). The Puritans, in the mid-seventeenth century, were worse still, even going as far as to ban the Christmas feast. There was no such thing as pure gustatory pleasure. To feast meant gluttony and gluttony, dear child, was a deadly sin.

Even my long-held view of English food as good, honest fare, of beautiful ingredients treated with care, was quickly shattered. 'English domestic cooking has never stood in high repute,' write J.C. Drummond and Anne Wilbraham, gloomily, in 1939, 'except perhaps in so far as roast meats are concerned. Its reputation appears to have declined during the nineteenth century, probably because we acquired from the Continent the knowledge how to grow garden vegetables [but] we did not trouble to learn how to cook them properly. It is one of the tragedies of English domestic life.'

All this sprang from just a mouthful of the wretched Woolton pie. Our attitudes to rationing provided an accurate snapshot of our attitude to food, which saw pragmatism mixed with creativity, the noble stirred in with the wretched, the good folded into the bad. The more I read, however, in recipe books and diaries, scrawled letters and formal orders, in the peace of the Imperial War Museum archive, the more I saw rationing as emblematic of the English attitude to food in general.

'Both materially and spiritually the future looks bleak,' huffed Dr J.P. McHutchinson, a staunchly Tory Scottish bachelor, in his diary of November 1945. 'VE day is now six months old, and yet ordinary conditions of living, food, clothing, etc, have improved not one whit … as a nation we have lost our soul … rations are even slightly tighter and every whit as lacking in variety. We are expected to celebrate the first post war Xmas with an extra ¼ pound of sweets!' James Lees-Milne, an assiduous chronicler of all things grand and titled, moaned, in November two years later, that 'everyone I meet complains of distended stomach and attributes it to the starchy food. The food in England is worse than during the war, dry and tasteless, even at Brook's.'

Yet amid the gloom there were moments of celebration too. An article in *The Land Worker*, 'the Journal of the National Union of Agricultural Workers', in 1945, talks of a particularly merry feast.

The Notton Branch, Yorkshire, celebrated its fourth anniversary and the passing of the 100 membership mark with a rabbit pie supper on October 17th. Men of a lesser breed would not have dared the dangers of the journey, but with vision of rabbit pie haunting his eyes as they strained to pierce the fog, Bert clung grimly to the wheel of his car, and in spite of mounting banks and other hair-raising experiences finally arrived at Notton with sharpened appetite. Although both he (Bro. Bert Hazell) and Bro. Robinson soon had what Bert described as a feeling of 'almost indecent repletion,' they managed to deliver bright and breezy speeches appropriate to the occasion. The South Milford Branch, Yorkshire, also had a supper when Bro. Hazell was the special speaker. There were none of the synthetic foods we poor Londoners have to put up with but real ham sandwiches, apple pies, gooseberry tarts, and other delicacies. One brother with a passion for pickled onions caused amusement by eating them with everything. He would take a bite of gooseberry tart, then pop an onion into his mouth and so on. In our native county, pork and apple pie was once eaten together, but gooseberry tart and onion seems a queer mixture. But the member ate the combination with evident relish and is even said to have patted the lower part of his anatomy with great approval.

Did these attitudes have any bearing on how we eat now? For any serious insight into this period, there's no better authority than Marguerite Patten, the food writer and historian. Now ninety-three, she speaks with clarity, wit and insight. 'I was still with the Ministry of Food when the war ended in '45. And in our innocence we thought that rationing would be ending within a year or so. Of course it didn't do anything of the kind. They told us we have to go on until '54. And we were rationed more than ever before. In 1947, the Ministry of Food became very, very unpopular,' admits Patten. 'During the war, we were happy to be given advice, we wanted advice. People came from all over to ask how to do it. We were fighting a war, so therefore we accepted that we should be dictated to and we should have to behave in the right and proper way. But after the government changed, the approach changed. I was always warned, from my very first radio broadcast, "Don't wag fingers, don't lecture people" and *they* began to lecture *us*. And I thought, well, maybe the Ministry think they're going to guide us for forever and a day. And maybe they were right, and we should have taken their advice and we wouldn't have obesity and the problems of today.' She laughs. 'Whilst that might well have happened, equally it might not.'

Would English food have improved if the ministry had stayed in charge? I think not. But rationing was just one part of a series of events that saw English food fall so low. What had started as my small excursion on English rationing had suddenly taken root and grown into a full-scale expedition into English food. A few days spent in the Imperial War Museum, in the air-conditioned somnolence of the British Library and upon the battered leather sofas of the London Library, were no longer sufficient to quell my hunger. I felt more voyeur than partici-pant, as if watching some invisible banquet, unable to join in – Tantalus tempted by ale and steak and kidney pudding. To really find out about the English and their food, I had to gird my belly and sharpen my knife. Most importantly of all, I would have to get out and eat …

Introduction

Englgrish food has never had it easy. On the one hand, it's the world's culinary whipping boy, the sorry butt of a thousand multilingual gags. 'An international joke,' wrote Philippa Pullar, 'as bad as any music-hall mother-in-law.' It's more comic stereotype than national cuisine, a deep-fried snort or a long-stewed giggle, up there with dodgy teeth, swinging vicars and Norman Wisdom. This hackneyed view is as predictable as it is pervasive.

'Every country possesses, it seems, the sort of cuisine it deserves which is to say the sort of cuisine it is appreciative enough to want,' writes Waverley Root in *The Food of France*. 'I used to think that the notoriously bad cooking of England was an example to the contrary, and that the English cook the way they do because, through sheer technical deficiency, they have not been able to master the art of cooking. I have discovered to my stupefaction that the English cook that way because that is the way they like it.'

Ask any foreigner from Paris to Port-au-Prince as to their views on the matter and they'll agree with Root. The

Americans and the French are the worst, earnest and infuriating. British cuisine is a wretched oxymoron, they sneer as one: grey, turgid and lumpen. There's no refinement, passion or beauty, just some barely edible, depression-inducing, overcooked mediocrity in a funereal flour sauce.

As far as the rest of the world is concerned, our contribution to global gastronomy stops at Marmite and the deep-fried Mars Bar. Oh, and jellied eels. Mustn't forget the jellied eels. The situation's so dire that even the lesser culinary nations, the Icelanders or the Dutch, peer down their noses at our food. Now it's one thing taking abuse from the Chinese or French, but quite another from a country best known for a hundred ways with rotted shark. The fact that the vast majority of these naysayers have barely left Omaha or Dieppe means little – the muck has been thrown so long that it not only sticks, but endlessly fertilises the tired old cliché too.

Yet the opposing view is equally galling, a damp-eyed vision of an Albion long gone, where jolly squires clinked flagons of foaming ale with slow-but-honest horny-handed sons of the soil. A grossly romanticised fairy tale where good eating was classless and universal, with hand-raised pork pies for all and as much pickle as you could fit on a shovel. One nation forever united by good beer, beef and bread. The perpetrators of this view argue we've always eaten well and heartily, making solid food for solid people. Certainly, the rich might have feasted on their roasted swan and neat's tongue in pastry, but the average peasant did all right too. Not for him the fripperies and fineries of court, but proper John Bull grub, a steak and kidney pudding to sustain him while he skipped through the medieval mud.

With a pig in the back yard and a vegetable patch for all those turnips, nothing could dampen the British spirit.

This is the view of those who see food as a nationalistic battering ram, the mighty rib of beef ready to smite down any lily-livered French fancies. The fact they bake their nationalism into a Victoria sponge makes it no less distasteful. Show them the most greasy and wretched of roadside breakfasts and they'd claim it preferable by far to the damned foreign muck of Johnny Frog.

In the past twenty years, though, a new attitude has crept in, the furrowed, angry brow replaced by a beaming, all-encompassing smile. These people joyously proclaim that we're living in the midst of a food revolution and that English food is undoubtedly the best in the world, now that we've rediscovered Bath chaps, Essex dunkles, rumbledethumps and flummeries, and that everyone, from the dwellers in sink estates to the lords of stately piles, is sharing in the pleasures of the new English food.

Both arguments are extreme and each is as misguided as the other. There's absolutely no doubt that English food – that is, the national food of the country rather than the food eaten every day – has improved beyond belief in the past two decades. A whole new generation of 'New English' restaurants pepper the land, from pubs using the best of local produce to Michelin-starred icons doing magical things with every part of the swine. Chefs study Eliza Acton and Hannah Glasse and Robert May, searching for information and inspiration in the way we once ate. The critics rave, the pundits applaud and we're proud of our food once more.

Yet this is hardly reflected on the international restaurant scene. How many English restaurants are there in Bejiing? Or Paris and Hong Kong? Aside from a few, crumbling, old-colonial clubs, relics of a past long gone, our international standing is still pitifully low. When foreign publications crown London 'Restaurant Capital of the World', only a precious few natives make the grade. The rest are the usual trans-global mêlée of French, Italian, Chinese and Indian. And although Gordon Ramsay has restaurants across the world, it is mainly the haute cuisine of France from which he draws his experience and techniques. While our drinking culture has spawned pubs across the world, our culinary exports are markedly less successful.

The irony lies in the fact that the best English food is easily appreciated by decent palates the world over. We're a country blessed with sumptuous produce. All food is a product of history, geography and climate, and a temperate, oft-invaded island filled with lakes and marshes, moor and pasture, is always going to be better supplied than the arid depths of the Gobi Desert. No other country has such a highly evolved pudding culture as we do. Roast meats too – we're masters of the art. In terms of raw material, we're every bit the equal of any other country. Thanks to a job that takes me around the world on the whim of my belly, I've eaten with the most exacting of Chinese, French, Italians and Americans, all of whom eulogised on the joys of roast bone marrow at St John Restaurant in Smithfield or the very sweetest native oysters at Green's in St James's. They've taken as much joy from a fresh crab sandwich or home-cooked Sunday lunch as they would from the most delicate of dim sum or most robust of bollito misto.

Good English food is undoubtedly criminally underrated, not least because so few visitors have actually eaten it. Imagine yourself a European tourist, first emerging from the tube stairs into Piccadilly Circus. You spot the welcoming banquettes of an Aberdeen Steak House and wander in, expecting the finest Scottish beef. An hour later, you stagger out, your sorry view of British food only reinforced. It's a similar story in all those pubs that promise 'Genuine English Fayre', but fail to point out that the shepherd's pie was made a month earlier in a Croydon processing plant, using New Zealand lamb and Spanish potatoes, fast frozen then blasted in a microwave for a few minutes. The unlucky eaters return home to the outskirts of Milan, or Rheims, or Nanjing, shaking their heads and sullying the reputation of English food further still. And can you really blame them?

The state of our national health is also worrying – morbid obesity is on the rise, along with Type A diabetes, both intrinsically linked to poor diet. The multinational, processed-food pushers get richer by the day and sales of ready meals are soaring. For all the Jamie and Nigella books we buy, for all the Gordon and Hugh we watch on television, the national waistline continues to expand. Because we're a nation of culinary voyeurs – we watch but don't do. Our appetite for ever growing portions of processed food is so voracious that experts believe the National Health system will soon buckle under the extra weight. And our pockets will be hard hit too, as taxes soar to pay for more beds. In fact, we haven't eaten so badly since before the Second World War.

To be sure, universally affordable food means that everyone can afford to eat, but the long-term costs could be catastrophic. Sometimes, I wonder whether all those books bought, and programmes watched so slavishly, are little more than culinary titillation. While I don't believe we're a nation uninterested in quality, the fact that so few of us now do cook means we're prepared to put up with mediocrity. What use are heritage tomatoes and organic goat's cheeses to people who cannot boil an egg? And can a cash-strapped mother of four, scraping by on dead-end jobs at all hours of the day and night, really justify buying an organic chicken at double the price of a standard one? There is no black and white with English food, just endless shades of grey.

'The trouble has been that having the finest materials in the world,' writes Rupert Croft-Cooke in *English Cooking* (1960), 'we take them too much for granted.' He was speaking to a nation still reeling from the deprivations of rationing, and in an era where anything foreign seemed impossibly exotic, borne in on a thyme-scented, Mediterranean breeze rather than smothered in a cloud of London smog. Who wanted dull old shepherd's pie when there was bouillabaisse and pommes dauphinoise? As an ardent devotee of good English food, I'd be a liar to deny some flutter of culinary patriotism. 'The cookery of a nation is just as much a part of its customs and traditions as are its laws and languages,' wrote my great-grandfather P. Morton Shand in *A Book of Food*. 'There is much to be said for preserving the purity of all four, and also a good deal that can be argued in favour of a properly controlled assimilation from appropriate foreign sources to replace incongruities and repair deficiencies.'

This sensible, pragmatic approach, written over eighty years ago by a man not noted for his delicacy of opinion, is all the more relevant now. A cuisine that stands still and stagnates, that refuses to adapt with the ever-changing times, is no longer a national food, but a relic of the past. There's absolutely no question that English food has evolved, like any other, from the fruits of the primitive hunter-gatherers to the cosmopolitan harvest of the global pick 'n' mix. So why is our national food still so mocked?

The food of centuries ago would certainly have lacked the pesticides, hormones and fertilisers so crucial to today's industrialised farming. England, some claim, existed in a permanent golden age of gastronomic bliss, before the juggernaut of industry came along and ripped us away from our pretty cottages and well-tended plots. Everything was organic and 'natural', God's own food. However, a few days spent in Victorian London would soon put paid to this myth. Sweets were made with clay and coloured with toxic copper, red lead lurked in cheese and sloe leaves were sold as tea. And that's just for starters. With no regulations, food adulteration reached epidemic proportions.

As for the lot of the poor, for most of the last millennium it was wretched: pottage, a dull, stodgy, soup-like stew was the staple, a far cry from the happy, feasting peasants of popular imagination. It's tempting to see the decline of English food as the end result of a long historical chain of events. The Enclosure Acts ripped the peasants from their common land, then industrialisation changed the country from mainly agricultural to primarily urban. If you add wartime rationing, the flight of women from the domestic kitchen, the rise of processed foods and the power of the supermarkets, you can chart what has happened to English food. This, though, is too scientific a method. It offers markers but no real truth.

It's too easy to lay all the blame on the supermarkets, although the case for the prosecution is strong. They suck the life out of small, local shops like vampires with an unquenchable thirst, draining the high street of life in their eternal quest for ever-increasing profits. They favour the cosmetic appearance and transportability of their produce over flavour, as anyone who has suffered the bland iniquity of a Dutch tomato will attest. They seduce us with their homogenised ready meals, those insults to the palate that are loved for their 'convenience' rather than their flavour. And they reduce the world of butchery into sirloin steak and chicken breasts, neatly cut and ready packaged. This is not a dead beast, they purr, this is a shiny product, wiped clean of blood and viscera, so you can sleep easy at night. My mother's blind Jack Russell knows more about the various cuts of beef and lamb than the average man on the meat counter, while my two-year-old daughter is positively well informed on the subject of British piscine life in comparison to the hapless fish-counter assistant.

But there is also the case for the defence. Bulk buying means cheaper food, so everyone can afford to eat fresh fish, meat, fruit and vegetables. It's all very well my deploring the quality of the meat but compared to a hundred years ago, at least everyone today can afford to buy and eat it.

Despite the average trip around the supermarket having all the excitement of a Mormon rave, they are not all bad.

Cheap food may not be the long-term answer, but it's democratic. Everyone now has access to good food, and it's more important that a child learns to cook from scratch rather than fussing about seasonality or local ingredients. Those concerns come later. By studying the past, though, would it be possible to find a clear path to the present? I want to find out the truth about English food, how it evolved and what went wrong.

Full English is as much about enjoyment as it is about disgust, about the past and the future, celebration and despair. Whatever your view on the subject, we're in a better place now than we were forty years ago. But is this really the dawn of a renaissance in English food? Or have we, a country eternally uninterested in the food we eat and produce, left it too late?

1

The West

On first sight, there's little to differentiate Manor Farm from any other dairy operation. The yard is muddy and expansive, the air thick with milk and manure. The farmhouse itself is rambling and lived-in, comfortably scruffy and sitting a few metres back from the main road running through the Somerset village of North Cadbury. In fact, this could have been any old working farm, the sort of well-oiled, faceless and resolutely unglamorous business that goes about its work with the minimum of fuss. Cows are milked, milk is sold and the seasons ebb and flow.

This place, though, is different, and I'd be a liar if I didn't admit a jot of disappointment, a hint of the anticlimax, at its apparent normality. I'd grown up around farms like this, made camps among hay-bales, chased the chickens and fired catapults, impotently, at scurrying rats. So how could this everyday, unassuming sprawl produce the finest cheese in the world?

Others may argue the strengths of an oozing Brie de Meaux, aged manchego, Colston Bassett Stilton or Mrs Kirkham's Lancashire. All are great cheeses but none, for me, reaches the blissful heights of Jamie Montgomery's unpasteurised Cheddar. While George Keen's Cheddar comes close, made just a few miles down the road, Montgomery's is the king of them all.

It is a light, elegant yellow in colour; the unpasteurised milk comes from Montgomery's own Friesian cows. The eighteen-month aged cheese starts off in the mouth tasting buttery, sweet and nutty. A few seconds later, these qualities are tempered by a fine lactic bite – forceful at first, then measured – adding balance and acidity. The flavour rolls across the tongue in stately waves, building to a perfectly pitched crescendo before fading into warm, creamy delight. It lingers, blissfully, for minutes, coating the taste buds with the quintessence of good milk. Even the French, not known for their gushing admiration of English cheese, have been known to pause thoughtfully upon tasting, and proclaim, 'pas mal'. If it were a person, Montgomery's Cheddar would be awarded a knighthood for services to the palate, and become a national living treasure, opening supermarkets and pontificating on Radio 4.

So where were the huge brown signposts to this Cheddar Mecca, proclaiming 'Big Cheese Bliss, just five miles away?' In America, even cheese in a can gets a gift shop flogging cuddly cows plus an overstocked concession stand pushing sugary drinks and ditchwater coffee. Yet in England, the opposite is true. In many cases, one has to seek out the best. There's no bloated marketing budget, no smooth-talking specialist drafted in to build the brand, just an inherent quality of product matched only by the passion of the producer.

I grew up in the West Country, near the once-typical market town of Chippenham. Now, its straightforward, Bath-stoned Wiltshire charm has been blighted by idiotic planning and corporate myopia, its bramble bushes and scattered copses buried under faceless business parks and graceless housing. In a few years' time, the town will be little more than a gloomy suburb of Swindon, its character ripped out along with the fish shops and butchers that once dotted its streets.

Despite a resolutely urban adulthood, I adore the West Country. The village names call out like old friends: Lacock and Berry Hill, Kington St Michael and Box. This is the land of the *Gazette and Herald*, with its tales of school fêtes and stolen chainsaws, harvest festivals and neighbourhood watch. The traditional food of the West found its way deep into my consciousness before I ever knew it. School trips were taken to cider farms and Cheddar dairies, and every time I went to play at my best friend's house we'd drive past Harris's sausage and bacon factory in Calne. Our daily, Mac, had come to us after it closed down and would regale me with stories of searing the bristles off hogs, or the constant, cloying smell of pig, which even the deepest and hottest of baths was unable to remove. So that Western holy trinity of apple, milk and pig was ingrained in my earliest years, long before food became my job. Start with what you know, they say, so it made perfect sense for me to set off for Somerset.

Back at the farm, I push open a small, creaky iron gate and wander up the short path to the door. I knock, softly at first, before hammering again. There's no reply. I look up and notice a pane of glass is missing from a window on the top floor. The whole farm is eerily silent, save for the odd, distant moo. For a moment I panic, thinking I'm in the wrong place. I decide to wander around the back, immediately regretting wearing trainers. Rice-paper slippers would have provided as much protection from the rural muck. Despite my having had an agricultural upbringing, where wellies were almost fused to my feet, the lure of the pavement had long since swamped any lingering inclinations in that direction. Now I tend to panic when too far removed from an easy source of shrimp paste, imported DVD stores and all-night garages.

'Up in London again, are we?' my parents still ask every Friday, incredulous that anyone would want to spend a weekend in the capital.

'Yup,' I reply, as if traipsing around a garden centre and tramping through a gale is a civilised way to spend one's Saturday.

It's a bugger of a day, though, the sky moody and aloof, as if unsure whether to open the floodgates and pour it all out or just sulk and seethe until nightfall. Too self-conscious to actually open the door and shout, I loiter, miserably, debating what to do next. At least I'm expected. When ringing the farm, I hadn't expected to be given Jamie's mobile number, still less that he would pick up the call. It was like calling up Virgin and getting old beardie himself.

Just as I am about to give up all hope, I see a tall figure striding through the yard and immediately know it is him.

Still, I go through the motions. 'Uh, excuse me, I'm looking for Mr Montgomery.'

The man is tall and broad of shoulder, boyishly good-looking with the sort of forearms that could both wrestle an incalcitrant cow and beat off an army of invaders. At the same time. He looks up and proffers a mighty hand. 'Yup, I'm Jamie. Come in.'

'I grew up on the farm, a third-generation cheesemaker,' he says in his warm, slightly tattered office. Piles of *Farmer's Weekly* and various other agricultural periodicals grow from the floor like glossy stalagmites. The effect is one of organised chaos and a life lived mainly outdoors. 'Mother's father bought the place in 1911. He made money in property and moved down here for the hunting. He wasn't actually a farmer but a huge fan of all things to do with engineering and mechanics. That's why he kept the cheesemaking going when everyone else was giving up. Of course, we stopped during the First World War. Everybody did. There were no men and women in the fields and all milk had to be sent towards the war effort.'

This was an uncomfortable time for the production of real Cheddar, when the future looked not so much uncertain as non-existent. Cheddar-making is an old English art, with Somerset its centre and its neighbours – east Devon, Dorset and Wiltshire – traditional secondary producers. The local climate tends towards dampness, creating lush pastures that produce a wonderfully fat-rich milk. Henry II was said to have bought eighty hundredweight of it, and Henry III, in 1253, granted a charter for a weekly market and annual fair that continued right up until the outbreak of the First World War.

Thomas Fuller, in the reign of Queen Elizabeth I, described the cheeses made at Cheddar as 'the biggest and best in England'. They were ruinously expensive, however, and Fuller went on to bemoan that they were 'so few and dear, hardly to be met with, save at some great man's table'.

During the Elizabethan period, Cheddar was mainly made in village dairies, created from a co-operative of local farmers' milk. As these farmers didn't produce sufficient to make a decent supply of their own farmhouse cheese, they pooled their resources. Their cows would graze the common land (soon to be ripped from the grasp of the ordinary man by a swathe of Enclosure Acts) and each man's milk was carefully measured, to ensure he got the correct proportion of profit from the cheese's sale.

The problem was that the resulting Cheddars were vast, up to 120 pounds in weight, often taking five years to properly mature. A mould used to make a cheese for Lord Weymouth at the start of the eighteenth century was said to be large enough to hold a girl of thirteen. Nevertheless, the cheese seduced all who were able to taste it. 'Without all dispute,' wrote Daniel Defoe in *Tour Through the Whole Island of Great Britain*, 'it is the best cheese that England affords, if not the whole world affords.' It is a view still shared by many of Jamie Montgomery's fans, as well as those of Quicke's and Keen's near by, two other fine Cheddar producers. The parish of Cheddar has always attracted huge numbers of visitors, all keen to marvel at the jagged limestone gash that is the Gorge and its labyrinthine network of caves, crammed full of stalagmites and stalactites.

I remember a school trip to the area when I was about eight. The caves were lit in eerie blues and greens, and there was a geological ghost train with its very own witch of Wookey Hole, an allegedly 'blear-eyed hag' who had issues with everyone from young lovers to local farmers and their crops. Apparently, she got a little trigger-happy with her evil eye, and damned be the consequences. It was up to the abbot of Glastonbury, who dispatched his best witch-slaying priest, a sort of proto-Ghostbuster, to sprinkle the old cow with holy water and turn her to stone. A few hundred years later, enter a rather windy young boy who had to be dragged, white knuckled, to see the allegedly petrified old bat. It might just have been a suggestively shaped rock but it certainly did the trick. Not even a swig of local knee-cracker Scrumpy, happily sold to the underage at the gift shop, was enough to soothe my tattered nerves.

The tourists who flocked in would try a slice of Cheddar at the local inn and decide to take some home. Hence this Somerset cheese became 'cheese from Cheddar' and the makers were only too happy to cash in on its nationwide fame. In a typically British way, there were no efforts made to protect the name. 'The honourable name of Cheddar has been given away to the world,' sighs Patrick Rance in *The Great British Cheese Book*, 'and is now equated in its home country with mouse-trap fodder by those who only know it through eating cheese which should never have borne its name.'

If anything sums up England's fraught and ambivalent relationship to good food, it is this. Here we have a tradition of great cheesemaking and hundreds of years of history (Cheddar was a great luxury in the seventeenth and eighteenth centuries, reaching up to three times the price of good Cheshire in London), only to be met, in modern times, with absolute indifference. In 1980, a bunch of locals opposed a new dairy in the village on the grounds that it might smell too much. Who needs local, artisan Cheddar when the supermarket shelves are filled with cheaper, imported blocks of sweating mediocrity? By the start of the 1980s, the market for real, regional Cheddar was in a truly sorry state.

'Many farms had gone out of cheese making during the First World War,' writes Rance, 'and many dairy farmers were only rescued by the advent of the Milk Marketing Board in 1933, which bought all their milk with a reliable monthly cheque, and sold it back to them on the farm at a lower price if they wished to make cheese from it.' During the Second World War, all hard-cheesemaking was centralised, a practice that continued well after the war. In 1939, 333 farms were registered as Cheddar-makers in the South-West, producing a fifth of the 117,000 tonnes produced in England, and all were made in the traditional way. By the start of the 1990s, you could probably count them on one hand. 'Not many people went to the trouble of cheesemaking after the war,' says Montgomery, surrounded by endless certificates declaring his cheese 'Gold Medal Winner' at the British Cheese Awards or 'Best Cheddar Cheese' or 'Best Traditional British Cheese', 'when they realised they could still sell the milk. That's the great tragedy.' Montgomery, like many of the other producers I would meet, is incapable of trite platitudes. To describe the man as passionate about his craft is like saying Casanova had an eye for the ladies. Montgomery possesses not only an encyclopaedic knowledge of the process of Cheddar-making but an ability to communicate this immensely technical craft in an easily digestible form.

'When I came back from college in the 1980s, it was a low point for proper Cheddar-makers. The supermarkets were in the ascendancy and a lot of people really believed that Sainsbury's and Tesco were going to obliterate the independent cheesemakers. It's only thanks to Randolph Hodgson, and the growth of his Neal's Yard Dairy, that I don't have to supply a supermarket. OK, so I do sell a tiny amount to Waitrose, about ten cheeses a month, but strictly on my terms. They get only the amount I give them, never any more. I state there must be no margin shaving. They must sell the cheese at the same price as independent sellers. If I see it on offer anywhere, I'll pull it. And I have the right of veto as to the stores in which it's sold. Of course, all the Waitrose outlets are local. For example, Ann-Marie Dyas, of the Fine Cheese Company in Bath, rang me to say that the Waitrose opposite her were selling my cheese. I don't want to take away business from her independent shop so I rang them and demanded the cheese was removed. To their credit, they were as good as their word and that's why I still continue to work for them.'

To take on the supermarkets, even Waitrose, which is less obviously commercial than most, takes determination and guts. To take on Sainsbury's, though, takes balls of pure granite.

'It was all very satisfying,' he says with a wry smile. 'In 1998, we were in Sainsbury's. They had to pay full price for my cheese and I could have all the wastage and cutting too. If you don't agree to these conditions, I said, I'll delist you.'

In the normal world, it doesn't work this way. Most small farmers and suppliers would snorkel naked through a lake of slurry just for a chance to get their product 'listed' with a supermarket, and will happily submit to all manner of price-cutting and ridiculous requests ('Can you get the apples more round, and the carrots more orange?' – that sort of thing) merely to remain on the list. If Tesco or Sainsbury's demand that, from now on, all work must be done in the nude and accompanied by an endless loop of Cliff's Christian Christmas crackers, most suppliers would accede. With those people who produce for passion, rather than profit, the battle lines are markedly different.

Montgomery is a perfect example, a small, artisan producer who sticks firmly to his principles. He admits that 'the cheese will never taste the same in supermarkets, thanks to their system of packaging', but he refuses to be bullied. 'They [Sainsbury's] weren't sticking to their side of the deal,' he says. Hence his threat to get out.

Sainsbury's retaliated fast, and hit below the belt. 'So the bastards came back and said, if you delist us, we'll delist everyone in your group. Now this included Clapp, Barbers, Longman, Tower Coombe Farm and another dozen cheesemakers. Thankfully, the press got hold of the story and took our side. And Sainsbury's backed down. I'm not sure they would have carried out their threat but I wasn't prepared to take that risk. It was very satisfying, though.' He smiles again at the memory. 'A couple of years back, Jamie Oliver wanted to come down with the Sainsbury's buying team. The idea was that if they arrived with Jamie, they would get into places they otherwise wouldn't. I said they were very welcome but nothing would make me supply Sainsbury's again.'

A few minutes later, clad in white wellies, hairnets and doctor's coats, we leave the office to get deep into the cheese-making process. 'Cheese was originally a way of using excess milk, and to be able to sell it throughout the year. Cheddar was historically made in the summer,' explains Jamie as we climb into our sterile attire. 'There was not enough good forage to get milk in the winter, just hay. You couldn't milk a cow on it. Stone barns kept the cheese relatively cool but hot summers back then were a bugger. This area around here has always produced milk and so there was a need for a cheese that could handle a decent quantity of it. With Cheddar, you can make big cheeses.'

We enter the first room, dominated by a long, rectangular steel bath at the top, where the milk is fed in directly, by pipe, from the dairy. He explains that he only ever pumps the milk in once, as it tends to smash the fat particles in the milk. This, it appears, is a bad thing. The milk is then warmed up with steam, to about 35 degrees Centigrade, and the starter added, made by A.J. Barber. 'It's very traditional,' he says, casting an experienced eye over the tanks, 'and taken from the best cheese.'

The juggling of acidity levels is an art and crucial to the cheesemaking. It has to be constantly monitored and, once the starter has been added, it takes around forty-five minutes for the correct levels to be reached. Then animal rennet is added to start setting the cheese and once the mixture has reached 'clean break' stage, the mechanical blades are lowered into the tank, stirring then cutting it all up. The smell in the room mixes the medicinal with one of milk that is slightly off, at times both fresh and nostril-twitchingly acidic.

'We need to cut the curd into chunks, without bashing it about too much. At the same time, the curd is scalded, up to 40 degrees.' Although I struggle to keep up with the science, the start of the process makes sense when explained by Jamie. He makes Cheddar-making sound as simple as boiling an egg but the devil is in the detail. Everything, from the time of year to the age of the actual cheesemaking room, is critical in moulding the cheese's eventual character.

I had heard tales of cheesemakers changing location and the quality dropping as a result. Was there something about a particular cheesemaking room, one that had been used for years, that improved the end product? Jamie nods his head emphatically. 'It's incredibly hard to start all over again. When I put in a new vat, I was worried. But the action is now smoother with the new mixer and the cheese more consistent. But a room, over the years, adds as much to the character as the milk.' This isn't some mystical tosh, rather straightforward science. All kinds of yeasts permeate the cheesemaking room and affect the nature of the cheese.

Once the curds become recognisably rubbery, like wobbling blocks of off-white crème caramel, the liquid is drained away and the curds taken next door to the Cheddaring room. Here, two men in overalls and bare arms manhandle great slabs of curd, pale and elastic, cutting it into blocks, piling and re-piling it, texturing the curd and releasing more moisture as the acidity continues to rise. It's hard physical work and they wear as little as possible while sticking to the rules of hygiene. In midsummer, the heat must be near unbearable. They constantly check the all-important level of acidity too and these readings are based on years of knowledge and experience, a world away from the computer-controlled trickery of the big producers. Once the acidity is perfect, handfuls of salt are thrown in to stop it increasing further.

'Very subtle changes happen at this point,' says Jamie, fingering the curd. 'To start, we just have crumbs but as it's stacked, it starts to look like a torn chicken breast.' Then into the shredder. 'Most Cheddars are put through a machine with sharp, rapidly rotating blades. The process is fast but produces standardised, glossy, cheese chips. Our machine,' says Jamie with obvious pride, 'the same one my grandfather employed, uses a shredder.' The chips are less standardised, giving the cheese its own idiosyncracies. 'I'm particularly proud of the metal addition I designed, a feeder, to speed up the process.' He casts a fond gaze over the machine. It's this obsession with the fine details, this stubborn adherence to old-fashioned, time-consuming production methods, that makes Montgomery's Cheddar such a unique product. 'My job is not to fuck it up,' he says to no one in particular. 'I'm looking after this cheesemaking, just as my grandfather did, to carry it on to the next generation.'

The salted, Cheddared curd is packed into cylindrical moulds and left to sit overnight. We move out of the Cheddaring room and into a small anteroom with a steel basin filled with hot water. The moulded truckle is dropped into the water for thirty seconds, heating the surface to create the beginnings of a rind. At long last, it's starting to resemble the Cheddar of my dreams. Pressed for one further night, the cheese is then bound with cloth and slathered with molten lard, which also helps create the rind, as well as letting the cheese breathe.

Just across the yard is the first cheese store. It's cool and serene, the air thick with lactic expectation. 'The store's Grandpa's and has a wonderful system that turns the cheeses, every couple of days at first, then every month. We try to keep the humidity at 90 per cent and the temperature at 10.5 degrees Centigrade.' The first store is supposed to mellow and settle the cheese, before it goes to the main maturing shed, a huge, warehouse-like barn filled with five-storey-high truckles of Cheddar, from the very young, pale and fragile to those over twenty months old, with full rind in place, dark and distinguished. The cooling fans shatter the silence but, again, the area has the feeling of an old church, damp and serene, a place well suited to worship. The mature Cheddars get twelve months here, the extra-mature eighteen.

'You want the cheese to catch the mould, and the mould to grow by eating the lard. The rind isn't that strong to start with but as it dries out, it gets more and more firm. The mould is absolutely critical in creating the rind. Now, have a look at this,' he says, beckoning me over to a microscope. I gaze down to see fat, maggot-like creatures with spindly little legs, milling frantically about. 'These are cheese mites, complete bastards. They make a hole in the rind and if they get in you're knackered. It takes three guys three months to clean them from half the store, so it's bloody hard work too. We're no longer allowed to use gas to kill the buggers, but I am considering a robot that brushes and hoovers automatically. Bloody expensive, though.'

With that, we've reached the end of the Cheddar process, at once so simple (milk to curds, cut curds, add salt, mature) and so utterly complex. In terms of taste and texture, it's as far removed from the dull, block stuff as Nabokov is from a Mills and Boon hack. There's a beautiful depth and complexity, yet the taste of the sweet milk is never drowned out.

'Cheddar was a cheese considered good enough for all the colonies to want to make,' Jamie says as we wander back towards the car. 'Canada, New Zealand, Australia, it's made everywhere. But the more muck out there that calls itself Cheddar, the better it is for those of us who make the real thing. We started a Slow Food Praesidium, the first, for Artisan Somerset Cheddar. I do it alongside Keen's and Westcombe's, in association with Neal's Yard Dairy.'

To qualify, the cheese must be made in Somerset, with milk from farmers' own herds, to ensure quality. The milk must be used raw, as this allows the true flavour of the milk to shine through, something that is erased by pasteurisation. Pint starters, directly evolved from cheesemaking farms all over the country, are mandatory, each with its own unique character. The rennet must be animal, the Cheddaring must take place by hand, the truckles must be cloth bound and the cheese matured for a minimum of eleven months. Only by sticking to these stringent standards can the future of real Cheddar be guaranteed.

'Our biggest growth in the last three years has been in Europe. This is good, making us feel that Slow Food makes sense. The process is constant, seven days a week, but it's worth it. It was sometime around 2000 that the name, Montgomery's, was first used without qualification or explanation. People were expected to know what Montgomery's was and, if not, to find out. It was hugely satisfying to see that.' With that, he wanders off towards the main house, the Cheddar crusader behind the world's finest cheese.

However, before this descends into a one-sided paean to the culinary beauties of the West in particular, and English food in general, a measure of balance is necessary. There is no doubting Jamie's passion and experience, and the beauty of his end product. Nevertheless, it would be all too easy to waft around the country on a fluffy cloud of pear drops and optimism, declaring England to be in the midst of a food revolution, claiming that English food, once so drab and reviled, has been revitalised, shot through with lightning like Dr Frankenstein's monster. In fact, like the fictional creature, modern English food is made up of many ill-fitting and opposing parts. All that extra time, effort and devotion costs more money. I'm convinced that, given the choice, in a blind tasting between Montgomery's or Keen's or Westcombe's and your classic, shiny lump of dull block muck, the former cheeses would be triumphant. All the latter have to offer is that they are cheap.

In most European countries, the food culture is sufficiently strong and ingrained into society for consumers to understand that good food costs more, because it takes more input, time and manpower to produce. Artisanal, old-fashioned methods are on the whole, extremely hard work … compared to the heavily mechanised forces of mass production. With industrialisation came progress, as the mechanised superseded the manual. In terms of manufacturing engines and the tools of empire – bricks, planks and tanks – this was superb progress. I certainly don't share those loony, 'back to agrarian' beliefs that everything was better when done by hand, and artisanal food production simply couldn't sustain the UK's population, let alone that of the whole planet. The upside of artisanal food, though, is that you eat or drink a beautifully idiosyncratic product, be it ham, cider or cheese, that is of its area, its *terroir*, shaped by the particular soil, climate, even water. These sort of products tend to taste magnificent.

The English, in contrast to their continental counterparts, are still a nation in thrall to value. Not value in the sense that a tenner for a wedge of Montgomery's Cheddar is a serious bargain, when you calculate the pleasure it gives, and the work and passion that has gone into its creation. No, English value, when buying food, is more about the deal, conditioned as we are by the massive buying power of the supermarkets.

How many times have you fallen into the supermarket trap, picking up three lettuces instead of one, simply because you are offered three for the price of two? You need only one lettuce, for that night, yet the idea of getting something for free is difficult to resist. The supermarkets exploit this, which leads to a third of the food we buy in the United Kingdom being thrown away. While I'm as guilty as the next man of over-shopping, that figure is nothing short of disgusting.

There is such endless guff about England becoming a nation of food lovers – and this is a country where arguments rage in the street as to the merits of chips fried in dripping over those fried in oil, where perfectly respectable ladies come to blows over their differing recipes for Lancashire hotpot, or there are running battles fought over the superiority of the Colchester native oyster over, say, the Helmore. Despite all this, the majority of our population still eat a diet that is only marginally more nutritious than that of our ancestors many centuries earlier.

That's not to say that we were always a nation of kitchen retards, cack-handed, iron-palated dullards who didn't know a spoon from a spatula, who judged happiness on price, not flavour. Our taverns, hostelries and inns were generally admired and although the French were usually seen as born gourmands, not everyone agreed that Gallic was God. Frank Harris, the priapic gourmand and author of *My Life and Loves*, published in 1922, had little time for French niceties.

The French have the democratic idea of cooking and are continually tempted to obliterate all distinctions with a democratic sauce. They will serve you potatoes in twenty ways, all of them appetising, but none of them giving the true potato flavour: in fact you don't know half the time what you're eating in France; it's the sauce you taste! Fancy serving a partridge aux choux! The whole exquisite flavour of the bird lost, swamped, drowned in the pungent taste and odour of the accursed cabbage! Compare this bourgeois mess with the flavour you get of an English partridge roasted before a fire by a cook who knows the value of the jewel he is asked to set.

This is the essence of good English food, albeit a somewhat romantic, moneyed view. During the interwar period only the rich could afford to eat such luxuries. 'I often said that the English ideal of cooking was the best in the world: it was the aristocratic ideal, the wish to give every single thing its own peculiar flavour … Beef should be roasted before the fire and served lightly cooked. Everyone of any position in my time in London knew that grouse lightly roasted and eaten cold with a glass or two of brut champagne made a lunch for the gods.' Sadly, such expertise had become all too rare and even Harris admits that 'there are so few cooks in England and nearly all who merit the name are French.'

Yet the public cookshop of earlier centuries was an urban institution, especially in London, a place frequented by both rich and poor alike. Monsieur Misson, a splendidly merry Frenchman who travelled to England at the end of the seventeenth century, delighted in what he found. 'Generally, four spits, one over another, carry round each five or six Pieces of Butcher's Meat, Beef, Mutton, Veal, Pork and Lamb; you have what quantity you please cut off, fat, lean, much, or little done; with this, a little salt and Mustard upon the side of your plate, a Bottle of Beer and a Roll; and there is your whole feast.' He was an early advocate as to the quality of our beef, too. 'The English Beef is reported [to] excel that of all other Countries in the World,' he notes, before going on to eulogise on the English as a nation. 'The English eat well,' he declares, with a metaphorical rub of his belly and a smack of his lips.

Never again would a Frenchman write so well of English food. There is, of course, plenty of evidence to the contrary. 'Roast beef and mutton are all they have which is good,' wrote Christian Heinrich Heine, the German Romantic poet and journalist, in the nineteenth century. 'Heaven keep every Christian from their gravies ... And Heaven guard everyone from their naïve vegetables which, boiled away in water, are brought to the table just as God made them.'

Joaquim Pedro de Oliveira-Martins, a nineteenth-century Portuguese politician, was less than impressed by the food at the newly opened Simpson's-in-the-Strand. 'Certainly the climate requires hot and strong nourishment. These are traditional, as I went to see them in the classic tavern of Simpson, the real one, in the Strand. They gave me a slice of meat swimming in fat, a piece fit for Pantagruel, cut out on the spot from a sanguinary heap carried about among the tables.'

Even 200 years back, the debate as to the inherent quality of English food still raged. Just as in any other country or culture, you could eat magnificently – and very badly. In a strong food culture, the former becomes more likely than the latter.

The next leg of my journey is only a few miles from Jamie Montgomery and his blessed Cheddar, this time to visit someone dedicated to the art of real cider. As I drive deep into Somerset, the roads become increasingly narrow and winding, while the sky above threatens still more rain. The low light makes the hedges and fields almost neon in their luminescence, lending the landscape a surreal, other-worldly feel. So entranced am I by this brooding glow that I shoot past the entrance to Pass Vale Farm, home of Julian Temperley's Burrow Hill cider.

The yard is more chaotic than Jamie's, with dogs and farmworkers threading purposefully between ancient tractors, building works and apple crates. It's a cider farm as imagined by J.R.R. Tolkien and H.E. Bates – buildings jostle and crowd each other, some romantically run-down, others resolutely modern, clad in green corrugated iron. Such is the rambling nature of the place that, initially, you're amazed anything manages to get produced at all. The view is stunning, acre upon acre of apple trees stretching into the distance. Even in the bleakest of midwinter weather, with the trees gaunt and bare, the place oozes charm.

I'd met Temperley before, when he came on a television show I co-present to talk about cider and cider brandy. Broad-shouldered, good-looking and with a thick shock of light-grey hair, he's a mixture of rogue and master craftsman. Ted Hughes meets Puck. His pale-blue eyes glitter constantly, as if on the cusp of some barely contained mischief.

His Shipwreck cider brandy is as good an introduction to the man as anything, highlighting his mix of businessman and buccaneer. When the *Napoli* was shipwrecked off Branscombe in Devon in January 2007, the small town was flooded with looters, all determined to grab whatever was going. Temperley went down and found some empty Allier oak barrels lying on the beach, destined for a vineyard in South Africa. He logged his claim with the Receiver of Wrecks ('strictly legal, not like the bugger who nabbed the motorbike') and took them back to Somerset, where he uses them to finish his Shipwreck single-cask cider brandy. The reason the barrels were in such good nick? 'Protected from the elements by a large shipment of bibles written in Zulu.' He roars with laughter. The story is classic Temperley, a man who cloaks a profound knowledge of his craft behind a jovial, slightly scruffy exterior.

'You'll have to forgive Julian,' explains Di, his beautiful wife, 'but he's had a bad case of flu for a few days.'

'Nonsense, nonsense, I'm absolutely fine,' he says with a sniff, wandering into the kitchen. His blue eyes seem a little cloudy and his voice slightly hoarse, but one mention of cider and he's off.

'This farm has been making cider for about 150 years, and it's gradually taken over everything. I arrived in the early 1970s and there was a large wooden press and some cider sitting in the barn when I arrived.' He pauses to sip some of Di's home-made soup. 'We started with nine acres of orchard and now have 150, producing over 100 tonnes of apples. We never use apple concentrate like the big boys, although if I did I could produce cider all year.'

I take a mouthful of his Burrow Hill medium-dry cider, a wonderfully balanced drink with good acidity and a fantastic finish.

'When I started, the business was very agricultural; people would go to work with a gallon of cider. Now, the whole market is so much wider.' But like Jamie Montgomery, Temperley is interested only in quality. Actually, when he does buy in extra fruit, Jamie supplies Julian with apples from his farm. Both share the same *terroir* of south Somerset and both produce world-class products, as much a product of the geography and climate of Somerset as Chateau Lafite is of its part of Bordeaux. Neither man is in the game for a quick buck, rather for the love of the game itself.

'The cider market has evolved so much. Historically, cider consumption goes up when we have a war.' He pauses to chew a piece of eel, smoked a few miles down the road at Brown and Forrest. 'Especially with the French. We used to get very patriotic, and all the boats carrying wine were sunk on the way to the UK anyway.'

Cider has long been linked with patriotism, 'a symbol', in the words of James Crowden in *Ciderland*, 'of Englishness and independence from Europe and Catholic France'. A matter of national pride, then. Over the past twenty years, cider's stock has sunk pitifully low, as it transformed from a farmhouse artefact, traditionally made with pressed apples from the owner's orchard, into an industrialised, standardised product, made from a concentrate containing a mere 30 per cent juice. 'Heav'n's sweetest blessing' had fallen on hard times. I remember swigging sickly-sweet, lukewarm supermarket cider from a three-litre bottle at school, hidden away on the banks of the Thames. The initial delirium slowly and inevitably mutated into a dry mouth, barely coherent mumbles, a spinning head and the final ignominy of splattering the towpath with the contents of my gut.

Historically, in the West at least, cider was every bit the equal of beer. 'The planting of large-scale orchards in the seventeenth century following the bloody Civil War laid the foundations of the cider world we see today,' continues Crowden.

That this was happening predominantly in the west of England is no surprise, because the monasteries there had once held cider in great esteem and built great tithe barns that housed large cider presses and ranks of wooden barrels. The new land-owning families, who had taken their place at the helm of rural England, saw it as their duty to provide their own Garden of Eden, a spiritual paradise on their doorstep, which provided not only cider but rural employment and helped the economy in times of crisis. So marked was the improvement that the whole of the West Country, from Cornwall to Herefordshire via Devon, Dorset, Somerset and Gloucestershire was simply referred to as 'Ciderland.'

So cider was not only a drink but a source of employment and social edification.

Temperley, for his part, is rather embarrassed by his prominence in Crowden's book. 'Not sure why I got so much space,' he shrugs. 'Certainly don't deserve it. Anyway,' he says, pulling on his coat as we face the gloom outside, 'we have about 20,000 trees with forty different varieties. The real art of cider-making is blending different varieties of apple. That's the key.' I ask what he thinks of the new trend, moving towards single-apple ciders, like the Kingston Black from Sheppy's, near Taunton. 'I think the single variety has had its day, although Sheppy's does do it exceptionally well. But they're an exception. The idea of the single-variety cider is essentially a heresy. The blending of different apples is the whole reason for what I do. We need our forty varieties. The job of the cider-maker is to make a drink that is drinkable.'

When Julian started making his cider, the usual choice was between farm scrumpy, often rough and ready, packing a mighty alcoholic punch, and the refined, bottled and draught ciders from the likes of Bulmers and Coates. As concentrated apple juice, rather than fresh, became the mainstay of commercial production, the gap widened between the home-brewed, knee-cracking stuff and the sweeter, fizzier and more commercial brands. Temperley sits firmly in the middle, producing high-quality farmhouse cider.

Since the end of the Second World War, many local farmers gave up cider-making and sold their apples to big companies. Just twenty years back, a farmer could guarantee to be paid about £120 per tonne and take on long-term contracts, up to thirty years, with their orchards. Now, the price of apples sits around £90 per tonne and the markets have been ruined by a flood of cheaper foreign fruits. However, the success of Magners, thanks to a brilliant advertising campaign, has seen cider become cool once more. And despite the Magners being very much a mass-produced, sweet cider, with little interest to the aficionado, the knock-on effect means that the likes of Temperley benefit too. The Temperley cider bus has long been a Glastonbury favourite, manned by his daughters (one of whom, Alice, is a world-renowned fashion designer) as well as various supermodels on their day off. The success of ersatz cider, though, has sparked a resurgence of interest in 'the real thing'.

Of course, the choice of apple is key. Temperley likes the local 'Jersey' apples, not from the channel island but from 'jaisy', meaning bittersweet, cider apples. The apples grown are specially suited to their *terroir*, their soil, climate and conditions. Kingsbury Episcopi is actually one of three vintage areas of Somerset ciderland. The names of the apples are as evocative as they are beguiling – Yarlington Mill, large and conical with sweet, slightly astringent flesh; Dabinett, with green, red and yellow flesh, the biggest and most important apple in Temperley's view; Harry Masters Jersey, late mid-season and bittersweet, Coat Jersey and Chisel Jersey too, all three from south Somerset; Stoke Red and Brown Snout, both bittersweet. He tells me about a local farmer, Frank Yandle, for whom he pressed cider. 'Frank just wanted to see every colour of the rainbow going up the elevator to be pressed, lots of variety. And you know what, he was right. He understood the art of cider-making.'

The actual business of harvesting and pressing is hard work. Julian never presses too early, believing that the fruit of November and early December are the best, but the picking is labour intensive and, when in full swing, the presses have been known to run from six in the morning until ten at night. He now uses an automatic belt press, rather than the slightly more romantic hydraulic press, which still sits in the barn. The apples are cleaned, then ground in a traditional hopper and pressed. Once the juice has been released, it's fermented in vats, the real skill of the process, where yeast is added.

'There are so many variables that it can be argued that there is no one right way of fermenting a vat of cider apple juice,' explains Crowden. 'It is, after all, a natural process and fermentation is at the mercy of natural phenomena.' This is what gives the Burrow Hill cider, and other proper farmhouse ciders such as Sheppy's or Thatcher's, such depth and complexity. 'In the large companies they just press the relevant buttons and the computer does the rest.'

Like Montgomery, Temperley is also a member of Slow Food, which he views as far more relevant to what he does than some spurious 'organic' certification. He feels, as I do, that although organic farming is admirable at heart – a fundamentally sustainable system of agriculture – it's been hijacked by transnational businesses that ship food across the globe, whether organic or not, at huge environmental cost. He, like many other farmers I meet, is pragmatic. 'We use the minimum sprays possible and no artificial nitrogen. And we use traditional methods of fermenting juice in autumn.' Why in any case should he have to jump through bureaucratic hoops to become organic? The quality of his cider speaks louder than any label.

But there's one more, apple-based string to Temperley's bow. He also uses his apples to make Somerset cider brandy, one of the great digestives of the world. Many a night has been wasted with my friend Mark Hix, extolling the virtues of Alchemy, Temperley's fifteen-year-old aged cider brandy. It's stunning stuff, smooth and mellow, yet possessed of a depth and seriousness that puts it up there with the very finest Calvados and brandies.

'This is Josephine and this is Fifi,' he says, introducing me to two Heath-Robinson-esque, French-copper, gas-fired Calvados stills. The former is rather austere and proper, a reliable workhorse, the latter a touch more coquettish. He smiles. 'I brought the ladies back from France on the back of my Land Rover.' These continuous stills can, when fired up, go for hours transforming cider into 70 per cent brandy. The end result is a clear spirit but the real magic takes place when it's put into barrels, mainly Limousin with some Pedro Ximenez sherry as an experiment, and using the shipwrecked barrels too. The bond, 'where it all happens', is a huge, modern warehouse, smelling of musty apples and oak. Again, it had that stillness, the sense of gentle transformation that I felt at the Montgomerys' cheese store. The atmosphere is benign, a place for spirit and timber to meet, in which the former transforms entirely, in colour and in taste.

'Cider brandy is the crown jewel of the cider industry,' exclaims Temperley. 'You put in a plain spirit and, a few years later, out comes a richly coloured drink. Amazing.' He shakes his head in admiration. 'There is rather a lot of evaporation as the spirit ages, and we probably lose about £500–£800 a day through the wall. But we call it the angel's share.' The temperature is constant, with the barrels kept well away from direct sunlight. 'We're somewhere, I suppose, between an Armagnac and a Calvados,' he says, 'but we're different from Calvados. We've avoided, at all cost, any rivalry with the French. I love them dearly, have huge respect for their Calvados, always will. But we are Somerset cider brandy. This is not like some English champagne, or English Calvados. It's a proper Somerset product.'

When we get back to the house, he pulls out *The Here-fordshire Pomona*, a great and learned tome of 1885. 'See, look,' he jabs excitedly at a paragraph, 'orchard brandy was being made there all those years back.' He goes on to explain that 'cider brandy' was first mentioned in John Worlidge's *Treatise on Cider* in 1676. It was the Moors who brought distilling to Europe, along with a taste for dried fruits, sweet and sour flavours and all manner of nuts. 'But there's been cider brandy for as long as there have been apples.'

The three-year aged has quite a kick and a real tang of fresh apples, while the five-year-old has more pronounced oak, and the edges are a little smoother. As to the fifteen, it's liquid bliss, beautifully balanced and elegant, the ultimate expression of the apple's appeal. Temperley, like Montgomery, is not a pioneer, rather a keeper of the flame, a protector of a specific tradition in a particular part of England. Neither the cheese nor the cider would be the same if made, say, in Bury, or Birmingham. They're products of the West, more specifically south Somerset. And that night I was off to wassail, a tradition as ancient as the apple itself.

At first sight, a wassail is a trifle unnerving. Hundreds of folk mill around a great bonfire, until a troupe of black-faced Morris dancers weave through the crowd, dancing with a fair young maiden held aloft on their shoulders. At times, one feels like an unwitting extra in *The Wicker Man* and at any moment expect to see Edward Woodward dragged, screaming, 'Dear God, no,' towards his flaming doom. The reality, though, is rather more palatable. Wassailing is an ancient fertility rite, held either on Twelfth Night or the Pagan New Year, which falls on 17 January.

My wassail took place at Stewley Orchard, home to Gaymer's Orchard Reserve. Although they're responsible for the distinctly average, mass-market Blackthorn and the faux-glam Babycham perry, the Orchard Reserve, made entirely from the orchard's apples, is a fine cider, full bodied with lots of fruit and a decent tannin kick. Wassail, which is Old English for 'be well' or 'good health', was supposed to frighten away any bad cider spirits and appease, with various offerings, the cider god. In this age, where chemicals and technology have taken the place of good old-fashioned polytheism, the ceremony might seem a little anachronistic. Yet it made perfect sense in days when the entire fate of a community rested upon the success of its harvest. The atmosphere tonight is as much piss-up as ancient rite and, despite the biting night air, the cider is salve against the winter's chill. 'Cider is very much part of wassailing,' explains Julian, who arrived a few minutes earlier, 'but it's about fertility for everything, the wife, pigs and apples.' He winks and empties his glass in one.

The Morris men jingle and skip in first, their faces blackened and clothes bedecked with gaudy rags. However, this isn't some rural branch of the black-and-white minstrels, and the black face has nothing whatsoever to do with race. Traditionally, when the Morris dancers wanted to earn an extra bit of cash in the winter, they'd conceal their identities behind a thick coat of black paint. All the same, I've never been entirely comfortable with Morris dancers. Certainly, they represent a link to the past that should never be forgotten or ignored. Folk music is every bit as important as local food in creating the identity of a region. Given the choice, though, of watching them smack sticks, whoop and skip, I'd rather listen to Razorlight. Or Keane. Even Enya. It's that bad, I'm afraid.

Anyway, in they come, the Wassail Queen aloft on their shoulders. Cider is poured on the apple tree's roots as an offering and then the chanting starts. 'Old apple tree, we wassail thee,' we sing, 'And hoping thou will bear, / For the Lord doth know where we shall be, / 'Till apples come another year.' The song finishes, and a piece of toast soaked in cider, an offering, is placed in the boughs. The singing is meant to wake the trees from their winter slumber. Then all hell breaks loose. Three hundred sticks pummel the earth, each one accompanied by a frenzied bawling; pans bash pans, voice-boxes crackle and roar, and any spirit not scared off by the thought of 300 half-cut cider lovers must be either desperately dumb or three sheets to the wind themselves.

As a final precaution, a volley of shotguns is fired into the tree. The effect is both surreal and strangely moving, although my rapidly swelling emotions have as much to do with the four pints of cider poured down my neck as any romantic affection for times long past. And as much as I would like to relate tales of apple bobbing and cider lore, local brews and spit-roast pig, my memory is decidedly hazy. I remember talking to Julian and Di, and him telling me the difference between Devon and Somerset cider. 'The former is simple and sweet, rather like Devon folk. Somerset is slightly more dry.' Various indecipherable squiggles filled my notepad and I could just about make out 'Charles Baughan ... big tache … fucking fine sausages.' And 'spelt … the new wheat? Might get a mention in *Private Eye*.' And 'bedtime soon, one mooore drink'. And, strangest of all, 'Marcus Trescothick, big fella. Not very talkative. Strong accent.' Little wonder he didn't want to speak to a swaying outsider with a skinful of cider, especially as I vaguely recall peppering him with questions as to his abrupt departure from the England cricket side. The hangover, as I drove back up to London the next day, was suitably fierce.

Wassailing is not just a link to the past, but a bringer together of communities. One can talk as long as one likes about rustic charm but really, the serious side apart, wassailing is a celebration of the seasons, of the New Year and the chance, of course, to get hog-whimperingly pissed.

Talking of hogs, the pig has always been at the heart of the West Country. On first impressions, there's little to thrill about Swindon. It's the birthplace of Diana Dors (born Diana Fluck), which is of only mild interest, and of Melinda Messenger, which is of none at all. The town is also notable for its roundabouts, states one local guide, which just about sums up the place. A prolific but determinedly B-list star, a perky ex-glamour model and lots of roundabouts. Oh, and the Oasis Leisure Centre (there are endless leisure centres in Swindon) that supposedly provided inspiration for a band formed by two brothers, Noel and Liam Gallagher. Whether or not that's an urban myth spun by the County Council, I don't know. It certainly had some fairly mean waterslides. The Shaw Ridge Leisure Centre was also a place where I spent an inordinate amount of time, either blasting zombies in the arcade or avoiding their local descendants in the car park.

Despite all this, I hold Swindon dear, mainly for all those leisure centres and shops. It was the best that urban Wiltshire could do. Bath was too pretty, Bristol too far, although many millions would disagree. For most people, Swindon is little more than two junctions on the M4, the Slough of the West (it's not coincidental that the other branch in *The Office* was situated in Swindon), an ever-expanding, amorphous, concrete mass that seems, these days, to start near Hungerford and infect the land as far as Chippenham.

Swindon, however, was once known as Swine Down, home to a bunch of continental immigrants called the Beakers. They were some of the first settlers in the country, around 1800 BC, and the glorious pig was central to their lives. A pagan people, whom many think responsible for Silbury Hill, the Avebury stone circle, even Stonehenge, they depended on this animal for everyday sustenance, and the pig has been central to the region ever since. The English, rich and poor alike, have long adored bacon or salt pork. The rich could feast upon it all year round, while for the poor, it added much needed excitement to their dull, daily diet of pottage, a thick soup made from oats and anything else that might be lying about. The sheep, in later years, became the more important beast in terms of trade. With the wolf extinct, the sheep had no natural predator and thrived. In the Middle Ages the majority of England's riches were gleaned from wool. In the eighteenth century, Wiltshire was seen as the land of wool, cheese and bacon, but as the wool trade declined, pork, or more accurately, cured pork, flourished. Even today, there are Wiltshire hams and cures of bacon.

'Wiltshire's association with commercial bacon,' writes David Mabey in *In Search of Food*, 'is largely a commercial accident.' Geography is the key; the country lies between the kingdom's great port and its capital. In the eighteenth century, before the coming of the Great Western Railway, pigs were imported from Ireland and were driven along the main road that hews its way from west to east. Calne became a natural stopping point, about halfway between Bristol and London. The men would down a few pints, while the pigs were fed and watered. Sarah Harris, owner of a shop in Butcher's Row, would buy pigs as they arrived in the town and transform them into bacon, pies, fresh meat and sausages. By 1808, Sarah's son John had opened a second shop. And when his son, George, travelled to America in 1847, he was deeply impressed by the bacon technology there. Thanks to the use of icehouses to keep the meat cool, it was possible to cure all year long. A few miles down the road in Trowbridge, the Bowyer family were setting up a similar factory. By 1856, the Harris family had created their own icehouse (the ice came from the Calne canal and ponds, and was stored in thatched sheds) and business flourished. It continued to do so right up until 1983, when the factory was closed. I remember driving past (or rather, being driven past) the derelict building, vast and imposing. For many years after its closure, it sat there, lonely and unloved. Then, a few years back, it was demolished. Very recently a whole new complex appeared, with shops, housing and a library taking its place. As ever, the new buildings are a garish mess, totally out of sympathy with the surrounding area. At least there are books. The closure of the Harris's factory, though, caused an economic slump in the town, as it employed up to 20 per cent of the population. The only visible reminder now of this great bacon-making past is a charming bronze statue of a pig in the middle of a small shopping arcade. Sadly, it's become the headquarters of the local disaffected youth, who use this memorial to a once-thriving town as target practice for their spit and cigarette butts.

Roger Keen knows the area around Calne as well as anyone. He grew up on Sandridge Farm, before marrying Rosemary. 'I've always lived here,' he says, gazing out towards the Wiltshire Downs. His face is weathered and ruddy, but like Temperley, his eyes twinkle. My initial impression is of a serious, businesslike man with an encyclopaedic knowledge of his trade. While the latter part stays true, it takes only a few minutes for the more gleeful, irreverent side to emerge as we sit down to a lunch of thick, sweet slices of their own smoked ham, cauliflower cheese and roast parsnips straight from the garden. William, Roger's three-year-old son, eyes me suspiciously.

'My father would look down the track and defy the world to come in,' says Roger. 'He fought in the First World War and wasn't at all sociable. I wanted to get out to the public. As a teenager, I sold eggs all around the area. But it was the bloody Sixties, and all the women were off at work, so there was no one around to buy the damned things.' He smiles and chews silently on a piece of ham. 'We opened the farm shop in '68. It was revolutionary then. Rose used to make gateaux and éclairs with cream from the local dairy, which you couldn't do now, as it was fresh and unpasteurised. Back then, we had five different local cheeses in the area. The main one was Wiltshire, bright orange, from marigolds, they said. I've heard that someone started to make it again. I wanted to make it myself at one point but thought, I can't do everything. We started curing our pork in 1968.'

Another silence, broken only by William's cry for more ham. 'He knows quality, that boy,' says Roger and carries on.

'Not so long ago, every town in Wiltshire used to have their own bacon curer. There was the Royal Wiltshire Bacon Company in Chippenham [which was also famed for its molasses- and juniper-cured Bradenham, jet black on the outside, that is now produced by Keen under the new name of Brumham]. Then Bowyer's in Melksham, and Harris in Calne. Harris once had a good reputation, back in the 1920s, but then they started injecting their bacon with water for extra weight and it got worse and worse, real second-rate stuff by the end, while I wanted to keep proper Wiltshire bacon going. So I went to the closing-down sale at Harris's. Everything was way too big for the size of my operation but I did come away with the factory manager.' He grins.

'Bacon curing is a wet, cold job. Nowadays, I employ mostly Polish workers [a pattern repeated across the land] as the modern English don't want to work in those sort of conditions. Anyway, we supply lots of farm shops and butchers in the area and did once flirt with Waitrose. They wanted a huge whack of our bacon, yet tiny amounts of our sausages. If you know what you're doing, which we do, you can supply the bits everyone wants, the chops and the fillet, and also get rid of the other parts on the carcass that aren't so popular. That is key, otherwise within three months you could go bankrupt. So we said no. I have a price I sell things at and if it doesn't sell, it doesn't sell. Of course, our salesman is rather more flexible.' He smiles again. 'But we do have to be firm with the butchers. It's all about balance. Yet we offer them a personalised service. If they want more fat or more lean on their bacon, we can supply it. We have around 200 accounts and have never received a single complaint about the product.'

If you're looking for purely rare breed or organic, Sandridge Farmhouse bacon is not for you. But then if you're judging food strictly on those narrow criteria, rather than tasting the end product, then more fool you. 'We've aimed for the middle ground,' says Roger as we leave behind the warmth of the farmhouse, and the apple and blackcurrant pudding, and step out into a crisp, bright Wiltshire winter's day. 'We felt we could cure with a sensible approach to production. We try to supply a good-quality product at a price that is fair to all. You just can't sell to everybody. Sure, I supply shops and markets right down to Somerset, Hampshire and Dorset, but despite constant requests we've resisted London. The cost of all that hanging about pushed that to one side.' His voice is soft, with a pronounced Wiltshire burr, for me one of the most attractive of inflections. 'My main ethos, apart from the quality of the end product, is to produce at a price that people can afford. My sausages and bacon are not as expensive as the supermarkets' "Premium" selection and they are better too.'

The pragmatic farmer is generally the successful one. It's all well and good to drool over biodynamic sausages, made from Lops and Tamworths fed on a diet better than that of most schoolchildren, but this is a niche, expensive market. I have huge belief in both the organic and the biodynamic systems of farming, but the more I learn, the more I realise that taste conquers all. I love rare-breed pigs, and the different flavours and characteristics they have, but in the real world, there has to be a balance between quality and price.

'There's no way I can compete with the supermarkets in terms of price, convenience or advertising. So I go for quality. And if people want bacon made from British pigs (not Danish bacon that is just cured over here, which allows it to be called British on the packet; and remember the Danish own two of the massive bacon curers anyway) you have to be able to trace your meat back to the source. Here, you can do just that. What ruined English food manufacturers,' he mutters as we tramp over the flint-hard earth towards the pigsties, 'is the moment when the accountants came in, looking for profit, not flavour.' He shakes his head, his smile rueful and eyes distant.

'I mean, look at Harris's. During the last war, it was made into a central processing plant, taking all the regional pigs. Then they filled the place with management types; too many chiefs, not enough Indians.'

The same could be said of food businesses across the country, of excessive management and needless health and safety criteria, taking us away from the art of producing good-quality food. My objection to European meddling is not nationalistic, rather it's because I believe that a central system is not suited to the governing of so many disparate countries. In Italy, Spain and France, there tends to be a somewhat more laid-back approach to health and safety regulations. Inspectors and consumers alike know more about the agricultural processes involved in food production, and there are ways of getting around the more stringent regulations. No one suffers and any individuality is unstifled by red tape. In England, not only do we stick more firmly to the letter of the law, but the official himself couldn't tell a knuckle from a hock. Keen, like most farmers, is especially good on the vagaries and by-roads of European food legislation. For the time being, however, he's happy.

'We've got a really good inspector this time. She knows her stuff and we work together. The last one, God, she was a nightmare.' It seems petty and pathetic, not to mention counter-productive, for one person to have so much power over a producer. The cured-pork trade, along with everything from cider and Cheddar to pickles and preserves, should be allowed more freedom to regulate itself. The most knowledge is, after all, concentrated among the producers and practitioners. The last Minister for Farming (or Secretary of State for Environment, Food and Rural Affairs, as they're now known) to have more than the barest inkling about farming was William Waldegrave, Minister of Agriculture, Fisheries and Food, in 1994. As for his successors, a sorrier bunch of ladder-climbing numbskulls (at least when it comes to farming) I've yet to find. Give the likes of Keen, Temperley and Montgomery a voice and the power to back it up, and English farming would be in a better state.

We wander down to the pigsties while Keen explains why his pigs aren't free range. 'If I had the right soil conditions, they'd be outdoors all year around. But my land sits on heavy clay and in a wet winter, the pigs hate it, their hooves and legs get clogged and they all hunker down back in the sheds. In those conditions, they refuse to go out. So they're outside all summer, then kept in here for the worst of the winter months.'

Before I arrived, I had the impression that any pig not classified free range was one of those wretched beasts that spent their short, miserable lives huddled together on concrete floors, with a bland diet and bugger all to do but bemoan their own existence. For me, the welfare of animals is as important as the flavour, so the continental treatment of the pig, especially by the massive companies, is nothing short of disgusting. The quality of the end product is wretched too. At Sandridge, there's plenty of space in the pens, which are clean, warm and comfortable. The pigs – some blacks, saddlebacks, Large White cross, some with a touch of Duroc – jostle and fight to get close to Keen, and he knows many by name. The fact he is so happy to throw open the doors of his sties is testament to his care for their welfare.

He makes his own feed too. 'It's a mixture of Yeo Valley yoghurt, from not so far away, and whey from Barber's Farm, where they make cheese. Some ice cream goes in too, and brewer's yeast from Wadworth's, the local brewery. And milk from a co-operative near Portsmouth. All that dairy produces a harder fat, which the butchers like as it makes for a better display. I reckon it tastes better, too. The pigs love it. We spend very little money on medication, but do vaccinate some of the pigs when needed. If you have good stockmanship, and feed and look after them well, you're 99 per cent there.'

As we walk back towards the bacon-making barns, he shows me a couple of liquid-storage tanks, about twenty-five feet high. 'I got them from Greenham Common, many years ago. They were used for fuel storage. I drove them home in a truck and halfway back this car started beeping and flashing. What the hell, I thought, and slowed down. "The telephone lines," he said, "you've hooked the telephone lines." And bugger me, sure enough, I'd managed to snag some overhead wires. Well, I thanked the man, untangled the lines and beat it back home as fast as I possibly could.'

The actual bacon-curing takes place in a succession of old sheds, all carefully joined together. Here I meet Kevin Royston, a young Zimbabwean farmer who was thrown off his family's land in Africa and escaped to Wiltshire. He started off as a delivery driver and worked his way up to the top. The first room is where the pigs arrive as split carcasses, having been slaughtered not far away. The spines are removed and destroyed, the offal taken out, and the bacon sides (Keen also produces sausages and exceptional hams from the other parts) cured for seventy-two hours.

'The Wiltshire method is always the wet, or brine cure. The pork is put in a solution of water, salt and sodium nitrate. In the old days, before brining was discovered, bacon tended to be exceptionally salty, thanks to the dry cure, and had to be washed before it was ready to eat. The brine cure produces a less salty end product.'

The maturing comes next ('After salt,' says Keen, 'time is our most important ingredient') at controlled, cool temperatures, for at least four or five days, sometimes as many as fourteen. But as Royston points out, 'The butcher wants to keep it for a bit too, so after fourteen days here it gives him less time to sell it in the shop.' Some of the bacon is smoked over beech and oak chips, got from the local Derry Hill sawmill. This produces the Golden Rind smoked, available, like all the other bacons, in back, middle and streaky. It's the bacon of my youth, with just the right amount of salt and smoke to bring out the very best porcine twang from the bacon. And the Golden Rind ham is rich, luscious and properly piggy, washed through with the scent of oak and beech. They also make an unsmoked dry-cure bacon where, instead of brining, salt and nitrates are rubbed in, left for ten days at least, so the end result is dry, firm and rather more salty. An acquired taste, certainly, but wonderful all the same. Then there are wet-cured hams, the Devyses, cured in Devizes-brewed Wadworth's and air-dried and York-style ham, the Trubridge (in honour of Trowbridge). In everything, the taste of the pig is as important as the cure and texture. They're all first-class products and none the worse for not being organic, free range or anything else. What Roger Keen shows is that it is possible to make hams and bacons, to old recipes, at good prices without compromising on quality or welfare.

I left the West, quietly optimistic, with old traditions going strong, in the hands of masters of their trade, making not just niche, expensive products for the lucky few but food for everyone. My travels here had given me hope for the rest of the journey. First, I had to be at a long-overdue reunion with Wimpy, a few hundred miles up the M1 heading towards my next port of call: the North.

PIGEONS IN CIDER WITH APPLES

This comes from Theodora Fitzgibbon's *Traditional West Country Cookery* and would work especially well with Burrow Hill Kingston Black Cider and a cooking apple such as Peasgood Nonsuch or Arthur Turner, although you could also try Lord Derby or Glass Apple. It is a perfect Somerset dish, using local apples, cider, birds and butter.

Serves 4

4 young, plump wood pigeons
salt and freshly ground black pepper
1 lemon, halved
2 onions
450 g (1 lb) cooking apples
175 g (6 oz) butter
pinch ground mace
good slug (about 5 tbsp) dry cider
150 ml (5 fl oz) single cream

Preheat the oven to 180°C/160°C fan/gas mark 4. Wipe the birds inside and out. Season with salt and pepper, and rub with half of the cut lemon. Set aside while you slice the onions, and quarter, core and cut the apples into thick crescent-moon wedges.

Heat half the butter in a big frying pan and brown the pigeons all over (you may need to do this one at a time).

Remove from the pan, add the rest of the butter and when the foam dies down stir in the apples and onions. Cook for 2–3 minutes until slightly softened. Season with the mace.

Spoon half of the cooked apples and onions into a casserole. Lay the pigeons, breast down, on top and spoon the rest of the apples and onions around them. Deglaze the frying pan with cider, stirring and scraping up all of the meaty sediment and juices. Add the cream, salt, pepper and a squeeze of lemon juice, and pour all into the casserole.

Lay a circle of greaseproof paper directly on top of the birds and cover with a lid. Slip into the oven and cook in the preheated oven for about 1½–2 hours, or until tender.

BRAWN

As culinary descriptions go, brawn is a bit of a bugger. Utilitarian, lumpen and ugly, it frightens off all but the most adventurous pig-guzzler. The Americans call it 'head cheese', surely one of the most unattractive descriptions of all time. Many people remember it as too visceral by half, with chunks of sticky fat and lumps of bristle-covered gristle.

Done well, though, brawn involves the sweetest, most tender parts of the pig's head (as well as the hock and trotters), held in glorious suspension. The end result should be as pretty and delicate as a Pompeian mosaic, light pink chunks contrasted with pale white shards, all set in a green-flecked jelly.

This recipe comes from Martin Blunos, a greatly talented West Country chef. Serve with some pickled shallots.

Serves 6 to 8

1 pig's head, singed of all hair, cut in half
1 slated ham hock, singed
2 pig's trotters, singed
3 large onions, peeled and cut into large chunks
4 carrots, left unpeeled but trimmed and washed
2 leeks, trimmed, washed and sliced
3 sticks celery
1 head garlic, split
2 bay leaves

1 tbsp whole black peppercorns
handful parsley stalks
5 whole cloves
1 stick cinnamon
handful curly-leaved parsley, chopped

Salad
handful flat-leaved parsley, roughly chopped
2 shallots, finely chopped
good slug olive oil
salt and freshly ground black pepper

Wash the meats and soak overnight in plenty of cold water.

The following morning, lift out the meats, drain and put in a large pan. Cover with cold water. Add the onions, carrots, leeks, celery, garlic, bay leaves, peppercorns, parsley stalks, cloves and cinnamon. Bring to the boil and reduce the heat to a gentle simmer for about 4 hours, skimming often.

When the meats are soft, remove the ears from the pig and set aside.

Drain all the solid ingredients from the pan and set aside to allow to cool, discarding the vegetables. Reduce the cooking juices by half, skimming as you go.

Pick over the meats, chopping the fat into tiny chunks. Cut the larger pieces, such as the peeled tongue and hock meat, into bigger chunks.

Add the curly-leaved parsley to the meat, season well and then return to the pan of reduced liquor. Stir to combine.

Ladle into a lined terrine and set aside until it reaches

room temperature, then cover with cling film and put it in the fridge overnight to set.

When ready to serve, make the salad. Dress the flat-leaved parsley and finely chopped shallot with olive oil and salt and pepper. Remove the brawn from the terrine and slice into thick pieces. Serve with the parsley salad.

CHEESE TOAST OR ENGLISH RABBIT

This comes from Florence White's *Good Things in England* and is listed as a 'savoury'. Dishes like this were traditionally eaten at the end of a dinner, an eminently civilised finale for those not in thrall to pudding. There were many such savouries: scotch woodcocks (anchovies, eggs, cream and bread), marrow toast, and cod's roe to name just a few.

This is a version of cheese on toast, similar to Welsh rabbit (never rarebit, by the way), although there is no ale, which is a traditional ingredient. Jamie Montgomery's Cheddar would be perfect for the dish.

I've adapted the recipe for the modern kitchen but its soul is still there.

Serves 2

4 tbsp milk
2 tbsp breadcrumbs
2 eggs
1 tsp English mustard
pinch salt
decent pinch cayenne pepper
200 g (7 oz) grated Cheddar
4 slices good bread (a bloomer loaf is perfect), toasted
    and buttered
slug Worcestershire sauce
big pinch chopped parsley

Preheat the grill to a medium heat. Heat the milk but do not allow it to boil. Soak the breadcrumbs in it. Beat the eggs in a separate bowl and stir into the milk and breadcrumbs. Season with the mustard, salt and cayenne. Over a low heat, add the cheese and stir until melted.

Have the toast ready. Spread on the toast quite thickly, covering the edges so that they don't burn. Place under the preheated grill and cook until browned.

Sprinkle with chopped parsley and a dash of Worcester-shire sauce, and serve immediately.

APPLE AND RHUBARB CRUMBLE

This is a rather modern English invention, said to have come about during the Second World War and the strictures of rationing. Normal pastry would use too much precious flour, fat and sugar, so the crumble was invented, using less of all the ingredients. I love it not only for the contrast of crunchy crumble and sweet, soft fruit but because it is so bloody easy to make. No mucking about with cold hands and even colder surfaces, murdering puff pastry. Making crumble, pinching the butter with the flour and sugar, is as soothing as cooking gets.

The addition of rhubarb is not strictly seasonal, as it is very much an early spring dish, but it makes for a fine combination. Serve with double cream or custard.

Serves 4

Filling
450 g (1 lb) Bramley apples, peeled, cored and sliced
200 g (7 oz) rhubarb, washed and sliced
knob butter
75 g (2¾ oz) light brown sugar
pinch cinnamon
splash cider brandy
2 cm (¾ in) fresh ginger, peeled and grated

Topping
100 g (3½ oz) unsalted butter, diced
200 g (7 oz) plain flour
pinch ground ginger
50 g (1¾ oz) demerara sugar

Preheat the oven to 180°C/160°C fan/gas mark 4. First make the filling. Put the apples and rhubarb into a greased oven-proof dish and dot with butter. Mix the sugar and cinnamon together and sprinkle over the fruit. Pour over the cider brandy and sprinkle with the freshly grated ginger.

Next, make the topping. Put the butter, flour, ground ginger and half the sugar into a bowl. Rub the butter into the flour until it resembles coarse breadcrumbs. Spread the crumble over the fruit and scatter with the remaining sugar.

Bake in the preheated oven for 45 minutes or until the top is golden and crisp. Serve warm.

2

The North

There was a time, at the dawn of the Eighties, when Wimpy had more allure for me than mere golden arches. Admittedly, McDonald's had yet to reach Swindon and the numbers of hamburger-flogging, Happy-Meal-purveying, fast-food joints were rather thin on the ground. All the same, the invitation to a birthday party there was only a step or two down from Jim fixin' it for you. When I was a child, it was a prospect more exciting than a day trip to Barry Island or Zippy slicing up Bungle into a thousand quivering chunks.

Back in those far-off days, Wimpy was as much a part of the English culinary landscape as chippies and the Fray Bentos pie. With determinedly grumpy service, watered-down fizzy drinks and a decidedly inferior burger, this was American fast food the English way. Hardly the most attractive of marriages but, God, did we adore it. The first opened in the Lyons Corner House in Coventry Street in 1954 and was so successful that by 1970 there were over 1,000 restaurants in twenty-three countries. But as McDonald's, Kentucky Fried Chicken and Burger King arrived on the scene, all gleaming smiles and 'Have a Nice Day', poor old Wimpy, huffing and puffing, was left behind. A chubby beefeater knocked senseless by a slim and sinister clown, it was bought and sold like some wretched slave. The Nineties saw its eventual decline and now only a few remain, squatting forlorn and lonely, cast adrift in a vicious modern world.

A cursory glance at the official website offers up some tantalising high points of their history. In 1985, 'Wimpy was the first burger chain to offer a vegetable burger – the original and still the best Spicy Beanburger.' Some boast, but it gets worse. In 1997, they celebrated becoming 'The first chain to offer a Quorn® based product on its menus.' Now it's one thing to come up with the veggie burger, even if the filling bears a worrying resemblance to a deep-fried Birkenstock. But Quorn? The less said about this reprehensible, ersatz sludge, the better. The last entry, sadly, is in 2004. 'Fifty years of Wimpy excellence,' they crow. The rest is silence.

During my childhood, though, Wimpy was a pleasure dome to beat Xanadu, especially in the grip of a sugary, post-cinematic buzz. The usual birthday party routine involved a trip to see *Superman II, Clash of the Titans* or, most aptly, *Popeye* (featuring the burger-addicted J. Wellington Wimpy, after whom the chain was named). There were balloons, streamers and, best of all, a bargain-basement version of the McDonald's Happy Meal toy. Rather than some slick, ultra-branded movie tie-in, you'd get a bendy straw or a crap plastic yo-yo. I still have a badge from one of these trips, with the eponymous fatty balanced precariously on the back of a Venetian gondola, as part of his world tour. I wanted him bursting out of Manhattan on a speedboat but there was little chance of prising the badge from my friend's clammy grasp.

Nearly thirty years later, driving up to Blackpool on the M6, I see a familiar sign featuring a small, red-and-white burger and, like one of Pavlov's dogs, the saliva floodgates open. A few minutes later and I am queueing (well, not exactly, as I am the only customer there) for a taste of my long-lost youth.

It's less of a restaurant proper and more a cut-back concession counter, stranded in a service-station limbo between the main entrance and the loos. The burger menu is mercifully short (although the 'Bender in a bun', a vast, curled sausage, probably needs rebranding), with the usual cheeseburger, bacon and cheese or quarter pounder. The ordering process involves interrupting an animated chat between two Eastern European servers, although once in work mode, they're chirpy and charming. 'Sorry, we haven't had straws for a few days,' one smiles, as she hands me a sealed cup. 'Just sip without lid,' offers the other, helpfully. I thank them for their advice and sit down, alone, in the middle of the service-station foyer.

'Didn't know Wimpy were still going,' I hear one man tell his wife.

'They were always a bit of a joke,' she replies with a shudder. They both look at me with pitying eyes.

Even in a nation where dull, mass-produced muck is devoured, nay, enjoyed, daily by millions, this food takes some beating – the chips are dull and flaccid, tasting of stale oil and regret, and the burger is pitiful, not only sub-football van but beneath contempt. Even a ravenous hound would pass it by. The meat is grey and underseasoned, the texture like grit-encrusted cardboard. I feel my taste buds ripping away from my tongue and hurling themselves down the chasm of my throat in disgusted despair. The bun is stale, the lettuce limp and God only knows what went into the 'Special Sauce'. Three bites are all I can endure. I leave the lovely ladies to their chat, climb into the car and head north, stopping only at the pumps to cleanse my mouth with diesel.

Bury promises more enlightened gastronomic relief, home of the famed market and the even more revered black pudding. Blackpool is my ultimate destination, where I am to meet up with friend and fellow food writer Matthew Fort. The omens are not good. Early that morning, an uncharacteristically sombre voice had groaned down the line: 'The sodding trains have all been cancelled out of Euston and I don't think I'll make it.'

Surely there must be some way, I coo, attempting to soothe his ragged mood. This is a man of such easygoing charm that the occasional black rant comes as somewhat of a shock.

'Not really. It all looks pretty screwed. I may as well bugger off back to Gloucestershire and bury my head back under my pillows.'

Think of the fish and chips, I implore, appealing to his baser instincts. I was desperate not to lose his company, both as companion and walking gustatory reference book. Despite his having covered every culinary tale in the country, at least twice, he could still approach something as well worn as fish and chips with unique joy and gusto.

He's also a world-class raconteur and, even if I have heard a couple of the tales more than once, they do, like good claret, improve with age. Four subjects in particular fuel his fire, being, in no particular order: Heston Blumenthal, regional Italian food, offal and sausages. Great friends with the first, authority on the next, committed guzzler of the third; and, in his view, world expert on the last. Brave would be the man who professed an admiration for a little rusk in his breakfast banger (as is the traditional English way). And you'd be taking your life into your own hands if you so much as whispered a preferred meat content of less than 89 per cent. I know, because I've foolishly argued both. Without any form of resolution. In reply, Matthew would shake his head imperiously, harrumph and turn on his heel.

His family offal feasts, held annually at Le Gavroche, are legendary. Alongside the usual brains, blood, heart and tripe are dishes adorned with coxcombs and cock's balls: 'Magnificent,' he later told me, eyes gleaming greedily. 'Just bloody magnificent. Michel [Roux] excelled himself.'

There are few men more committed to their calling, and he's a great and much loved figure of British gastronomy. So the thought of him giving up on the trip is too awful to bear.

'I could come back and pick you up,' I offer, secretly praying he'd say no. I am well north of Birmingham by now.

'No, I'm galvanised by the thought of an exquisitely edible afternoon. I'll get there, even if it involves a horse-drawn carriage.'

That's the spirit, I think, as I circle Bury on the orbital road, getting more and more lost by the moment.

About eight miles north-west of Manchester, Bury was once a small town of 300 inhabitants. The arrival of the Manchester, Bolton and Bury Canal Navigation Company and, with it, the construction of the canal, completed in 1808, changed all that, bringing wharves, warehouses and offices. Bleaching and the manufacture of woollens were Bury's traditional trades, with calico printing introduced by the Peel family (and Sir Robert Peel is the town's most famous son).

It was also known for its ox roasts. 'Ox roasting ceremonies were held at every opportunity during the Napoleonic era,' writes Fred Campbell in *Oxen, Oat-Cake and Ale*. 'An ox was roasted whole and the beef was cut up, accompanied by an abundance of soft oat-cakes and great quantities of ale … Ample slices of juicy beef were distributed to the people around and sufficient dripping was left to last a day or two for the poorer families.' The feasting went on through the night and the pub doors never closed. Bury, at the start of the nineteenth century, was booming, with water-powered wool mills springing up all around. But as the cotton industry declined, so did the fortunes of the town. Bury's expansion was a result of the Industrial Revolution, an event that transformed the country from a primarily rural society to an overwhelmingly urban one. It brought a population growth, or, rather, explosion, from 9 million people in 1801, doubling to 18 million in 1851, and doubling again in the next half-century to 36 million in 1901.

Despite the Northern boom, the first half of the eighteenth century saw widespread poverty and unrest among the entire working class. By the end of the Napoleonic Wars in 1815 England was spent, a situation made all the more deadly by the poor harvests of 1817 and 1819. With the introduction of the Corn Laws of 1815 – which kept the farmers and landowners happy by guaranteeing a high price for domestic corn, yet near destroyed the workers who no longer had land on which to grow their own food – the times became desperate. Food prices rose, while wages sat stubbornly still. 'The labourers seem miserable poor. Their dwellings are little better than pig-beds, and their look indicates that their food is not nearly equal to that of a pig,' wrote William Cobbett on 7 November 1821 in *Rural Rides.*

The Acts of Enclosure continued to cause widespread poverty, as they had during Queen Anne's reign, when around 12,000 acres were converted under two such Acts. While George III was on the throne, a whopping 3 million acres were stolen from the poor; over 4,000 Acts passed between 1750 and 1850, and, as was traditional, the villagers were powerless in the face of the Establishment. Although they had the right to lodge objections regarding the loss of the common land, and rights of appeal too, the problem was that you had to have at least some knowledge of the enclosures to do so. All the landowner had to do, before 1774, was to submit a petition for enclosure, have it made the subject of a Bill, and get it legalised. What chance did the mainly illiterate rural peasant have against the conniving, rapacious lawyer?

Nonetheless, attempts were made. *Lost Voices of the Edwardians* cites a 1797 Northamptonshire community pleading its case:

the Petitioner begs leave to represent to the house that
… the Cottagers and other Persons entitled to Right of
Common on the Lands intended to be inclosed, will
be deprived of an inestimable Privilege, which they now
enjoy, of turning over a certin [sic] number of their
Cows, Calves, and Sheep, on and over the said lands; a
Privilege that enables them not only to maintain themselves and their Families in the Depth of Winter … but,
in addition to this, can now supply the Grazier with
young or lean Stock at a reasonable Price to fatten and
bring to Market at a more moderate Rate.

Yet as Drummond and Wilbraham wryly note in *The English-man's Food*, 'It was indeed a rare event for the land to be saved
for those who lived by it and whose forefathers had tilled it
for centuries past.'

At the close of the seventeenth century, Gregory King, in
his *National and Political Observations and Conclusions upon the
State and Condition of England in 1696*, reckoned that there
were around 330,000 farmers in the country, half of whom were
tenants and the other half small farmers, owners of the property
they farmed. But it was the class below, the cottagers and farmworkers, who really suffered as their grazing rights were torn
away, leaving them with no way to fuel a fire or feed themselves
and their families. There was nothing left for them, save immi-
grating to America or moving to the ever-swelling cities where
if they were lucky they might find a job in the factories.

In hindsight, one could argue that the enclosures were an
absolute necessity for the modernisation of Britain, and that

they passed land over to men with capital and expertise, who were better placed to extract the greatest value and return, as opposed to the simple, uneducated peasant. And, as you'd expect, the landowners of the time were in full support. 'The idea of having lands in common, it has been justly remarked, is to be derived from that barbarous state of society, when men were strangers to any higher occupations than those of hunters or shepherds,' thundered Sir John Sinclair, in his 1795 'Address to the Members of the Board of Agriculture on the Cultivation and Improvement of the Waste Lands of this Kingdom'. Sinclair was the first President of the Board of Agriculture, founded in 1793. Arthur Young, author of the hugely popular *Annals of Agriculture* and Secretary of the Board of Agriculture, agreed: 'No small farm could effect such great things as have been done in Norfolk. Great farms are the soul of Norfolk culture; split them into tenures of a hundred pounds a year and you will find nothing but beggars and weeds in the whole county.'

The enclosures impacted in other ways. 'The cottagers and farm labourers who moved to the industrial towns had no means to buy food or even cook it, so those habitual daily recipes which had been a central part of their life must have been lost within a few years,' writes Colin Spencer in *British Food*. 'These people were for the most part illiterate, so the recipes that had once been passed on from generation to generation now vanished.' This was a fatal blow to rural British food, yet the repertoire of the poor was hardly thrilling. A few pease puddings, scraps of bacon and cheap, gritty bread. The ox roasts of Bury would have been anticipated with heady excitement, anything to break the glum monotony of their dreary daily bread. The diet was base and unrelenting: bread, cheese and pudding when times were hard, and as much meat as could be crammed into their bellies when it could be got. It was a diet made up, in the words of Richard Jefferies in a series of letters to *The Times* (1772), mainly 'of bread and cheese, with bacon twice or thrice a week ... vegetables are his luxuries, and a large garden, therefore is the greatest blessing he can have. He eats huge onions raw; he has no idea of flavouring his food with them, nor of making those savoury and inviting messes or vegetable soups at which the French peasantry are so clever.'

The French peasantry, on the other hand, were always viewed as being more creative with what little they had.

> In Picardy I have often dined in a peasant's cottage [Jefferies goes on] and thoroughly enjoyed the excellent soup he puts upon the table for his ordinary meal. To dine in an English labourer's cottage would be impossible. His bread is generally good; but his bacon is the cheapest he can buy at small second-class shops – only soft, wretched stuff; his vegetables are cooked in detestable style, and eaten saturated with the pot-liquor. Pot liquor is a favourite soup. I have known cottagers actually apply at farmers' kitchens not only for the pot liquor in which meat has been saddened, but the water in which the potatoes have been boiled – potato liquor – and sup it up with avidity. And this is not in times of dearth or scarcity, but rather as a relish.

It would be easy to over-eulogise French peasant food, but at heart it was made up of soups, vegetables and *bouillies* (boiled grain). There were regional specialities, the pot-au-feus and daubes, but these were not eaten on a daily basis by every peasant, for whom meat was still a luxury. 'The people themselves revel in good food, and the love of something, anything in fact, is the main requirement for producing it,' writes Philip Oyler in *The Generous Earth*.

The British poor, in contrast, never seemed to delight in their food, and with good reason. The peasant fare of England had always been desperately dull, stodgy and uninspired, even, as Jefferies notes, when times were good. There could be no blossoming of English peasant cuisine in a day-to-day hell of mere survival. Never had the gap between the rich and poor been more pronounced.

There were those who saw the industrialisation of Britain as the end of our food culture, in which industrial towns such as Manchester, York and Bury, along with London, like vampires sucked the blood from the country, turning previously healthy peasants into starving vagrants. There's absolutely no doubt that rural decline and unrest were intrinsically linked with the rise of the factories, but this wasn't the sole factor. 'The rural skills: the domestic brewing and baking, had disappeared ...' wrote William Cobbett in the early nineteenth century; 'there was mass evacuation to the factories and towns, where not only was fuel scarce, but women who had put in a hard day's work in the factory did not have the time, or the energy, to cook large meals.'

Writing about the English love of pre-prepared food, he could just as easily be ranting against the supermarket ready meal today. 'Nowadays, all is looked for at shops. To buy things ready made is the taste of the day: thousands who are housekeepers buy their dinners ready cooked.'

Those romantic souls who claim that convenience food is a twentieth-century invention, that all the folk in the good old days cooked everything from scratch, are misguided. Everyone could but after the coming of the Industrial Revolution not everyone did. We've had a long tradition of buying ready-made food from cook- and bake-shops through to fish and chips, Wimpy burgers, curries and kebabs. The English used cookshops originally because most poor houses lacked an oven and fuel was expensive. But it's a core part of our culinary culture and perhaps proof that we didn't place as much importance on the home kitchen as did our European neighbours. The downside is an erosion of national cooking prowess.

It was not industrialisation alone that snuffed out our national palate, or drove us into the arms of the bake-shop, although it increased the urban population and made the country far more reliant on imports, especially canned and preserved goods. The true catastrophe lay in its side effects. The woman's realm had always been in the house and, more specifically, the kitchen. Even the very poorest families, eking out a miserable existence on bland pottage and gritty bread, were able to cook their own food. They had a basic culinary knowledge that was passed down, in largely verbal form, from mother to daughter. One might argue that the recipes would have made pretty uninspiring reading and eating, yet each generation ensured their survival by sharing them with the next.

However, with the advent of industrialisation, the working-class wife moved into the mills and factories, and no longer had the time to spend all day cooking for husband and children. Working long and exhausting hours herself, she craved convenience, and would buy dinner in the bake-shop rather than cook it herself. In Europe, industrialisation was not as widespread, with more women remaining at home. On the Continent, lunch breaks ran to two hours, allowing wives and mothers to both cook and eat. There was no such consideration in England. Bake-shops in the industrial age were the Sainsbury's ready meal of today, that bland salvation of the harried career woman. The result was that English working-class women of the time forgot how to cook. 'At first the bake-shop existed as a compromise between a working wife's factory hours and her husband's midday hunger,' writes P. Morton Shand in *A Book of Food*; 'its survival has become the shibboleth of her increasing incompetence.' Given the middle-class dismissal of culinary responsibility (in that the servants took over), and the moneyed classes' obsession with French food which, as we will see later, was closely connected to snobbery and social climbing, it's little wonder that by the end of the nineteenth century English food was in such a parlous state. And things were about to get worse still.

Soldiers returning to England after the First World War brought with them a taste for tinned food, bully beef in particular. The name came from the French *boeuf bouilli*, or boiled beef, and these tins revolutionised military eating, making provisions portable, nutritious and long-lasting. Even George Orwell, a rabid detractor of all things canned, was forced to admit that 'The Great War … could never have happened if tinned food had not been invented.' It wasn't just bully beef that kept the Tommies fighting, but Spam, corned beef, hard cheese and jam, all sealed in their metal jackets.

It was Nicolas Appert, a French chef and confectioner, who, at the end of the eighteenth century, perfected a method of preserving soup and boiled beef in gravy. Of course, he was not the first to attempt this, and fruits had been preserved in jars since Roman times; they were simply heated in a sealed container. Appert, however, managed to give food a longer keeping life without sullying the taste or ruining the texture. He published a book in 1810, detailing his findings. His only problem was that glass bottles were fragile and took up considerable space.

Across the Channel, a few months later in the same year, a London broker by the name of Peter Durand was granted a patent for a remarkably similar process, which he sold to Bryan Donkin, an engineer, for £1,000. Durand was happy to admit that his patent was an 'invention communicated to me by a certain foreigner'. Donkin, along with his partners John Gamble and John Hall, adopted Appert's method but used tins instead of bottles, making them the pioneers of canning.

The first proper trial took place in November 1812, when Durand sweet-talked Captain George King into taking tinned meats and soups aboard the *Mary and Susannah*, which was embarking on a round trip to Jamaica. They were a resounding success, with the captain fulsome in his praise: 'the meats and soups I opened during the voyage, were as good as when first put up, and I have no doubt will keep in all climates.' The navy took note, the company flourished and tinned food was upon us.

Surprisingly, until after the First World War, canned food-stuffs were expensive treats, found in the likes of Fortnum & Mason. Tinned pheasant, turtle soup, truffles and artichokes had little part to play in the diets of the everyday worker. Meanwhile, the rather cheaper meat, flooding in from Australia and South America, was tainted with scandal. In January 1852, *The Times* revealed that out of 2,707 large canisters of meat opened in navy depots, only 197 were actually edible, and even those were made up of the 'roots of tongue, pieces of palate' and 'ligaments of throat'. This did little to endear tinned food to the English, although by 1880 we were importing around 16 million pounds of the stuff.

In 1922, just three firms in Britain produced tinned foods, yet by the start of the 1930s there were eighty, preserving peas, carrots, cabbages, plums, damsons, spinach and anything else that grew, sprouted or fruited. Ambrose Heath even dedicated a book to the subject, *Open Sesame: The Way of a Cook with a Can*. In it, he listed 90 kinds of fish, 218 types of meat, 100 vegetables and 97 varieties of fruit.

Some people, though, saw the advent of food technology as the root of all ill health. George Orwell, in *The Road to Wigan Pier* (1937), remembers the crowds at the funeral of George V. 'Puny limbs, sickly faces, under the weeping London sky! Hardly a well-built man or a decent looking woman, and not a fresh complexion anywhere,' he despairs. And these weren't just the usual hollow-faced, sunken-eyed workers, but 'the shopkeeper-commercial-traveller type, with a sprinkling of the well-to-do'. He admits the physical average has been long declining in England, countrywide, though these shrunken frames compare badly to the hearty specimens of his youth. 'Where are the monstrous men with chests like barrels and moustaches like the wings of eagles who strode across my childhood gaze twenty or thirty years ago? Buried, I suppose, in the Flanders mud.'

P. Morton Shand, a fellow Old Etonian, though a man many miles to the right, agreed.

> Chemical nutrition, the *esculents minérales* so confidently forecasted by Brillat-Savarin as the gastronomic achievement of future generations, had come to stay, but in a form he could scarcely have dreamed of in the most troubled of his many nightmares. Preserved and adulterated had begun to have much the same significance without anyone realizing there was anything unwonted in this confusion of terms.

He saw the preservation revolution in aesthetic terms too, as something visually monstrous that forever ruined our green and pleasant land, a cursed technology riding roughshod over Nature:

> the next [effect of free trade] was the advent of tinned foods, an innovation that came from America [it was actually an Englishman, William Underwood, who first introduced the method to the USA in 1817] ... which soon rendered the refuse heaps of our great

cities as desolate as the slag-heaps they supplemented, and more forbidding and degraded than a stretch of the war zone in France still defying cultivation.

Orwell went further still, barely able to suppress his disgust. He blamed not only the Great War for having wiped out a whole generation of the country's finest, fittest and most able men, but also 'the modern industrial techniques which provide you with cheap substitutes for everything. We may find in the long run that tinned food is a deadlier weapon than the machine gun.' While Orwell was wrong, of course, the effect on the palate, rather than the population, was ruinous. And he was prescient as to the effect of processed food upon the British. It wasn't, in the end, tinned foods that conspired to destroy our national sense of taste, but their nebulous descendants, the micro-meal, boil-in-a-bag, Pot-Noodle rubbish that continues to infest our supermarket trollies. His statement about 'the English palate, especially the working-class palate' now rejecting 'good food almost automatically' might have had some truth at the time, yet for a writer capable of such brilliant and precise detail (such as the 'astonishingly dirty' Mr Brooker with his black-thumb-printed bread and butter), he can often descend into the indulgently general.

Who's to say that the miner, when offered a plate of spanking-fresh peas or foamingly fresh milk, wouldn't jump for joy and renounce the sins of the tin? But then again why should he? Although the fresh might be healthier, he's perfectly entitled to prefer the tinned variety, to relish the grainy texture or more pronounced vegetative depth. Tinned fish can be easily equal to the fresh variety; it's just different, just like the difference between fillet steaks and shin of beef. A tin of Ortiz tuna is far superior to that dried-up scrap of old protein that festers on some second-rate fishmonger's slab. And give me a can of Campbell's consommé over some wretched carton of supermarket soup, where more money seems spent on marketing than on ingredients. At times, Orwell, for all his card-carrying Socialism, seems as much of a tub-thumping food snob as the most pompous of our culinary bores.

His anger, though, comes not from social superiority but resigned desolation. In general, Orwell and Shand are right. 'In the highly mechanised countries,' writes the former,

> thanks to tinned food, cold storage, synthetic flavouring matters, etc, the palate is almost a dead organ. As you can see by looking at any greengrocer's shop, what the majority of English people mean by an apple is a lump of highly-coloured cotton wool from America or Australia; they will devour these things, apparently with pleasure, and let the English apples rot under the trees. It is the shiny, standardised, machine-made look of the American apple that appeals to them; the superior taste of the English apples [is] something they simply do not notice. Or look at the factory-made, foil-wrapped cheeses and 'blended' butter in any grocer's; look at the hideous rows of tins which usurp more and more of the space in any food-shop, even a dairy.

Had Orwell been alive today, wandering through the strip-lit aisles of his local Tesco Metro and gazing upon the endless rows of Sunny Delight, Cheesy String and microwave burgers, he would have shaken his head in despair.

It is raining as I park in Bury market, wedged between a supermarket and the main road. Matthew had just rung to say that the fates had smiled upon him, and Blackpool was back on. A Bury black pudding would make his journey all the sweeter. At first sight, I am disappointed. This looks like any other English market, a warren of stalls selling everything from cut-price DVDs and scratchy frilly knickers to the sort of frying pan that would melt on contact with heat. A nagging drizzle makes the market subdued, with grey faces in the Stygian gloom. As long as the black puddings are there, though, the weather is all but impotent to ruin my day.

Bury has long been famed for its puddings, a beguiling mix of pork fat and blood, oatmeal and onions, salt, pepper and seasoning. However, if you describe them as a blood sausage the average English eater would wrinkle their nose and politely decline. It's their loss, as the finest black puddings are sublime and surprisingly unvisceral. There's evidence of their having been made in Bury from at least the start of the nineteenth century (although they'd probably been in domestic production many centuries before that), cheap and filling comfort food for the new influx of urban poor.

And they weren't just a Northern treat. You'd find versions of black pudding wherever pigs were killed. At their best, they contain the essence of the pig, rich and comforting, a hint of the dangerous made soft with spice. As to those spices, the exact amounts are usually a closely guarded secret. Bury was known for adding marjoram, thyme, pennyroyal, mint and celery seed; Staffordshire liked pimento and coriander; while Cheshire added caraway. Even forty years ago, in 1970, United Cattle Products, the main tripe producer in the country and the owner of an offal-related chain of restaurants, sold 5,000 pounds of pudding per week. Unlike tripe, black pudding sales are still going strong, especially in the North. How anyone with even the slightest leaning towards sausage could fail to enjoy a decent black pudding, I don't know. Tripe, though, is an altogether harder sell.

January is hardly the finest month for English produce, unless you have an especial penchant for brassicas. But alongside the cabbages and swedes there are more recent arrivals: plantains and habanero chillies, coriander and sweet potatoes, edible testament to the multinational make-up of modern England. A bakery is filled with fresh fruit teacakes and large barms (or buns), oven bottoms, muffins and scones, alongside cheap loaves of industrial plastic bread. As a nation of bread eaters, we seem to have a blatant disregard for quality. Yet there's something appealing about cheap white bread, and a proper bacon sandwich is unthinkable using grander stuff.

Opposite is an old-fashioned sweet shop, Lawson's. I stop to peer at the endless jars, brimming with sour apples, sherbet lemons and cherry drops, a mouth-puckering traffic light of sugary delight. Sweets, another area in which the English traditionally excel, never lose their appeal; Pontefract cakes, rhubarb and custard, cola cubes and raspberry crystals – a decade back, these old classics were in danger of dying out. However, such is the English hunger for nostalgia that they made a comeback and internet sites such as Cybercandy and aquarterof.co.uk have ensured their survival for a few more years yet.

I must have gazed, mouth agape, for a moment too long because I am brought back to Bury by a sharp tap on my shoulder. 'Can I help you?' asks a stern-faced man.

'Uh, no thanks.'

'So why the pen and notebook then? Writing a book, are we?'

I immediately feel guilty and blush, simply confirming his suspicions. 'I am, actually.'

He looks me up and down, his eyes narrowing to slits.

'Seriously,' I stutter, 'I'm here for the black pudding.'

His face crumples into a smile. 'Well, that's all right then. So sorry. It's just that we've had problems with competitors nicking our recipes.'

I don't dare point out that the commercial spy would be far better off buying a selection of sweets, rather than loitering with intent.

His whole manner changes and he shakes my hand. 'Black puddings you're after, eh? You want Mary's, oldest and best. Take a left, wiggle round, then right past the shoe stall and you're there. Better still, I'll take you halfway.'

And off we go, past Bollywood posters and outsized bras, dog food and crocus bulbs.

He points into the distance. 'She's just over there. She does proper black pudding. Anyway, happy eating.'

Just before I reach Mary, I find a van selling hot boiled

potatoes and steaming black peas. Doused in vinegar and white pepper, they taste of sun-warmed earth. 'Are these still popular?' I ask the man behind the counter, my breath billowing in the cold air.

'Ay, proper Northern food, cheap and filling. I get through bags of peas when it's busy. Bit dead today though.' I ask what he thinks of Mary's black pudding. 'The best. Really, there's nowt better.'

When I eventually find the Bury Black Pudding Co., aka Chadwick's Original Black Puddings, there's a queue, ten people deep. Next to the dozens of black puddings is a glass-fronted cabinet filled with wobbling tripe and cow heel, off-white, waxy-looking, cartilaginous lumps. But the vast majority of people are here for the puddings. Some buy them fresh and hot, the black, horseshoe-shaped sausage split open and slathered with mustard, then eaten on the spot with a plastic spoon. Others buy them uncooked, to be taken home, sliced and fried for breakfast.

One mother feeds her toddler son with hot morsels and he eats with obvious relish. 'Start 'em young,' she says, when she sees me looking on. 'Make 'im strong too.'

Reputed to be the oldest stall in the market, it first opened in 1929. Eventually, I reach the front of the queue and ask the lady behind the counter, quiet and modest, where I could find Mary Chadwick. 'Yes, that's me,' she says, her voice guarded and low.

I buy a few puddings, fatty of course, as the lean ones, without the chunks of fat, seem to miss the point. Also, if I turn up and present a lean one to Matthew, the disappointment might send him mad. The sausage is tied together at the ends into a tight, black horseshoe, which is a trademark of the Bury pudding. Mary's is actually black in colour, rather than a brownish hue just wrapped in black plastic. The original recipe is said to date back to Joshua Thompson, who made the original Bury version in 1865. When Mary's father, Edwin, a butcher, bought the business in 1972, he named them 'Bury Black Puddings', or 'berries' as they're widely known.

Once she's established my motives are pure (meaning I don't work for the competition), she opens up a little. 'Oh, I've been here a few years, about thirty-seven in all. And seasoning is the key, although the recipe is secret.' She stops to serve another customer. 'Oh yes, everyone still eats them. Sales are the same as they've always been. And, of course, they're all handmade. Tripe, though,' she points to the bleached cow's stomach and shakes her head, 'that's not so popular now. It's only really the old who come in and buy it with any regularity. Same with cow heel. It's cheap, tasty and nutritious, great in a pie. If you've been brought up with it, as so many around here were … you eat it. But if you've never tried it, you won't touch it at all. I don't think it will die out altogether, because people do come and buy quite a bit, but it's true to say that it's not as popular as it was.'

Her puddings are magnificent, rich and deeply piggy. Matthew, I know, is about to fall in love.

My Northern odyssey had taken me by way of Yorkshire, in search of that English rarity, a tripe dresser. The name evokes nimble-fingered craftsmen, delicately plying their trade on great flaps of cow stomach. The reality is a little less romantic, although they are very much a dying breed.

There are probably better times to visit the town than on a damp winter Wednesday and there's little chance of Dewsbury being described as the jewel in the Northern crown. The streets are all but deserted, shrouded in a dull, relentless mist, as if the whole town has its face turned against the world. Broken windows and dilapidated wool mills provide a gloomy backdrop, and there's a feeling that the glory days have long since passed. There are moments of unexpected beauty, such as a handsome Victorian town hall, built during the wool boom. Cheap imports from Australia burst that particular bubble and Dewsbury slipped into a gradual decline. There are pockets of regeneration, not that they are of much interest to many residents.

'What do you want to go up there for?' asks one incredulous resident, sucking the last scrap of smoke from a soggy roll-up. 'There's fook all to see round there.'

It seems fitting that Dewsbury is home to the Ideal Tripe Works, as both town and cow stomach share a similar downward trajectory. The place isn't so much grim as unloved and at times feels like little more than an afterthought of Leeds and Bradford, a few miles to the north. Furthermore, Peter Sutcliffe, the Yorkshire Ripper, was formally indicted in the town hall in 1981; a twelve-year-old girl was charged with attempting to hang a five-year-old boy in 2005; and in 2008, in Dewsbury Moor, Shannon Matthews was abducted. (In a scenario that would be high comedy were it not so wretched and depressing, her mother, inspired by the McCann family appeal and the money they raised, decided to get together with Michael Donovan to fake her daughter's disappearance. They failed, of course.) Dead and missing children, alongside serial killers: hardly the best advertisement for a small town. Were it not for the tripe works, there'd be little reason to visit.

But as I wander through the town, it is possible to get a taste of the town as it once was, its grand buildings and façades squeezed between discount shops and crammed behind chain pubs. After an hour or so of trawling the soggy pavements, I finally find the factory, tucked away in a small industrial estate.

The first thing you notice is the smell. It doesn't so much creep up my nostrils as cosh them, a viciously warm mix of rotten fish, boiled meat, sulphur and shit. I try to block my nose and smile, breathing gulps of air through my mouth. But to no avail, as the stench just pours down my throat until I can taste it in the pit of my stomach. Tripe is still the great divider of British food – most of us abhor the stuff but once under its wobbling, slightly gelatinous spell, there's no going back. Inexpensive, sustaining and deeply comforting, it's also a badge of the old North, up there with flat caps and racing pigeons in the regional stereotyping guide. The smell is just one of the many factors that make tripe so widely despised. Combine that with a gelatinous texture, a slight squeak between the teeth when chewed, a ghoulish appearance and a pretty forceful taste, and you have a piece of offal that is capable of offending all five senses.

My conversion to tripe was hardly instant; for years I didn't even bother to try the stuff, such was my aversion to these smelly folds of cow gut. It took a French dish, *tripes à la mode de Caen,* eaten in Les Vapeurs in Deauville, to convince me of its charms. Cooked over a low heat in a sealed casserole, with cider, apples, carrots and herbs, the end product both soothed and thrilled. That slippery texture became delightful, the deeply meaty savour the very essence of bovine heft. All the same, it will be a few more years before I embrace cold tripe with vinegar and white pepper. Still, it does little to deserve such a vile reputation and is very much more sinned against than sinning.

The Ideal Tripe Works is one of the last tripe dressers left in the land and the optimistic name seems incongruous with the low, industrial buildings before me. 'Don't talk tripe,' runs their slogan. 'EAT it!'

I'm met by Chris Hey, owner of the family business, R. Hey and Sons. He's tanned, with porcelain-blue eyes and a warm smile.

'Seventy per cent of our market is abroad these days, Eastern Europe, China and the like,' he says in a warm Yorkshire growl, as we escape the smell in the comfort of his office. 'They want it cleaned but not cooked. It's all changed since my father's day.' He smiles. 'I started back in 1969, but my father began after the Second World War. He couldn't get a job as a butcher, as there was still meat rationing. So he started work for a tripe dresser in Dewsbury. Anyway, he ended up buying this company in 1953, a tripe dresser called Whitakers in Leeds. I was one year old, and he needed to make more than a fiver a week to keep us all fed. He borrowed the money off my uncle and got on with it. I remember my father telling me, he used to fetch the tripe from the abattoirs, process and boil it, then sell it down Dewsbury Market. In those days the stalls were open until ten-thirty, so we could sell tripe to people coming out of the pubs. It was a much loved late-night snack. Around here, and in Lancashire, we liked it cold, with salt and vinegar. In the south and north-east parts of York-shire, they prefer it cooked.'

Tripe, like black pudding, cow heel and other offal, was hugely popular in the industrial North, although the condi-tions of its preparation were often far from ideal. J.P. Kay, in *The Moral and Physical Conditions of the Working Classes* describes one manufacturer in Manchester: 'a low cottage, which was in a state of loathsome filth. Portions of animal matter were decaying in it, and one of the inner rooms was converted into a kennel and contained a litter of puppies ... Offal was allowed to accumulate with the grossest neglect of decency and disregard to the health of the surrounding inhab-itants.' The Ideal Tripe Works might smell of hell, but there is no question as to the cleanliness of the place.

'In 1969, there were six tripe dressers in Dewsbury alone,' says Hey. 'In Bolton, there were about forty, mostly one-man bands, each selling ten tripes (or stomachs) per week. Now, I reckon there are just four left in the country, one in Newark, one in Liverpool, us and a little one in Padiham, near Burnley.'

Back in 1924, Lancashire had hundreds of tripe dressers, from Richard Abbott, at 90 King Street, Blackburn, to W. Young, at 3 Eagle Street, Accrington. United Cattle Products, a company formed in Manchester in 1920 by fifteen Lanca-shire tripe dressers, quickly became the king of them all. At the start, they were wholesalers but as orders grew (with 200 tonnes sold per week just before the Second World War) they started opening restaurants in Manchester, Blackpool, Oldham, Bolton, Rochdale, Southport, Macclesfield, Bury, Wigan and many other towns, each adorned with the famous UCP oval sign. The shops had inviting, red-painted fronts 'in order to brighten up the grey streets!' The interiors were smart and modern, with tablecloths and even the odd water feature. Prices were low. The menu, as expected, was heavy on tripe (not just the usual honeycomb, but 'jelly' and 'black' too), with cow heel, pork belly, elder (or udder) and trotters equally popular, alongside ice creams and coffee.

'Tripe has long been a target for comedians,' writes Marjory Houlihan in *A Most Excellent Dish: Tales of the Lancashire Tripe Trade*, 'but as one tripe dresser remarked, "People think tripe is funny for some reason – for folk in the trade I can assure you it is a very serious matter indeed."'

As a nation, we've just lost our taste for the extremities and offal, tripe and pig's foot alike, seeing them as rough and visceral, too texturally bizarre to ever be accepted again. We're a country reliant on shoulder of lamb and cheap ham, seeing anything else as too strong-tasting or slippery or grotesque. In a country so obsessed with class, upward mobility is not just about bigger houses and better schools. Often, it's about escaping the food of your earliest years. While the older generation still adore tripe and offal as a reminder of their childhood, the younger are more cosmopolitan and global in their tastes. They also believe that, in flight from the privations of their youth, they have little reason to go back to the cheap cuts of meat. Gastro-snobbism, if you like. So it's not only the taste, appearance and texture of tripe that sets it against the modern world, but its history too. At the start of the Edwardian era, though, often erroneously viewed as some form of golden age, the poor were barely even able to afford tripe.

A hundred years ago, the poor were experiencing starvation and hardship on an unimaginable scale. 'It is no exaggeration to say that the opening of the twentieth century saw malnutrition more rife in England,' said Drummond and Wilbraham, 'than it had been since the great dearths of medieval and Tudor times.' A Sheffield survey of 1900 shows that many children still existed on a diet of just bread and jam. Rickets and tuberculosis were commonplace; among the poor, meat was a rarity, food was generally expensive and unemployment was widespread. Out of every nine men inspected for military service, just three were fit and healthy. Another two were ailing, three were totally unfit and one was barely breathing.

The English working-class urban diet was astonishingly meagre. As the Victorian Age gave way to the Edwardian, there was such a shortage of healthy men for the South African war that the minimum height restriction was lowered to five feet. Infant mortality in the working-class areas was a horrifying 1 in 4. Worse still, the wholemeal bread and butter once enjoyed by the working classes had been replaced with white bread and margarine, washed down with tea. The latter combination has half the calcium of wholemeal bread and butter, less than a quarter of the iron, 2,000 times less vitamin C, ten times less vitamin B1 and fifty times less vitamin D. With tea now the drink of choice rather than beer, the calorie count dropped lower still. It was little wonder that a third of the population lived in a state of near-starvation. This, at a time when England presided over her vast empire, when debs waltzed around gilded ballrooms with enough diamonds in their hair to feed the Dewsbury poorhouses for weeks.

At least back in medieval days, there was common land on which you could graze your own beast. Those in the country were marginally better off, growing produce in small gardens, and maybe having even a pig or two. Agricultural workers ate better than most of their class, while the small farmer was comparatively well fed.

Jack Larkin was a waggoner's mate in a rural area at the start of the twentieth century, helping drive a farmer's cart. In *Lost Voices of the Edwardians* he recalls, 'The farmer always had a barrel of beer in and we had small beer for breakfast, ale for dinner and small beer for tea. The only time we had hot tea to drink was on a Sunday. Breakfast in the morning was a darn great lump of fat pork, half a loaf of bread and, if they'd got plenty of milk, a jolly great bowl of milk … I lived on fat pork for twelve months. And sometimes it wasn't done properly and when the knife went through it you could hear it sort of crunch. Pork fat not done properly is awful.'

Gertrude McCracken, working at the same time, remembers that 'Most cottages in those days kept their own backyard pig, feeding it on household scraps and vegetable peelings boiled up in the copper and mixed with meal … nothing was wasted from the pig – the offal and the fleck, the tummy lining, made faggots, with brawn from the head and trotters, and black pudding from the warm blood. The sides were cured and hung up in the back kitchen. The fat was rendered down for lard, and we children ate the scraps that were left after the lard was melted.'

These people were the lucky exceptions. Traditional English food might have been thriving in the middle and upper classes, and among the farmers too. But the poor – overworked and underpaid, crammed into slums unfit for human habitation – were lucky to get a small snippet of imported mutton on a Sunday. It would be difficult to see what joy they took in this apparently golden age.

In 1901, B. Seebohm Rowntree, the third child of Quaker chocolate magnate Joseph Rowntree, published a damning report, *Poverty – A Study of Town*, about conditions in York. It's a serious sociological work, bursting with charts and figures, that throws an illuminating insight into the life of the very poor. He defines 'Class A' families as 'the poorest people in the city', who were mostly unemployed. One husband is described as 'Out of work. Married. Five children. Drinks. "Chucked his work over a row". Very poor; have to pawn furniture to keep children.' Near by is a charwoman, living in a two-roomed house with her son, aged twenty, a casual labourer. The husband is in a workhouse: 'Dirt and drink in plenty. This house shares one water-tap with six other houses, and one closet with two others.' Rowntree's conclusion is that 'the wages paid for unskilled labour in York are insufficient to provide food, shelter, and clothing adequate to maintain a family of moderate size in a state of bare physical efficiency ... no allowance is made for any expenditure other than that absolutely required for the maintenance of mere physical efficiency.'

The basic wage was so low that it left not a farthing to spare for anything other than basic existence. Out of the question were notions of travel, or newspapers, or the music hall, or postage, or dolls, or marbles, or sweets. There was never enough cash for beer or fags, for doctors or even graves (the poor were buried by the parish in the event of their not being able to pay for a proper funeral). Not that this meant that they didn't spend cash on booze or cigarettes. Who wouldn't? It just meant even less money for food. 'If any of these conditions are broken, the extra expenditure is met, and can only be met, by limiting the diet,' concludes Rowntree.

The slum houses themselves were filthy hovels, oppressively small and crowded together into narrow alleys that caught barely a beam of natural light. Up to ten families, sometimes more, shared one common tap and one loo, the raw sewage passing directly under the tap. Rubbish scattered the common area, ash pits overflowed and the stench was near unbearable. 'Inside the rooms are often dark and damp, and almost always dirty.'

John William Dorgan's experiences were typical. 'In 1900 I was going to school and my parents were very, very poor. I knew poverty right to its limit. I was brought up on rice pudding and broth. These were the cheapest meals anyone in our position could get. I can't remember ever having any meat in my schooldays.'

Ethel Barlow remembers, 'In them days we had oranges but we didn't stop to peel them. We ate them with the peel on. We were hungry – always hungry. I remember buying chips and a lovely lump of fried fish, and when we got home and started to eat, we found about six big cockroaches all fried up, but we just made a joke out of it, and kept on eating.'

May Pawsey's experiences were the same. 'We lit a fire once a week. We only had meat on Sundays, so usually it was just soup with a slice of bread.'

The 1906 Education Act helped matters somewhat, in providing free meals for needy children. Again, the standard of cooking would be horrendously low, with scant consideration given to flavour or culinary experience on the part of the cook. (The same was true at public schools, where the main thing was to stuff the budding empire builder with as much bread, porridge, meat, potatoes and suet pudding as possible, with little regard for taste, never mind the inclusion of milk, fruit, vegetables or salads.) The problem was that the Act was funded by increasing local rates and it was difficult to raise money in the poorest areas, where nutrition was the most burning issue. Nevertheless, by 1911, 200,000 children, those who needed it most, were at least being fed one proper meal a day.

You'd imagine, nearly a century on, that this sort of poverty was long gone. A relic of a dirty past. Yet last October, the *Blackpool Gazette* reported that 'almost two thirds of children in Blackpool live in poverty'. Poverty is defined 'as a couple with two children living on less than £312 per week after housing costs and a single parent with two children living on less than £231'. Conditions and benefits may have improved, but poverty is still rife, alongside poor diet.

As a city, though, there's something rather magical about Blackpool, even in the January off-season, when the lights are off, the hotels boarded up and the revellers long gone. As I wiggle towards the Esplanade and the Palace Hotel, I pass posters for long-forgotten comedians, all-day strip clubs and 'blue' reviews. In winter, Blackpool's a city not so much resting as fast asleep. The hotel is dull and monolithic, a once-great institution now tired and curling at the edges. The less time spent in this dusty timewarp, the better. It broods ruefully over a bleak Irish Sea, where dirty breakers wet a dull-beige sand, making it hardly the most beguiling of places.

Yet despite the out-of-season shabbiness, the place has a latent energy bubbling just beneath the tarmac, as if all the vomit, spilt beer and discarded chip wrappers permeate its very soul. The town might be dead for now, but its heart still beats loudly. Hitler was so taken with Blackpool that he ordered the Luftwaffe to stay away during the Second World War. Apparently he had visions of the swastika fluttering atop the tower and his Nazi troops parading down the Golden Mile. Even if the unthinkable had happened and Hitler had won, I can't see the Lancastrians rolling over without a fight.

It is now mid-afternoon and I haven't eaten for hours. My hunger has changed from a niggling itch to a full-blown obsession. So when Matthew strides through the door, overcoat flowing and brown fedora balanced jauntily on his head, my belly turns cartwheels of joy. Despite the occasional childish spats over life-changing issues such as seasoning steak (he reckons there's no need to salt meat), I adore him and his company.

'Fucking trains,' he spits, removing his hat and smoothing down his bristles of white hair. 'I mean, really, the whole bloody system breaks down just when I need to get up here.'

He's researching fish and chips for an article and I've shamelessly tagged along, because when it comes to the best fish and chips in Blackpool, and Lancashire as a whole, you need focus and laser-like precision. Everyone has their own favourite and they'll defend their choice to the death.

Matthew's mood, already darkened by the vagaries of the British rail system, is made all the worse by a flare-up of gout. 'Now, Tom, gout is not the payback of a lifetime of wine, women and song. It's a genetic thing, not,' he pauses for dramatic effect, 'any reflection on my appetites.' The pain was so severe that he's had to give up booze, shellfish and offal, 'my three bloody favourite things', for a month. To make things worse, his car broke down earlier in the day, and then he 'slipped on the ice and landed smack on my arse'. So he's hoping the fish and chips will lift his spirits. For both of our sakes, I pray they do, too.

As for me, I'd eat my fist with a splash of vinegar. My hunger is starting to actually hurt. I even contemplate risking my life on one of the hotel's sandwiches but to waste my appetite on a wet, slippery flap of ham, squashed between two margarined slabs of dried bread, would be an admission of defeat.

Shaking with barely concealed fish-and-chip lust, we climb on to the tram on the Esplanade and set off towards Fleetwood, a town a few miles north of Blackpool. 'You know how Londoners view Blackpool,' says one passenger, upon hearing our destination. 'Well, that's how we look at Fleetwood.'

It used to be a huge fishing port, but business is somewhat slower these days. Matthew, ever the arcane fact fan, is delighted to find out it once had the highest divorce rate in the UK. 'All those days at sea didn't do much for their sex lives, I suppose,' he muses as we rattle past castellated concrete battlements and the Fisherman's Friend factory, complete with a whiff of menthol and camphor.

We're supposed to be meeting up with a local fisherman, but he's proving elusive. His demand for a fee did little to endear him to Matthew ('The bugger must be joking,' he spluttered) and the nearer we get to Fleetwood, the less likely an option the meeting seems. It's dusk and the tram, the oldest system in the UK, passes a never-ending row of guesthouses, from the Buona Vista to the Robin Hood Hotel. Talk turns from obstreperous fishermen to jellied eel, Matthew's memories of eating grouse in the dining car bound for Scotland and the horrors of the Virgin Train menu.

'I mean, really, Welsh Cumberland sausage? Lincolnshire Cheddar? Is the world going mad?' He then proceeds to tell me, in his cut-glass Eton accent, that he is a Northerner. 'Northern to the core,' he declares, much to the amusement of the other passengers.

Such is the intensity of my hunger that I don't even attempt to argue. Even the most grotty fish and chip shops, the ones that sell curry and chicken chow mein alongside battered cod, take on a mystical appeal as we pass. Ten minutes later, we step off the tram. It's dark now, and bitterly cold. The negotiations with our fish-catching friend have reached an impasse and end abruptly. The only good piece of information to come from him relates to his favourite chippy, Shakies. Day boats leave from Fleetwood, and trawlers too.

There's even a small fish market, opening before dawn. But this is an industry that's long since passed its prime, although the ladies in Lakeland Seafoods, a proper wet-fish shop, restore our faith in humanity once more. There are Dover soles, and gleaming mackerel, John Dory, with their startled faces, fresh crab, Manx kippers and herring melts.

'It's nothing like it used to be,' says Debbie, a smiling, attractive lady in her forties. We ask how near Shakies is. 'Definitely a cab ride, love, over t'other side of town. Don't worry, I'll ring you a cab.'

'Is Shakies any good?' I ask.

She nods. 'One of the best. Everyone knows Shakies.'

Indeed they do. Our cab driver agrees. 'Everyone knows Shakies. I mean, there are probably ten chippies in town but most, including that one,' he says as we pass another, 'are utter crap.'

That one fish and chip shop could inspire such fervour is ample proof that we, as a nation, can talk food with the best of them. Why is it that we can debate batter thickness, chip-cooking mediums, freshness of fish and colour of mushy peas, yet be so seemingly uninterested in anything else related to food?

Like a thousand other fish and chip shops, Shakies is little more than a white Formica counter, a couple of fryers, a jar of pickled eggs (does anyone actually eat these mouth-puckering ovoids?) and particularly lurid soft drinks. In fact, the fish and chip shop is the place to find fizzy drinks long since extinct in the outside world: cherryade, Panda cola and those crenellated plastic pots with the foil lid that were once the staple of my local cinema.

Jackie, a small lady in her fifties, mans the till while Chris Pittounikos, the owner and a second-generation Greek Cypriot, batters the fish and drops them into the bubbling oil. The smell of fresh fish and chips is among the most intoxicating in the world – hot paper and crisp batter, warm vinegar and fried potatoes. I remember being barely able to control myself on the way home from our local chippy, the tightly wrapped bundles on my lap scenting the car and driving me mad with desire. At their best, fish and chips are a world-class fast food – protein and carbohydrate, sea and soil, crisp and soft.

A regular customer wanders in. 'Evening, Joan,' say Chris. 'All good?'

'Oh yes, all the better for being here. Large cod and chips, please.'

I ask her what makes Shakies so great.

'Oh, everything. But the batter is ever so important, and here it's nice and crispy.'

'You've got to throw the oil away every day,' adds Chris, checking on the fish, 'otherwise everything is tainted with that old greasy taste. We use the very freshest fish and cook everything to order.'

As anyone who has suffered a soggy piece of fish cooked six hours previously can attest, good fish and chips need to be freshly cooked. That way, the batter stays crisp and hot, and the fish within delicately steamed.

'We cut our own chips, Maris Pipers, and double-cook them to get that proper crunch.'

By this point, Matthew is eyeing the battered black

pudding and haggis while our fish bubbles away. 'I think I'll hold back on those two,' he declares, his appetite for once overruled by his head. 'But battered black pudding. Now there's a thought to chew on.'

The lights are harsh, but the shop is warm, the window fugged up by the chill outside and our ears serenaded with the soothing fizzle of cooking fish. Only a decent pub can offer a similar welcome. For the first time that day, we both relax.

The chips are superlative, tasting of good potato, fluffy within and crisp outside. 'In Yorkshire, they use dripping, but here we use veg oil.'

Matthew's face drops. 'Dripping still makes the best chips,' he whispers conspiratorially, his mouth filled with fish.

The batter is light, the cod firm and sweet. There's very little more you can say, save that a dousing of vinegar and a blizzard of salt make this dish one of absolute perfection. If it's not the best I've ever eaten, it's certainly in the top ten. The mushy peas, too, are fresh made and a steak and kidney pudding, ordered as a 'snack', has good suet crust and a fine gravy to boot. By the time we leave, the queue snakes outside the door. A few hundred yards away, another place, very much open, stands empty. Say what you will about Fleetwood, the residents are a discerning bunch.

Our next stop is Seniors, a couple of miles outside Blackpool. This is a rather more modern, even lavish affair. There are tables, for one thing, a wine list and even John Dory, monkfish and silver hake on the menu.

'Looks a bit posh,' mutters Matthew as we wander in. Yet haddock and cod are also there, both under six quid a portion.

'Our mission,' proclaims the cheery sign above the door, 'to bring the Fish Experience to as many people as possible. Fresh fish daily from Fleetwood,' it goes on. 'Insist on using our quality local produce, and serve our customers in a quality environment.'

The place is owned by Rick Horasin, a cheery, ebullient fellow who takes obvious delight in what he does. He's a former fish merchant and buys his fish direct from the trawlers.

'This place started life in 1923 as a corner café, very successful until the war. Then after that, it became the Victory chippy, then Seniors. I took over in 2000. I'm just the custodian of this place. Got to keep the momentum going. Now, you must try everything.'

My hunger now abated, I am able to sit back and take a rather more laid-back approach to the fish, chewing slowly rather than forcing it down my gullet like a deranged pelican. The John Dory comes first, dipped in an ethereal batter, halfway between tempura and the traditional stuff. It is sensational, elegant and thin, flattering the incredible sweetness of the fish, each bringing the other to greater heights of edible beauty. It is an exemplary lesson in the art of fish frying.

'We used to make our own batter with French flour but we couldn't guarantee consistency. So we use a commercial mix, whisked up by hand.' If every commercial mix is this fine, then so be it. Handmade doesn't always mean superior quality. The chips are decent, too, although not quite up to Shakies' level.

'With Maris Piper, you don't really get the real ones any more. So four years back, I worked with a seed merchant, and we have the Cabaret variety, then Victoria in season. All the potatoes are grown within three miles of the restaurant.'

Even in the off-season, the place is packed. Then comes the old-fashioned fish and chips, cod and haddock, all luxuriating in their batter shell. The quality is flawless; the contrast between hot, crisp batter and fresh, pearlescent fish sublime. Not forgetting the 'Lancashire caviar' or mushy peas, fresh made every day.

Two fish and chip shops, markedly different but both obsessed with quality. 'Knowing where the fish comes from is important, as is the whole issue of sustainability,' Rick says, 'but I get a real buzz from selling really good fish.'

The industry is huge, and there's barely a town in the land without its own chippy. I once spent a long January day, holed up in the bowels of some blandly corporate hotel, as part of the judging panel of the UK Fish and Chip Shop of the Year. I'd signed up, expecting a day of cramming endless chips and battered cod into my gob. Instead, we sat through ten thirty-minute presentations from the finalists, concentrating on everything from food hygiene to sustainability and customer education. Although the complex technical chat went right over my head (optimal oil temperatures and the like), it was a fascinating few hours, seeing quite how advanced the industry now is.

'Have we another food-catering trade so national in character as the fried-fish trade?' wrote journalist John Steven in 1933. 'I doubt it. Fish landed by British ships, manned by British fishermen, searching the seas from close inshore to the Arctic regions, in fair weather and foul; potatoes grown on our home farms, dripping from home cattle, ranges made by British labour in British factories, and the fuel, coal or gas, from British mines.' Almost a century later, the same is broadly true. OK, some of the lesser fish shops might use pre-cut chips and imported potatoes, while others might rely on the reach of the Nordic fleets. But this is a dish inexorably entwined with our national identity, even if the shops, as John K. Walton writes in *Fish and Chips and the British Working Class*, 'expressed ethnic diversity as well as simplistic solidarity, from the strong East End Jewish element in the early days of fish frying in London, through the strong Italian presence in the trade from the turn of the century, in urban Scotland and Ireland especially, to the growing importance of the Chinese and Greek Cypriots in the post-Second World War decades'.

There's little doubt as to the popularity of fish and chips, eaten by dukes and gravediggers alike. You'll find it neatly plated up in the likes of The Ivy and Scotts, central London glamour magnets, as well as tucked away in shabby shopping precincts, wedged between a pawnshop and Pound Saver. Historically, though, fish and chips has been working-class fare, and among the few foods not to be rationed during the war.

Fried fish has long been street fodder, ever since the middle of the nineteenth century, in London, where it was a speciality of the Jewish community, as well as in the bigger industrial cities of the North. Cooked potatoes were also popular, although sold separately. Henry Mayhew, in *London Labour and the London Poor*, written in 1851, talks of the fish fryers he meets. 'Fishy' had been in the trade for seventeen years. 'I'm known to sell the best of fish,' he tells Mayhew, 'and to cook it in the best style.'

During the nineteenth century, there was a glut of North Sea fish, supplied from Barking, a hugely busy port. Between 1799 and 1823, the supply of North Sea fish to Billingsgate Market rose from 2,500 tonnes to over 12,000 tonnes. The freshest fish would fly off the counter, while the slightly more stinky stuff would be battered in a flour-and-water mix, fried in shallow pans and usually flogged cold. A few steps down the road from 'Fishy' was a baked-potato seller, one of 300 in the capital at the time, who baked his potatoes in a baker's oven and kept them warm in four-legged, water-heated contraptions, sometimes very ornate. Often bought just to warm the hands on a freezing morning, baked potatoes were eaten by every level of society, but, according to Mayhew, 'the working classes are the greatest purchasers.' So while it's probable that fried fish and baked potatoes were eaten together, at what precise moment the baked potato became fried and joined up with the fish no one is entirely sure.

Recipes for fried potatoes were widely available in cheap cookbooks during the Victorian period, such as Alexis Soyer's books *The Modern Housewife* (1849) and *Shilling Cookery* (1855). So there was no exact moment of union, no cry of eureka or moment of clarity. The Lancastrians will claim the dish as their own, as will the Londoners. William Loftas, Manchester frier, fish-and-chip journalist and guru, wrote under the name 'Chatchip' in the first half of the twentieth century. He pinpointed Soho in London as the birthplace of the fried-fish trade, with the Jewish community who lived there as responsible for starting it all off. Conversely, the Lancastrians, he says, were the originators of fried potatoes. 'Lancashire was the birthplace of the chipped potato trade in England as London was the birthplace of fried fish, and just as in London the fried fish trade was carried for years without potatoes, so in Lancashire was the potato trade …'

The argument could rage on for ever and probably will. All that is certain is that fish and potatoes came together some-time towards the end of the nineteenth century and captured the English appetite. In Preston alone, the number of shops rose from twenty-two in 1885 to 155 by 1936. So despite this being a national dish, the marriage of the battered fish and the fried potato certainly had its roots up North, although its true genesis is Jewish and French. Not, then, as genetically English as popularly believed, but for the armies of industrial workers needing cheap, satisfying sustenance, it fitted in perfectly. 'In these close-knit communities,' writes David Mabey in *In Search of Food*, 'the fish and chip shop was as much a meeting place for gossip as a source of food.' The same is true today.

The journey back into Blackpool is a little more muted than the voyage out, thanks to a bellyful of good fried food. Any normal person would have collapsed into bed, moaning gently while chewing handfuls of Xantac. We, however, are made of sterner stuff, determined to cram as much of Lancashire as we can into our rapidly expanding guts.

Next up is dinner with Reg Johnson, Nigel Haworth and Paul Heathcoate, the three wise men of north-west food. Reg farms poultry in Goosnargh, where his famed chickens were the result of Paul's desire for a first-class bird. Reg is a brilliant raconteur, genial and eloquent, telling tales of rugby nights long past where he'd take twisting back roads to avoid the police. His jokes are so filthy, they'd make the Marquis de Sade blush. He can certainly hold his drink, as I've found down in London to my detriment. The moment your pint glass empties, another appears, as if by magic. 'Don't want to lose momentum,' he'd say. We usually end up back in some friend's house in the early hours, me comatose and Reg hardly breaking a sweat. Loved by chefs and fellow producers alike, he's a one-man encyclopaedia on Lancastrian food, history and all things poultry. He'll quite happily spend a whole night, lying on the sitting-room floor, surrounded by diagrams and jottings, creating a new, portable, free-range chicken shed. 'I bloody cracked it in the end, too,' he says with evident pride.

Paul Heathcoate trained under the likes of Michel Bourdin at the Connaught and Raymond Blanc at Le Manoir Aux Quat' Saisons. He went on to open the Longridge Restaurant in 1990, serving up proper English food with local Lancastrian ingredients. By 1994, the place had two Michelin stars and Heathcote settled into his role as restaurateur, opening a whole slew of restaurants. Fit and with a fresh tan from his skiing holiday, he's quick and funny, a brilliant cook and an equally brilliant ambassador for the area. As is Nigel Haworth, broader than Heathcote but fit as a butcher's dog. All three are open and generous and, when together, become more of a well-honed comic trio, relentlessly joshing and teasing, than Northern food saviours. Once they move on to the subject of food, however, they get serious and there are few who can match either their knowledge or their passion.

Nigel owns the Michelin-starred Northcote, as well as a trio of pubs in the area, serving local food and excellent beer. Reg supplies both of his friends with his birds and, together, they've done more for the food of the North-West than any half-baked government initiative. They know every supplier, be it Peter Gott's stunning pigs and boars up in Cumbria, Andrew Sharp's Herdwick mutton or Peter Ashcroft's purple sprouting broccoli. And no shard of gossip, however banal or irrelevant, ever passes them by. Woe betide the black-pudding maker who adds flour to his sausage, or the farmer offering dodgy gear.

Matthew had been singing the praises of Haworth's pub, The Three Fishes at Minton, and it's easy to see why. Here is a blueprint for the entire country, a pub serving food cooked to traditional recipes, made using products from the surrounding area, and not at grossly inflated prices, either. There's Lancashire whitebait, Leagram's organic cheese soufflé, Bowland lamb Lancashire hotpot, Ribble Valley (the area in which we're in) steak sandwich. The cook has a sure hand, which you'd need in order to impress these three. There's no pretension, no forcing of information down your throat. Although huge focus is turned on the producers (there's even a map pointing out the locations of the thirty-one suppliers, from Mrs Kirkham's famous Lancashire cheese to Andy Roe's tomatoes in Southport), there's none of that fluff showboating where menu descriptions not only tell you the name of the cow you're eating, but its star sign and favourite member of Take That too. All three travel the country, introducing their suppliers to other chefs, singing the praises of Lancashire produce, of Lancashire food. If the rest of the country could follow their lead, the oft-cited revolution would happen that much faster. As ambassadors, they're unrivalled.

Passionate as they are, they never resort to cheap provincialism at the expense of other counties. Yorkshire excepted, of course. As proud as they are of their Lancashire roots, they're fighting for national, rather than regional, change.

'We're incredibly lucky to have such a profusion of incredible producers, and we're proud of them,' says Haworth.

We're sitting at a table with their wives and the mood is suitably merry. Matthew, in between filling his cheeks with Forager's cured collared pork and home-made pickles, looks a touch glum, missing out on Worthington's White Shield, a legend among India Pale Ales.

'Right, Tom,' says Reg, who had driven into Blackpool to pick us up. 'Tomorrow, you're getting the Johnson Ribble Valley tour.'

'Even better,' says Matthew, 'you'll get the Winnie Johnson breakfast. Reg's mum, and she's a mean cook.'

Having just tasted a slice of 'Winnie Swarbrick's corn-fed Goosnargh chicken liver pâté', a star attraction on the menu, I could see why. And when Matthew mentions her Eccles cake, I swear his voice wavers a millisecond too long. 'Just make sure you're hungry,' I'm warned by everyone.

Fat chips, fried in dripping, arrive, and potted shrimps, beech- and juniper-cured smoked salmon, an impossibly rich rag steak and kidney pudding, all melting meat and soft suet crust. I force it all into what tiny space remains.

This is pub food at its finest, a direct descendant of the

coaching inn and hostelries that brought England such acclaim. The last thing you'd expect to hear in the kitchen here is the ping of the microwave, as it disgorges yet another molten-hot, pre-frozen lasagne. Yet the prices are on a par with any chain hell-hole. If pubs like this could exist in every county, serving the sort of food that would appeal to all but the most herbiverous, then the traditions of English regional cooking would be in safe hands.

There are similar establishments, like Emily Watkin's Kingham Plough in Gloucestershire, Tom Kerridge at The Hand and Flowers in Oxfordshire and Stephen Harris at The Sportsman at Seasalter. The latter two are Michelin starred but still rely on local produce and traditional recipes. Forget the cloched idiocy of silver service. These places are godsends for the serious, committed eater.

Both Heathcote and Haworth are highly successful businessmen, Johnson too, adored and respected wherever they go, true food heroes and pioneers. It's only sad that other regions don't pool resources like Lancashire and the North-West, working together rather than being bogged down in petty horse-trading and barely concealed rivalries.

The next morning, I escape Blackpool to meet Reg at Swainson House Farm, perched on the edge of the Ribble Valley. It's the home of the Goosnargh duck and chicken, although there's little sign of avian life as I crunch down the drive. His mother, Winnie, is every bit as formidable and opinionated as I'd hoped, but with a warmth, charm and wit that immediately put one at ease. Her recent knee operation does little to cramp her style. 'I'm supposed to use a walking frame, but it's really not that bad.'

A mug of tea arrives, then black pudding, cooked in a sandwich toaster so it resembles coal-black roadkill, or part of a shredded tyre. Topped with a brace of fried eggs and some decent bacon, it is a breakfast upon which empires could be built.

Winnie peppers me with questions as I eat, chatting about the time Paul Heathcote got married a few years back, when there were a dozen chefs in her kitchen. 'One lovely fellow, big lad, is apparently quite famous now.'

'Heston Blumenthal, Mum,' says Reg.

'Oh yes, nice fellow. Just another chef among many that morning, though.'

You get the feeling that it would be near impossible to really impress Winnie and, despite her small frame, bold would be the man who picked a fight with her, verbal or otherwise. She shares Reg's all-encompassing generosity, and her mind is undimmed by age.

Her son, and Reg's stepbrother, Bud Swarbrick, wanders in and settles down behind another mountainous plate of Winnie's breakfast. Reg's partner in the business, he's tall and solidly built with a shiny, pool-ball pate. More introverted than his mother and brother, he walks with a slight limp and is taciturn and slightly guarded. Reg looks after sales and development while Bud takes care of the animals.

'He has a natural affinity with all animals,' says Reg as we prepare for the tour. 'They all adore him, and he can deal with any of them.' Bud chomps on in silence.

Kara, Reg's daughter, strolls into the room, a mixture of all three, with Reg's bone-dry humour, Winnie's strength and Bud's slight reserve. Her Lancashire accent is broad and languorous. She works as the front for the company, the first point of contact for any client or chef. She also keeps the men on their toes, quickly shooting down any tall story or exaggerated tale. The cliché of Northern hospitality is a tired one and the generosity I was shown in the West was astounding. Here, though, I almost feel part of the family. There is such an easy acceptance of the stranger and nothing is too much trouble. All three are immensely proud of what they do, and are only too happy to share it with an ever-scribbling hack.

Reg has to spend a few minutes in the office so Bud takes me to see the duck barns. Where Reg is garrulous, Bud is laconic, offering information only when asked. Like the Sandridge pigs back in Wiltshire, the chicken and ducks here are not free range. A few years back, I would have condemned this without a moment's thought. Surely, I can hear myself saying, the bare minimum standard of poultry welfare is free range, in that the animals have space, the chance to move and to scratch about outside. Anything else involved the appalling battery system of farming, where wretched birds led short, dismal lives, wading hock deep in their own shit, barely able to stretch their wings, let alone cluck and fuss in their usual way. But as I look in at the hundreds of cheeping ducklings, tottering around a wide, airy and spacious shed, it is immediately obvious that these are contented quackers.

'They're an Aylesbury and Pekin cross, for ultimate flavour and texture. And we far exceed the Defra rules in terms of maximum space. We give them 50 per cent more space than the average.'

Reg saunters up behind us. 'We use no antibiotics or growth promoters, and kill at around sixty days. Our clients (which include everyone from Heathcote and Haworth to Mark Hix) depend on the quality of our birds. We make our own feed and ensure the poultry is comfortable and well looked after, because a miserable bird does not make good eating. I get so fed up with everyone bleating on about free range and organic, without realising that there are other ways to produce good chickens and ducks.'

We stroll over to the chicken shed, where a similar mob of chicks run in manic circles. The shed is artificially warmed and has that slight tang of ammonia, not overpowering but immediately evocative of my childhood spent on a farm.

Reg is a pragmatist rather than a romantic, with strong views on any subject you happen to bring up. What about GM food? Is it the future, I ask, or dangerous, untested technology about which we know nothing?

'If we don't have GM foods in the next few years, we're in big shit. Look, GM has been developed to eliminate the need for chemicals. That's a good thing.'

Even when the main investors are the very same multinational that makes billions from flogging chemicals, companies that dream of hooking Third World farmers on one GM strain of corn or maize, thus ensuring the poorest farmers are utterly dependent on their seeds?

He acknowledges that there will be problems, but insists it's necessary. 'Look, I produce poultry to the highest possible standard, and all the chefs and customers keep coming back. I'm a huge supporter of local food, and seasonal food too. It's just plain common sense. And so is the use of GM crops, you mark my words.' With that, he climbs into the Land Rover and we head off into the Ribble Valley.

It's impossible to spend more than a few minutes with Reg and not feel a rush of hope for the future of English food. He is such an evangelist for Lancashire produce, and every farm, house and field we pass is part of some story, another piece of the jigsaw. I try to keep detached, to remember that not every inhabitant of the Ribble Valley buys their vegetables and meat at the farmhouse gate. As we whizz through local towns, there is the usual bland rash of Greggs the Bakers and dreary cafés serving reheated rubbish. They're busy, too, and I can't believe that there's a whole area, a Lost World, if you like, hidden in some ancient valley, where people ignore the edible strictures of modern life, eschewing fast food and processed meals in plastic containers for the joys of locally grown produce. Reg admits as much but as I sit in our Land Rover bubble, while the Ribble Valley flashes by, it's pretty easy to believe the romantic view. It will be all right, I keep telling myself; we are a nation that fundamentally knows how to eat well. We've just forgotten. Then I pass a group of children, downing chips and cheap fried chicken, and the gloom descends once more.

The Ribble Valley stretches as far as the eye can see, not as stunning and desolate as the Yorkshire Dales, but quietly picturesque without resorting to the chocolate-box bland. Thanks to a dampish climate, the fields are lush and verdant, favouring brilliant dairy herds, as in Somerset. The River

Ribble snakes down the centre with the Hodder running parallel for a few miles, before joining the Ribble.

We start a mile down the road from Reg's place at Sheard-ley Farm where 950 goats are farmed. Goat's cheese is possibly the only food I abhor and, however hard I try, I can't get beyond the feeling that eating strong goat's cheese is akin to licking a particularly filthy farmyard floor. But you can't help but warm to the goat, at once dumb and inquisitive, impudent and comic. 'We tend to be very adaptable around here,' says Reg as we arrive. 'It's called survival.'

The goats cluster up to the fence, bleating and joshing, their straggly beards waving in the wind. I try to feign interest, praying I won't be asked to try a sip of their ghastly milk. It gets sent to Butler's near Inglewhite, Preston, where it's transformed into Kidderton Ash and Beacon Blue. The cheeses are said to be exceptional but I'll never know. And I'm happy to leave the tasting to those who can get it down their throats.

'The goats are a mixture of Tollenburgs and Alpines, whose milk quality is first rate,' says Reg as we walk back towards the car. I begin to skip as I realise there's no tasting involved. And when he declares that our next destination is Mrs Kirkham's, one of the legends of English cheesemaking, I become positively skittish, prancing into the car with goat-like glee.

As Lancashire cheeses go, there is none to equal Mrs Kirkham's. It's a great British cheese, delicate and crumbly, lusciously buttery with a mild taste and a finish that is both full and generous. 'There's no doubt it's the king of Lancashires,' says Reg as we pull up at a small, unprepossessing farm. 'It's made with full-fat unpasteurised milk, the only true way.'

Graham Kirkham, Ruth's son, now runs the cheesemaking, although his mother is still very active. She's off shopping, though, much to my dismay. Still, Graham knows as much as it is possible to know about Lancashire cheese, and he's a fantastic teacher, warm and friendly. He seems rather embarrassed by my gushing adoration, shrugging modestly as if to say, this is what I do. Like Jamie Montgomery, he is proud of his product while not given to unthinking hyperbole.

'As you know, the cheese industry was traditionally a by-product of the surplus summer milk. The extra milk was made into cheese during the summer, matured and sold in the winter.' He takes me into a large, new shed, the place where it all begins. 'We've been here a few years now, but it did worry my mother and me. I mean, look.' He points to a small, slightly decrepit brick shed near to the main house. 'There's thirty-five years of cheesemaking history in there, all of it impregnating the roof, the floor, the wall. We managed to produce sixty tonnes a year. And there's something magic in that shed.'

Jamie Montgomery had talked of the importance of the cheesemaking room and here was proof. Fi, who also helps Graham make the cheese, nods. 'We moved in in May 2008. Although the luxury of space was amazing, the cheese's character comes from the age of the room. We did worry at first, although it's good again now, thankfully.'

They use milk from a herd of ninety Friesians, which graze the surrounding meadows. They're well looked after, even getting mattresses in their barns. 'It makes them calm and relaxed,' says Fi with an indulgent smile, 'meaning they produce the best-quality milk.'

'Occasionally,' writes Sarah Freeman in *The Real Cheese Companion*, 'to enhance the taste of the cheese, she [Mrs Kirkham] goes out to plant extra meadowsweet; she also encourages dandelions and clover (rather than daisies, which she does not think add to flavour).' Mrs Kirkham comes from four generations of cheesemakers and the cheese is started using curd from the previous two days. 'It's a 200-year-old traditional recipe,' says Graham. 'Back then, the smallholders would produce milk every day and the excess was made to curd. And after three days of this, there was enough to make a cheese.'

He hands me a thick slab and, once back in the car, I break off a chunk. There are hints of lemon and yoghurt, all tempered by that famous Lancashire tang. Reg describes the texture as 'buttery crumble' and I can only nod my agreement. I stare out across the fields flashing by and thank them for their grass.

This is a whistle-stop tour and at times I feel like a Japanese tourist, being rushed from attraction to attraction. It's entirely my fault, as I had to drive down for a food judging that morning. We drop by Ye Horn's Inn, built in 1782, which gets through about seventy of Reg's ducks per week. 'See, even a small restaurant can't get enough of the ducks.'

As we're driving through the lush pasture of the valley ('This area is mainly dairy, as it doesn't drain too well and the crops don't like it') he points out small stone houses along the way.

'All these,' he says, 'were once small dairy farmers. Back then, they were all protected, insulated, by the Milk Board. They had a guaranteed price for their milk, and it was the same with egg farmers. The EEC saw the end of the milk and egg boards and free trade was, for many, the killer. It's all well and good that food became cheaper but the countryside is the loser. The only way to make proper money these days is to own the super-farms, the massive places that centralise everything.' The alternative is to specialise in quality.

'We Lancastrians are a nation of entrepreneurs, and many of the towns, for example Longridge, which we're going through now, were built on the back of the cotton trade. The atmosphere is a little damper here than in Yorkshire, that's why cotton was so big here. It stretched in the extra humidity.' He slows down. ''Ave a look at that bus stop.' I peer closer. It's called Paul Heathcote. 'What other chef has his own bus stop, eh?'

He grins and we set off once more, stopping only at yet another cheesemakers, this time Bob Kitching with his Leagram organic dairy. Middle-aged, with a shock of greyish hair, he speaks fast, nuggets of information coming as fast as bullets. 'I make all manner of cheese for all manner of people. Some are flavoured with everything from ginger to Marmite and mustard. Here, have this.' He plonks a wax truckle in my hand. 'Oh, and this, our organic Lancashire, great taste and texture. And this, too.' By the time I leave, I'm staggering under the weight of proffered cheese.

I scribble furiously as he enters his demonstration rooms. 'I want to get children excited about making cheese. I make a fresh cheese on the spot. They love it.' His eyes gleam. I hear mentions of Lister and Melotte cream separators, cheese mixers and milk coolers. Despite being an almost one-man band (his daughter Faye runs the place with him), with many orders to fulfil, he happily takes half an hour from his day to pass on his passion. He wants to spread the word and has that messianic glint in his eyes, not from the idea of making money, or for laurels and accolades, just from a love of what he does.

I look up and Bob is enthusing about his day-old Lancashire goat's curd, so adored by Nigel Haworth. It's light and creamy, versatile enough to use in all three courses of a meal. For a moment, I feel a pang of envy. If only I could get on with the goat. In all, he makes twenty-five varieties, from Cheddar to Double Gloucester, but it's his crumbly organic Lancashire I love most, with a great texture and beautiful lactic kick. The creamy and mature are pretty fine too.

I'm loath to leave Reg, to head back down to London, but as I leave, he fills my boot with everything from Winnie's Eccles cakes and Goosnargh cakes (flour, sugar and butter, mixed and baked, then sprinkled with caraway seeds) to corn-fed chickens and ducks. Nothing I say will stem his generosity. As I drive down the M1, the Eccles cakes slowly disappear, sweet, rich and insanely addictive. As I pass Wimpy, I salute. Not out of respect but superstition, like passing a magpie and warding off bad luck. All that remains of Winnie's cakes are a few shards of pastry scattered across my knees and the odd errant currant. Matthew was right. Winnie really is in a class of her own.

LANCASHIRE HOTPOT

'The English cousin of Irish stew', in the words of Jane Grigson, and traditionally a proper working-class dish, using mutton. The purists tend to scream bloody murder if you dare to so much as add an extra sprig of thyme but back when oysters were cheap a couple were tucked under the potatoes. The key is to start with a tough, flavour-packed cut of lamb, traditionally neck or chump chops, although you can substitute the mutton for lamb if you wish. A good, deep, glazed earthenware pot or 'pipkin' makes the dish look all the more impressive.

This recipe comes from Margaret Costa's brilliant *Four Seasons Cookery Book*.

Serves 4

900 g (2 lb) best end neck of mutton (or lamb)
3 sheep's (or lambs') kidneys
salt and freshly ground black pepper
900 g (2 lb) potatoes, peeled
2 sprigs fresh thyme
1 bay leaf
sugar
3 onions
300 ml (10 fl oz) lamb or beef stock
25 g (1 oz) butter, melted

Have your butcher chop the meat into cutlets, trimming them and removing most of their fat. Depending on the size and shape of your casserole, either leave the cutlets whole or cut the meat carefully from the bones into neat pieces. Skin, split and core the kidneys, and cut them into quarters. Season the meat with salt and pepper.

Preheat the oven to 165°C/145°C fan/gas mark 3. Slice the potatoes rather thickly, about 8 mm (⅜ in) thick. Butter your casserole and put a layer of half the potatoes in the bottom. Season well with salt, pepper and a little sugar and sprinkle with a little thyme.

Stand the chops upright on top of the potatoes if you can, and pack the pieces of kidney in between them; put in the onion and bay leaf.

Alternatively, lay the chops or pieces of meat slightly overlapping one another on top of the potatoes; tuck in the bay leaf and cover with the kidney, followed by the onion.

Whichever method you use, season each layer well with salt, pepper, sugar and thyme. Finish with the remaining potatoes, overlapping the slices.

Pour in enough stock to come to the bottom of the potatoes. Brush the potato slices generously with the melted butter, cover the casserole and bake in the preheated oven for about 2½ hours. Uncover for the last 40 minutes or so of cooking time so that the potatoes can get really brown and crisp.

POTTED SHRIMPS

The brown shrimp, *Crangon crangon*, is one of the finest crustaceans in the world, small but intensely sweet. They used to be found in their millions in Morecambe Bay in Lancashire. Potted in good butter, they make one of the finest of all English dishes. Either serve cold with bread and butter, or hot, melted on toast. I still believe Mr Baxter makes the best of all. This is my approximation of his recipe.

Serves 6

170 g (5½ oz) unsalted butter
1 tsp freshly ground black pepper
½ tsp ground mace
½ tsp cayenne pepper
1 small bay leaf
450 g (1 lb) brown shrimps, peeled weight
salt
brown bread, to serve
3 lemons, cut into wedges

In a saucepan melt the butter, then add the black pepper, mace, cayenne pepper and bay leaf. Allow the mixture to cool until it is just warm. Remove the bay leaf and discard.

Divide the shrimps between 6 ramekins. Cover with the spiced butter and a little salt. Put the mixture into the fridge and chill until set.

When ready to serve, toast the brown bread on a griddle and serve warm with the potted shrimps and a wedge of lemon.

BATTERED TRIPE

Don't fear tripe. Seriously, the taste and texture are beautiful once you get over the initial revulsion. Rather than offer some soothing, milky method from Lancashire or Yorkshire (both regions use onions, milk, flour and butter in the recipes, but cooks from the former add a pinch of nutmeg, cooks from the latter a covering of cheese), I'm going for a battered tripe dish. I first tasted it with Fergus Henderson and have since found a recipe in a slim but fascinating pamphlet, *A Most Excellent Dish – Tales of the Lancashire Tripe Trade* by Marjory Houlihan. Among the usual recipes, it also has one for 'Tripe and Prawn Cocktail sauce – an unusual starter'. You're telling me!

I've changed the batter from the recipe into seasoned flour, a tip I learnt from Henderson. Serve with chips, malt vinegar or, even better, a chilli-spiked cider vinegar.

Serves 4

pre-cooked honeycomb tripe, about 800 g (1 lb 12 oz)
plain flour
salt and freshly ground black pepper
big pinch cayenne pepper
vegetable or groundnut oil, for frying

Cut the tripe into small squares, about the size of an After Eight mint, and dry on kitchen paper.

Tip the flour into a large bowl. Season with salt, pepper

and cayenne pepper. Dip each piece of tripe in the flour and shake off the excess.

Heat the oil in a deep-fat fryer or deep pan to 180°C and fry the tripe until golden, then drain on kitchen paper. Serve hot.

WINNIE'S ECCLES CAKES

These are the legendary Eccles cakes from Winnie Swarbrick, one of the country's finest bakers. When I left her farm, I did so laden down with ginger cake, chocolate sponge, butter biscuits and endless other tins. I promise you will never taste finer.

Makes 12

Pastry
225 g (8 oz) plain flour, sifted
pinch salt
175 g (6 oz) unsalted butter
125 ml (4 fl oz) cold water

Filling
115 g (4 oz) currants
15 g (½ oz) caster sugar, plus extra for glazing
freshly grated nutmeg
40 g (1½ oz) unsalted butter, melted
milk, to glaze

First, prepare the pastry. Mix the flour and salt in a bowl, then divide the butter into 4 pieces. Rub a quarter of the butter into the flour. Add just enough water for the mixture to form an elastic dough.

Turn the dough out on to a well-floured surface and use

a rolling pin to roll out into a rectangular strip. Brush off any surplus flour.

Cover two-thirds of the pastry rectangle with another portion of butter, dotting it evenly over the surface.

Fold the pastry into 3, bringing the end without the butter to the centre, then folding over the other third. Then press together the pastry edges, using your fingers or the rolling pin. Give the pastry half a turn so that the folds are to the left and right, and roll out again lightly.

Rest the pastry for about 1 hour, then repeat the process to use up the last 2 pieces of butter. Rest for about 1 hour in between each rolling.

After the pastry has rested for the final time, roll it out until it is 5 mm (¼ in) thick, then cut out with a round 5½ cm (2¼ in) cutter.

Now make the filling. Preheat the oven to 180–190°C/ 160–170°C fan/gas mark 3. Mix together the currants and caster sugar, then add the nutmeg. Pour the melted butter into the currant mixture and stir to combine, then leave to cool.

When the mixture is cool, spoon the filling down the centre of the pastry and draw the edges together. Turn the pastry smooth side up and then roll lightly to flatten. Make 3 cuts in the top to show the filling, brush with a little milk and sprinkle evenly with caster sugar. Bake in the preheated oven for 20 minutes, or until golden, checking after 15 minutes.

3

The Midlands

For a serious voyage into the heart of Birmingham's Balti Triangle, there's no better skipper than Charles Campion. He's an old-school trencherman, a patron saint of serious eating. And as one of the London *Evening Standard*'s restaurant critics, he's trodden the byways and backwaters of the English restaurant scene for many years. Whether in search of bigos in Balham, Sikh kebabs in Southall or unagi in Acton, he's the go-to man for the gustatory-minded. His *London Restaurant Guide* is a bible for the committed gourmand, a shining beacon of clean prose and uncluttered criticism.

Equally at home among the hushed tones and haute cuisine of the city's Michelin pleasure palaces as he is on a plastic stool in a shabby Wembley café, Campion is immune to multimillion-pound facelifts and vapid PR guff, eschewing frills, fripperies and foams to cut to the heart of the matter: does the food taste good? He will plough through endless plates of second-rate fodder, just so we don't have to. He eats, so that we may enjoy.

Charles is a commanding figure, tall and broad, with an appetite well honed from years on the road. He lives up in Worcestershire with his wife and two children, so on his weekly working trips to London there's little time to waste. When truly pushed, he's able to manage up to three lunches in a couple of hours, though he would say in his deep, sonorous growl, with typical understatement, 'That's not to be recommended.'

He's not given to gushing platitudes and insincere praise, and is incapable of a dishonest opinion. If a chef asks Charles what he thinks of the food, he can guarantee to tell the truth, however harsh. Nor will he be your best mate, arm draped over your shoulders, within a few hours of your meeting. For the first five years of my writing career, I only watched him from afar. He seemed imposing and gruff, tearing through tastings with a wit dryer than a Mormon wake. Once he feels you're 'an all right sort of chap', his true character comes out, warm and wryly funny. And with Birmingham and her baltis just a few miles from his home, Charles was the natural choice of guide.

You may wonder what balti is doing in a book about English food. Surely this is the food of Baltistan, a remote and mountainous region of far northern Pakistan? The landscape is dramatic, all towering peaks and plunging gorges, a place that, culturally, is nearer to Tibet than it is to the rest of Pakistan. And the food of the area, the famed balti cuisine, is said to be the high point of any visit, its fresh, vibrant curries cooked in the eponymous vessel (balti means bucket), a twin-

handled, round-bottomed pan. As emigrants left their homeland, sometime in the Sixties, and travelled to Britain – more
specifically Birmingham and the Midlands – in search of a new
life, they brought with them a splash of subcontinental bliss,
a taste of Kashmir just miles from the Bullring. It's a hell of a
story, as epic as it is romantic. A happy tale, too, of integration
and acceptance rising from the post-imperial ruins.

Birmingham City Council is only too happy to trumpet
this delightful fiction, as is the esteemed Curry Club of Great
Britain. The problem is that there's barely a scrap of evidence
to support the case.

'There's no such thing as balti in either Indian or Pakistani
cooking,' says Reza Mahammed, chef, food writer and owner
of the renowned Star of India in London. His fine, aquiline
features wrinkle in barely concealed disgust. 'Balti has nothing
whatsoever to do with Baltistan. I've spent years trying to find
out where the balti really comes from and, as far as I can work
out, it was invented in the Midlands a few decades back.'

Panikos Panayi, in *Spicing Up Britain*, agrees, describing
balti alongside tandoori dishes as 'two new fads, which essentially became marketing catchwords: tandoori dishes, emerging in London during the 1960s, and balti, invented in
Birmingham during the 1980s'.

That's not to say that balti cuisine is a sham, with barely a
link to Pakistani food. No one is claiming that fresh, cheap and
quickly cooked curries were invented just off the M42 at the
fag end of the Seventies. A large number of Kashmiri immigrants made their home in Birmingham and the surrounding
area, bringing with them the food of their region, hearty and

highly spiced. And one of the most popular cooking vessels, used across the subcontinent, was the *karai*, a wok-like cooking pot.

Baltistan itself, however, is a culinary anomaly, an area largely populated by subsistence farmers where the diet is plain and drearily basic. While food may be shared from a communal pot, the residents of Baltistan are far less likely to recognise what we call balti cuisine than their neighbours in other parts of Kashmir. The most likely explanation is that the first balti houses were inspired by this communal simplicity, were even named by a homesick native of Baltistan. Their origins in Baltistan, though, are more myth than cold hard fact.

The balti is now as much a part of modern English food as chicken tikka masala, another subcontinent-inspired English concoction. They're both Anglicised Indian inventions, created by emigrant subcontinental cooks to please the English palate, as are the likes of Madras and vindaloo curries. While the former would provoke blank stares if ordered in the eponymous Indian city, the latter has its roots in a real Goan dish. It was created by the Portuguese, who introduced it when they colonised this south Indian state: and the name comes from the Portuguese for vinegar and garlic – pork is cooked slowly with palm vinegar and chillies (which were also introduced to India by the Portuguese). In a curry house, the vindaloo is more a test of pungency prowess than anything else, a super-spicy sop after a night on the lash.

That's not to say a classic curry house menu is to be sneered at, or criticised for a lack of authenticity. As in any restaurant, there are both beauties and horrors. Some rely on a basic gravy slop for every dish, adding cream or extra chilli when moving from korma to phal (another invented dish). Others grind their spices fresh each day, carefully blending them into a house masala. But it's only in the past thirty or so years that real, regional Indian food has become popular: mustardseed-spiked fish curries from Bengal, or the Parsi dhansak. Right up until the end of the Sixties, Indian food was seen, by the English, as one homogenous whole.

'With few exceptions,' writes Christopher Driver in *The British at Table*,

such as the Tamil cuisine at the India Club in the Aldwych, such places [Indo-Pakistani restaurants] relied on Bengali cooks and Pakistani (Bangladeshi) Muslim owners. Since British Army and administrative experience of India had centred on the meat-eating Muslim north, this suited the market, and although there were still plenty of majors (retd.) who prided themselves on the 'heat' of the curries they could swallow without sending themselves up in flames, customers of tenderer years or sex were better pleased with the mild pilaus, sweet dhansaks and creamy khormas of north Indian cuisine. Late in the 1960s, tandoors – clay ovens – for dry-roasting of yoghourt-marinated and spiced chicken began to be imported. Apart from providing for British taste more rice and less of the various Indian pulses and breads – naans, chapatis, parathas – this type of cooking, whether in cheap student places or in elaborately 'Moghul' settings, continues to dominate 'Indian' restaurants all the way from Newcastle to north Soho.

The Balti Triangle is centred on the Sparkbrook, Balsall Heath and Moseley areas of south Birmingham. Early on a Monday night in February, the area is all but deserted, even though it is as much a subcontinental theme park as the touts and shouts of London's Brick Lane. A garish, neon-drenched tourist stop, it is jam-packed with hundreds of restaurants featuring identical menus and similarly smiling owners, willing you through their doors.

Charles is meeting us at New Street station, and Bill and I are slightly the worse for wear. Bill Knott is a friend and fellow food writer, formerly a chef, then restaurant critic for the *Telegraph*. Like Charles, his knowledge is deep and hard won, and his views are strong, making him the perfect companion on a trip such as this. There was little chance of this being a subdued evening as, after a few drinks, Bill and I tend to conclude arguments by each trying to drown the other out.

Bill had already warned me against the consumption of a pasty back in London ('Marathon, not sprint, old bean,' he counselled, 'and with Charles we need to be at the top of our game.' I made some pathetic argument in the pasty's favour. 'Well, it's between you and your oesophagus,' he said, ending the matter). By the time the train pulls into Birmingham, our spirits are certainly high, thanks, in part, to a surfeit of gut-searing National Express white wine.

'Good evening, gentlemen,' Charles growls indulgently, reclining in a monstrous Volvo like some benevolent despot.

'I see you're in the spirit of things already.' He raises an eyebrow and we shoot off through central Birmingham, eyes glazed and bellies a-flutter.

'Balti is the grandfather of the curry scene round here. It's both a style of preparation, and the thing it's cooked in. It's characterised by simple, fresh curry. The underlying principles are cost – it must be cheap – and speed of service. The price is very low, the food cooked quickly and brought rapidly to your table. And you share, eating with your hands, using naan bread instead of rice.'

We stop outside Al Frash and head inside. Within minutes, we're sitting behind a naan so vast that it covers the entire table. Hot, thin and covered in exquisitely charred blisters, this naan is bread from heaven, manna made whole. It has that blissful combination of the crisp and chewy, like proper pizza crust. Even the usual accompaniments – chutneys that are so often just lurid, sticky mango jam and vomit-scented yoghurt – zing with freshness, prepared to order (well, the chopped onion and raita, anyway) rather than left loitering in some dark enclave of the kitchen.

The joy of eating with Charles is a complete resignation of responsibility. You just sit back and let him do the work. A huge bowl of mutton bhoona karai arrives, shreds of sheep, well flavoured but not overpoweringly pungent, tempered and flattered by pickling spices. The texture is dry, the flavour a perfect balance of the sharp and slightly sweet. Tear square of bread, dip, scoop and eat. Then repeat until you're scraping the last splodge of sauce from the side of the bowl.

Balti lamb pathia comes next, spicy enough to pique the taste buds, sharp enough to pucker the mouth. And various ways with chicken too, all fresh, vibrant and zinging with life. Who cares about authenticity when the quality is this good? There is a freshness and immediacy to everything, rich but never cloying.

Just as we begin to settle in for the evening, Charles is ready to go. 'Right, time to move. On to the next.' I look at Bill with barely disguised dismay. Fast approaching middle age and still unable to control my baser instincts, I had flown out of the starting blocks, indiscriminately filling my cheeks with the food before me. 'Marathon, not sprint, Tom.' Bill's words echo around my head. The thought of my own weight in kebabs is more than I can bear, yet soldier on I must. The bill is less than £20 for a feast that would have floored King Kong. I wobble out into the street, bloodied but unbowed.

'Of all the legacies of the Raj, none is more firmly or more happily rooted in British popular culture than curried food,' notes David Burton in his brilliant book, *The Raj at Table*. But while curry is as popular as ever over here, our own culinary legacy to India was rather less exalted.

> Biscuits (packed in solid corrugated cardboard, with brand names like Britannia), second-rate white soda bread, omelettes, and English breakfasts of porridge, boiled eggs, tea, toast and marmalade … by contrast, from the time [that] the very first Seventeenth-century traders sat down with Mogul princes to dine off delicately spiced meats and saffron rice, the story of India's influence on the British diet has been vast, colourful and fascinating.

So much so that Anglicised-Indian food is now a firmly established presence in the English food canon, with chicken tikka masala leading from the front.

This is a dish about as authentically Indian as curry-flavoured Wotsits, yet it remains one of the nation's favourites, miles ahead of jellied eels and black pudding, more popular than pork pies, cottage pie and Dorset knobs combined. 'It's a quintessentially British dish,' agrees Atul Kochhar, the softly spoken master of spice behind the Michelin-starred Benares in London. 'The inspiration might have been butter chicken. What goes into the chicken tikka masala is purely the way the British would like to eat curry. It's like a blank canvas, adapted for the English taste. You can add a bit of coconut milk here, a spoonful of chutney there, but the basis is still tomato and onion. Any cuisine adapts to the country into which it arrives. It adapts and survives. And any Indian coming to live in Britain would use the local produce in their own way. It's true that Indian food has become more regionally based here recently but the curry attitude is hard to shift. I have a friend who owns restaurants specialising in the food of southern India. He'll have customers who come in and demand Peshwari naan, a dish from the North. And they'll walk out if he says he doesn't serve it.'

He smiles and shakes his head. 'You have to remember that British curry is created not just by Indians in India, but by Indians across the whole empire. Indians living in Ghana, say, or Zanzibar or Uganda. British curries, the type sold in curry houses, are more complex than just Indian. It's a real taste of the colonies.'

As is the case in dishes as varied as salade niçoise and eggs Benedict, the exact origins of this dish are obscured by the fug of time and a slick of PR. An astonishing 23 million portions of chicken tikka masala are dished out each year, which tells us either that we're a nation in thrall to sweet and spice or one with collectively awful taste. The fact is that chicken tikka masala is a wretched hybrid of a dish, a plodding dilution of one of the world's great food cultures. What's the appeal of cheap, imported chunks of desiccated chicken, wallowing in a sickly, cloying swamp of a sauce? Only the English could reduce the curry to such a turgid mess. I know parents of friends, children of empire, who still insist on sullying a fine curry with slices of apple and endless handfuls of raisins. This was an English colonial take on a curry, and there's nothing wrong with innovation. But when the newly evolved version is so inferior to anything that came before it, you wonder about the point of the exercise. It's Indian food for people in mortal fear of spice, second-rate nursery fare with an artificial whiff of the exotic, more *Far Pavilions* than *Passage to India*. It's little wonder that the Indians themselves have little interest in cooking it. Yet chicken tikka masala accounts for over 25 per cent of every order placed in an Indian restaurant.

As to its invention, there's a popular story about a Bangladeshi chef, in the Sixties or Seventies, depending on which version one believes (and, like most urban myths, the details are both sketchy and interchangeable), who has a portion of tandoori chicken returned to the kitchen in Glasgow or Birmingham, accompanied by an order for some 'gravy'. Being a resourceful sort of chap, he mixes cream with spices and a can of Campbell's tomato soup and behold, a legend is born. Some chefs today add cream, others use coconut cream, and the colour ranges from radioactive red to slurry yellow. Every restaurant will have their own take on the recipe, although its origins owe more to canny marketing than historical precedent.

We can, however, be certain that somewhere between the arrival of the first wave of subcontinental immigrants in the Fifties and its debut on the supermarket shelves as a ready meal – in Waitrose in 1983 – chicken tikka masala was born. The late Robin Cook, currying favour as politicians are wont, called it 'Britain's true national dish'. He was far too canny to cite roast beef, or steak and kidney pudding, for fear of the left branding him an old-fashioned patriot. This was more about political mileage than statement of fact. Had he called it 'Britain's true post-war dish', he'd have been rather closer to the truth.

Cyrus Todiwala is a man of strong opinions. Chef patron of Café Spice Namaste in the City of London, he's also an expert on Indian regional food. As he speaks, he fixes you with his dark, chocolate eyes and occasionally seizes your arm to emphasise a point. He arrived in England in 1991, after stints as a chef in the Taj group of hotels in India, and as a pastry chef in Switzerland. He's an ingredients fiend, travelling the country to find British Lop pork ('Oh my God, the fat, Tom, and the flavour. A king among pigs') and Ronaldsay mutton. His views on chicken tikka masala have softened somewhat since his arrival.

'When I first got here,' he growls in a baritone as rich as ghee, 'I came across this chicken tikka masala. And it really pissed me off. As did the fact that Indian food was seen to be made up entirely of curries. How the hell could something like this have come about?'

He hits the table with his clenched fist. I jump. We're sitting at lunchtime in his restaurant, on an early spring day so crisp that you could break it in half and dunk it in chutney. The room is bustling, even in the depths of a recession. I decide to incite more table thumping by mentioning balti. 'Wasn't it a great Indian dish?' I ask innocently. 'It was brought over sometime in the Sixties.'

Crash goes the table once more, as hand meets wood with astonishing force. The cutlery leaps into the air and the glasses quiver with fear.

'Good God, a balti is a bucket in India, used for washing your bum. People would come into the restaurant and ask for a balti and I wouldn't have a clue what it was. But as the years have passed, my views have softened, I suppose. I've accepted that chicken tikka masala and balti are British Indian foods. Well, they're practically English. What do you think of the chutney?'

As he talks, various bowls and plates are laid before me, fig chutneys pepped up with chillies, fresh poppadoms and various works in progress. As a result my mouth is full throughout the interview but, with Cyrus, this is hardly an impediment. Once he starts, the torrent of information and history, cooking technique and anecdote, gushes forth, both unceasing and fascinating too.

'Look, masala in India is chopped onions and tomatoes cooked with minced ginger, with various spices – coriander, fenugreek and the like – added. And yoghurt too. So if you had this sort of thing in Delhi, it would be dry. But the English version ...' Double crash. Bang. A side plate is so moved as to teeter on the edge of the table, shaking quietly. 'Ugh! A gloopy, boring tomato sauce with almond paste and Carnation milk.' Like Kochhar, Todiwala sees the close link between chicken tikka masala and murgh makhani, better known here as butter chicken. 'It's a classic from the old Oudh or Awadh region of India, in the central north of the country, now somewhere in the centre of Uttar Pradesh. The area was synonymous with a devotion to fine Indian food. You take a lot of tomatoes and cook them right down, then add chillies, cashew nuts, for the creamy texture, ginger, a hint of garlic and butter. It's then passed through a sieve.' On cue, a bowl of deep-red sauce arrives at the table. 'This is my version.'

I take a spoonful, and it's rich, fragrant, comforting, the spices discernible but subtle, the sauce coating the entire mouth. A world away from the oversweetened excess of your average chicken tikka masala.

'The history of Indian food in England is fascinating. Everyone assumes that the Bangladeshis, who opened the majority of restaurants in this country, were the first arrivals here. They were, of course, Indians from East Bengal who became Bangladeshi in 1947 with Partition. But the first economic immigrants were Parsees originally from Persia, like me.'

He goes on to explain how cooking food was seen by his community as infra dig, unworthy of their standing and utterly undignified. For the Parsee, 'proper work' involved 'real money, textiles, ironworks and the like, just like the average

Indian businessman'. So the Bangladeshis seized the opportunity and began cooking a version of Indian food. He stops the lesson to wave in some peri-peri squid, sweet and hot, coated with a fresh but fiery sauce. I chew slowly while he watches my face. His food possesses an honest gutsiness, a real depth of flavour which stems from its progenitor's fantastic palate and natural knowledge of how to spice. It's some of the best Indian food – and his dishes come from all over the country – in London.

'So the Bangladeshis cooked Indian food as they saw it. As with the rest of Bengal, their food contains a lot of fish dishes. So why didn't they cook their own, home-style food in the restaurants, rather than some watered-down hybrid? They were just pandering to perception, providing what they thought the English wanted. The Asians never bothered to properly educate the English about their food. God, imagine how different things could have been if they had cooked real Bengali food from the start. So much crap could have been avoided.'

He pauses and stares up into midair, as if to calm his nerves. He's become so involved in his argument, in the story of Anglo-Indian food, that his whole body takes part, feet stamping, arms waving, breath quickening. You can almost taste his passion and it's impossible not to be affected. After a few more moments' silence, he takes a deep breath and puts his hand on top of mine.

'I mean, take roghan josh, for example. Here, it's seen as a fiery dish, with chicken or fish, lamb or vegetables. In reality, roghan is the rendered, chilli-red fat from the mutton. It's a classic Kashmiri dish, made only with mutton, the saddle and shank, marinated in red chilli paste with yoghurt. Whole spices and salt are added, then it is put into a sealed pot and cooked for four or five hours, until all the meat is soft and falling apart, the fat rendered and chilli red. A great dish but here it's just like a vindaloo, basic curry gravy with added chillies.'

Calm once more, he points to a plate laden with Parsee scrambled eggs, thick with chillies and onions, and fried bread. It's indecently good.

I once did a piece for a newspaper, charting a week-long diet where I survived solely on eggs. Charles Saatchi, the art collector, had lost about six stone living on eggs for a year. God only knows how Nigella put up with him, as my wife had almost kicked me out of the bed after Day 3. My intestines became blocked, my gut was backed up to my throat. The only happy memory I have of that week, save coming to the end of it, was the thought of Cyrus's recipe at the close of each day. When I told Cyrus about my ordeal, he rolled his eyes. 'Christ, even a Parsee would have problems with that. Even a Parsee.'

But I'm keen to quiz him on the origins of the balti. We've established that the literal meaning is a pot, but I want more.

'Baltistan is very near to the Afghan border, and traditionally home to the dacoits and thuggees, famous bandits and murderers. What they would do is swoop down on caravans that were laden with all sorts of goods, plunder the whole lot, then disappear. They were always on the run, with a diet to match. Of course, you couldn't grow onions or tomatoes in the mountains. They need deep soil, which the area simply didn't have. But their way of living involved sharing from a communal pot, a cauldron or big *karai*. They'd cook meat on a spit and also share it out. The balti in England is obviously not from that region. What it is, though, is a perception of Kashmiri food, which is very evolved, and parts of the region are supremely fertile, very green, with lots of water, and wonderful vegetables and fruit. But just like the bandits, English balti – this entirely made-up style of cooking – involves communal eating.'

His attitude to such imposters having now softened, he seems more pragmatic about the bastardisation of Indian food. Although I can't see him ever using the dread word 'balti' on his menu, I tell him of my experiences in Birmingham. He nods. 'In the end, if it tastes good, that's what matters, Indian dish or not.'

I ask him what he thinks the British left to the Indians, real Anglo-Indian food, expecting another tirade, instead of which he just smiles.

'I love the Britannia biscuits. Bloody good they are, too. Then the Country Captain, a sort of spicy cottage pie eaten by the colonials at gymkhanas and polo matches. Bloody good stuff.' It's way more than just bloody good; it is, for me, the finest of the Anglo-Indian dishes, spicy, rich and warming, a taste of home made better with Indian spices.

Cyrus talks of vegetable mornays, which, although French, were 'brought over by you lot'. Hardly a cause for culinary celebration, then? 'Well, no, but still popular all the same.' As are plain roast chickens and rissoles, too, although for this last import I apologise profusely. While these gritty, gristly wartime horrors, mean and parsimonious, might have helped us through the war, they're best left there, alongside mock duck and Woolton pie. He shrugs. It's hardly a fair swap, I argue;

we get the spices and techniques of Indian cooking, they get biscuits and rissoles.

'OK,' he eventually concedes, 'we certainly gave you more, in terms of food, than you did us. But London is a far better place to eat these days, for real Indian food, than it was twenty years back. And Indian food can be made as English as you want it to be, as we see in the curry houses. It's just like anything else, from Italian to Thai to China and Malay. These cuisines are adapted to English taste, whether from the colonies or elsewhere. So if you ask me whether chicken tikka masala and balti are English dishes, I'd say yes, they are.' With that, he bangs me on the shoulder, pumps my hand and wanders off to the next table. 'Mr Bell, you old bugger. How the hell are you?'

Back in Birmingham, Charles is ushering us into Saleem's, a few doors up the road from Al Frash, and famed as much for its sweets as for its meat. My tooth has never been sufficiently sweet to enjoy the kulfi, gulab jamuns and rasmalais so adored by many Indians. I find it hard to get excited by any pudding, let alone one that makes the back teeth ache at their very mention. Thankfully, we are here for more balti, and kebabs too.

The room is bright and sterile, more institutional café than old-school Indian restaurant. The kebabs are dry and gritty, yet the naan hot and fresh, and the tarka dhal superb. The baltis are less exciting, lacking the fresh kick of Al Frash. Charles insists on buying a box of teeth-rotting sweets for the journey home, and probably wishes he'd jammed them in our jaws, such is the inanity of our chatter.

The English have long had a taste for spice. As David Burnett and Helen Saberi point out in *The Road to Vindaloo*, 'In England spiced food was growing in popularity long before the British arrived in India.' In fact, our love affair with all things fragrant has been raging almost as far back as the Roman invasion. 'For some two thousand years,' writes Elizabeth David in her preface to *Spices, Salt and Aromatics in the English Kitchen*,

> English cookery has been extremely spice-conscious, [which is] not surprising to anyone in the least familiar with the history of the spice trade in Europe and the part played in it, successively, by the Phoenicians, the Romans, the Arab conquerors of Spain, the Norman crusaders, the merchants of Venice and Genoa, the religious orders which fostered the arts of healing, medicine and distillery, the Portuguese explorers who opened the sea route to the Indies, the Dutch empire-builders who wrested the spice trade from Portugal, [and] the British East India Company whose merchants in their turn made London for two centuries the greatest spice mart in the world.

The court of Richard II, in the fourteenth century, was known for its lavish use of spices, with numerous recipes included in a compilation by the 'Chief Master Cooks of King Richard II'. 'A study of English recipes of the fifteenth century,' continues Elizabeth David, 'leaves one with the impression that to the cook the spices were a good deal more important than the food itself.' By the end of the sixteenth century, fortunes had been made on the back of the spice route and London was a well-established spice Mecca. The British first arrived in India towards the end of the seventeenth century, and many returned home with a taste for masala spices, along with a recipe for their own curry powder.

Hannah Glasse, in her *The Art of Cookery Made Plain and Easy*, included the first curry recipe published in English, in 1747, under the title, 'To make a Currey the India way'. It bears little resemblance to even the most basic of modern curries: meat is gently stewed with water, coriander seeds, peppercorns, butter and onions. Glasse was a fascinating figure in English food history. Many of the recipes in her book are shamelessly lifted from other works, including the anonymous *The Whole Duty of a Woman*, published in 1735. Nevertheless, it is still an important historical document, not least for that first inclusion of curry.

'Curry renders the stomach active in digestion – the Blood naturally free in circulation, the mind vigorous, and contributes most of any food to the increase of the human race,' proclaimed the (London) *Morning Herald* in 1784. By 1780, commercially produced curry powders were available for sale on the streets of the capital and in 1810, the first curry restaurant, The Hindostanee Coffee House, opened there. Owned by Sake Dean Mahomed, it served 'Indian dishes, in the highest perfection, and allowed by the greatest epicures to be unequalled to any curries ever made in England'. While its success was short lived, its influence was immense.

Now, there are nearly 9,000 restaurants catering to the national craving for curry. The likes of Meg Dods (the pseudonym of Isobel Johnston), author of *The Cook and House-wives' Manual*, and Eliza Acton were big fans of curry in the nineteenth century, with Acton's wonderful *Modern Cookery for Private Families* dedicating a whole chapter to the subject. She gives eminently sensible advice: 'With us, turmeric and cayenne pepper prevail in them [the curries] often far too powerfully.' In fact her whole book is far superior to the stolid recipes of Mrs Beeton, although she's often criminally overlooked.

And it wasn't just the masses that had a taste for all things Eastern. Queen Victoria was a curry muncher too. 'On her Golden Jubilee in 1887, Queen Victoria was presented with two Indian servants, Sheikh Ghulam Mustafa and Sheikh Chidda,' write Burnett and Saberi. 'Their job was essentially to wait on her but they were soon instructed to cook curries. The Queen was known to insist on curry being regularly prepared at Osborne House, her retreat on the Isle of Wight. Menus preserved there show that chicken curry was one of her favourites.'

Her grandson, King George V, had a similar taste for curry. Unlike his father Edward VII, a gourmand with gargantuan appetites, George was a lover of basic food, the sort of grub dished up during his nascent naval career. 'King George V had far simpler tastes than his father,' writes Gabriel Tschumi in *Royal Chef*, 'and we had heard that as Prince of Wales, he had shown little interest in any kind of food except curry and Bombay duck, of which he was extremely fond.'

At what point do foreign dishes become naturalised? Do curries have to sit through some half-baked 'Life in the UK test', answering questions on where the cockney dialect is spoken, or when their rubbish is collected? Or do they endure the Tebbit test, quizzed to see whom they would support in a cricket match that pitted their homeland against England? As we've seen, fried fish had its roots in the London Jewish communities, while chips, dare I say it, are probably a French invention (first recorded in 1795, in *La Cuisinière Republicaine*). Roast potatoes and buttery mash have their roots, quite literally, in the New World, while parsley, that most English of herbs, is native to the eastern Mediterranean.

'No cookery belongs exclusively to its own country, or its region,' writes Jane Grigson in *English Food*.

> Cooks borrow – and have always borrowed – and adapt through the centuries ... We have borrowed from France. France borrowed from Italy direct, and by way of Provence. The Romans borrowed from the Greeks, and the Greeks borrowed from the Egyptians and Persians. What each individual country does is to give all the elements, borrowed or otherwise, something of a national character. The history of cooking is in some ways like the history of language.

Dorothy Hartley, in her classic *Food in England*, agrees. 'English cooking is old-fashioned, because we like it that way. We do enjoy foreign dishes and admire Continental cooks, but when we cook the foreign dishes, the dishes, like the foreigners, become "naturalised English".'

And so it is with chicken tikka masala and balti. They're now every bit as English as roast beef and potted shrimps, marmalade and Marmite, regardless of their actual genesis. They were created for the English and have become assimilated into the English culture. That's not to say that any foreign-inspired food becomes automatically English just by dint of its being cooked in the UK. Jerk chicken will always be Jamaican, just as the hamburger is American to its meaty core. We see Branston pickle and Worcestershire sauce as quintessentially English, yet they're Anglo-Indian inventions, made our own by love and constant use. Regardless of your views on chicken tikka masala or balti, you cannot but accept their rightful place at the English table.

Panikos Panayi, in *Spicing Up Britain*, discusses the reaction to his eminently sensible statement that fish and chips might not be as English as once believed. 'The press release attracted attention among the extreme right in Britain, so that my name appeared on a Neo-Nazi website, with numerous public figures, under the heading "Know Your Enemy".' These rabid racist types, though, are so myopic in their worldview that they'd rather dance to bhangra than admit Albion is a land created and shaped by immigration and invasion. They must realise that its food, like that of any other country, is as much shaped by history as it is by climate and geography. Anyway, their ancestors are probably French.

I collapse into bed, to be awoken only by the smell of frying bacon. My head is a little sore and my temperament sensitive, but this is nothing compared to the angst of my gut, which churns as if flooded with molten lead.

'Morning,' says Charles, sitting before a pile of bacon. His wife, Sylvia, looks on indulgently.

I had forgotten the hours spent bending her ear when we arrived home, although she seems to have forgiven me my verbal diarrhoea.

'Right, today we're moving away from baltis and going in search of England's best pint. I kid you not.'

Fortified by a few slices of Gloucester black pudding, studded with big lumps of fat but lacking in oatmeal, and a kilo of bacon, I ready myself for the day ahead. The Campion downstairs loo, though, cannot pass without honourable mention. This should be preserved as a shrine to food lovers everywhere: an entire collection of Alan Davidson's *Petit Propos Culinaires* sit wedged between trout-fishing magazines, American food journals and the collected works of Simon Hopkinson, Nigel Slater and Waverley Root.

I return to the kitchen to find Charles and Bill locked in friendly debate. 'There are only thirty-seven food stories, and they're just redone in different ways,' says Bill. For once, Charles agrees. I sit in silence, as the realisation dawns that I'll be using at least fifteen of these on my journey.

'Nowadays, everyone has done everything, from elvering to umami. There's nowhere left to look.'

Christ, I really hope there is. With that, we climb back into the Volvo and set off to rehash one of those blessed thirty-seven stories.

'I don't know why I ever gave up on a map,' says Charles as he bashes his sat-nav into submission. 'Fucking machine,' he spits, hitting it once more for luck. 'Well, it's died and, with it, our chances of finding The Bull and Bladder.'

We're driving, rather aimlessly, round Brierley Hill, a Black Country town that used to be home to the Round Oak Steelworks. The factory's long gone and in its place sits a shopping centre. We wind through identical trading estates, passing a pub every 100 metres. I've never seen such a concentrated mass of boozers, and a pub-crawl here could turn into a dangerous sport.

Our balti journey over, Charles is determined to show us the best of the other Midlands food. 'It's not just balti. You can't leave without at least a sip of good beer. And scratchings. Damned good scratchings!'

'This was always a great glass-blowing area,' explains Charles, 'and all that puffing is thirsty work, hence the pubs.'

I'm not entirely sure whether he's being serious but it certainly makes sense.

Suddenly, Charles lets out a whoop of delight. 'Gotcha. We're just around the corner.' He glares at the sat-nav, which seems stubbornly frozen mid-action. 'No thanks to you.'

It's ten minutes before midday and the doors of The Vine (better known as The Bull and Bladder) are firmly shut. The pub is a handsome building, with wide sash windows and the sort of warm, unpretentious feel that is impossible to resist. It's a proper boozer, not some gussied-up gastropub with diver-caught scallops and Keane torturing the ears. And it's close to George Orwell's vision of pint-pulling perfection.

'If you are asked why you favour a particular public-house, it would seem natural to put the beer first,' he wrote in 1946, 'but the thing that most appeals to me about the Moon Under Water is what people call its "atmosphere".' Orwell's paean to his fantasy pub, first published in the *Evening Standard* in February 1946, is an eloquent evocation of the perfect English pub – the heart of the community, a home from home and an alternative church for a different kind of worship. He wants a welcome ('Hello, dear', never 'ducky') as warm as a seat by the fire, regulars who 'go there for conversation as much as for the beer', 'draught stout on tap', a beer garden and decoration in 'the solid, comfortable ugliness of the nineteenth century'. Yet proper boozers are an endangered species. According to the real ale society CAMRA, a staggering 1,409 pubs closed in 2008, with even more predicted in 2009. This makes for depressing reading. The smoking ban is part of the problem, with 175 million fewer pints sold in the UK since its inception. Given the cheapness of supermarket booze, a prohibitive tax on beer and the fact that the vast majority of our pubs (20,000) are owned by just three companies, the future of the proper boozer – all sticky-carpeted charm, where a three-course lunch means prawn cocktail crisps to start, pork scratchings as a main course and a bag of cheese and onion to finish off – looks bleak.

'Blessing of your heart: you brew good beer,' runs the Shakespearean bon mot printed across the front of the building, while the area above the door proclaims, 'Batham's Genuine Home Brewed Mild and Bitter Beers'. To the left of the pub is the Delph Brewery, small and nondescript. The pub sits on a main road, surrounded by the usual unremarkable suburban yawn. We could be anywhere from Chippenham to Market Harborough.

'It is the least likely location for a superb artisan brewery,' admits Charles.

We're all staring intently at the door, where a small crowd has gathered, chatting and waiting for the gates to open. There must be forty people, who seem to have emerged, like thirsty ghosts, from thin air. Evidently they know one another, and chatter softly, rubbing their hands to ward off the bitter Midlands cold. The icy air is soothed somewhat by the soft smell of brewing malt. Then the doors open and the crowd floods in, with us in close pursuit.

We settle in a small room in the front, with the queue at the bar already two men deep. All the talk, in thick Brummie accents, is about Villa's upcoming game versus Portsmouth.

'We'll start with the mild,' says Charles. One sip and the pilgrimage makes sense. It's slightly sweet and wonderfully mild, but with a richness that seduces the mouth. The finish is long and languorous, with a hint of hop and a mellow fruitiness that lingers delectably on the tongue. It's the sort of beer that would slake the thirst of glassblowers and steel-workers alike.

Just as impressive is the choice of three kinds of pork scratchings. If there's any better partner to good ale than salted, deep-fried pigskin, I'd like to meet it. Nuts are mere also-rans. Originally, the word described the crisp membrane left behind after the pig fat had been rendered. The fat would be cut into tiny pieces or minced, soaked, then melted over a low heat. What remained was cooked connective tissue, or scratchings.

Joseph Wright, in his *English Dialect Dictionary*, gives examples of the word being used from the Midlands right down to Devon. Anywhere that pigs were raised and lard was made, there would be scratchings, a delectable by-product that was sometimes baked into a cake (similar to the American 'cracklin' cornbread) or, in this area, chopped up, fried and eaten with salt and pepper. Nowadays, it's the skin rather than the leaf lard that's used, and it's baked, along with the layer of fat, until crisp.

Although many brands of pork scratchings harp on about their Black Country roots (there were a huge number of abattoirs in the area, creating a constant supply of by-products), very few actually use British pigs, rather importing cheap pork from abroad and simply processing it here. I've long dreamt of producing a proper British pork scratching, and giving a percentage of the profits back to the pork industry. Food for the soul that salves the conscience. Or something like that.

For me, porky perfection involves a teeth-shatteringly hard crust, in contrast to the soft, gloriously fatty bit beneath. I want them salty and deeply savoury, and I lick the bottom of the bag to extract those last crumbs of porcine bliss. The hairs don't bother me especially, although a thick thatch of piggy bristle is hardly alluring. They're classic British pub food, salty enough to induce a thirst, with the beer cutting through any excess fat.

The RTP Original Black Country Pork Scratchings are as traditional as you could find, a sort of business-class version of the classic Mr Porky. Less bristle, more soft bits. The second bag is see-through and contains a stern warning regarding one's teeth. Again, they manage with some aplomb the balance of the crisp (well, diamond hard) and the yielding. (I have since found a brilliant website, porkscratchingworld.com, which not only lists every possible variety but rates them all too. To you brave pioneers behind the website, I salute you.)

By this point, we have moved on to the bitter, and Charles was right. This is the best pint I have ever tasted, the colour of fresh straw and heavily hopped. At first, there's a sweetness that spreads across the tongue before the hops kick in with their sharp finish. This is beluga caviar to John Smith's avruga, the sort of pint that could convert bitter dissers anywhere. As much a product of the area as the Whitstable oysters are of north Kent, or the cider brandy of south Somerset, this is Black Country bitter at its very finest. And, as pubs go, The Bull and Bladder takes some beating.

CHARLES CAMPION'S CHILLI-PICKLED ONIONS

A truly fine pickled onion has it all – good, crisp crunch, a sharp, spiky acidity, followed by a touch of sweetness to soften the edges. It flatters the cheapest bits of ham or cheese, while never overwhelming the really good stuff. I have a taste for chilli, and love an extra kick of heat too. The best I've ever tried are made by Charles Campion and he's given me the recipe, very kindly, to share with you. It works just as well with whole shallots.

Use sterile jars and, most importantly, non-corrosive lids that are proof against vinegar – corroded lids will ruin the pickle. The heat of the chillies is up to you; the Naga is the world's hottest chilli and gives a decent belt of heat, but Thai bird's-eye chillies are also good. Keep for 2–3 months before eating, so that the chilli heat leaches into the vinegar and suffuses the onions.

Makes 3 small jars

1 kg (2 lb 4 oz) white granulated sugar
1 dssp salt
1 litre (1¾ pints) white 'distilled' vinegar
12 pickling onions
whole black peppercorns
2–3 cardamom pods per jar
3 hot red chillies

Start by making up the pickling vinegar. Put the sugar, salt and vinegar into a non-reactive saucepan and bring to the boil. If you want a pretty pink colour add a couple of sliced beetroot.

Peel your pickling onions and cut into quarters (vertically so that they can fan out, but still remain joined together by the core).

Pack each jar with quartered onions, adding a good pinch of whole black peppercorns and 2–3 cardamom pods. In each jar, thrust a small, whole, fiery chilli into the heart of the onions.

If using beetroot, remove and discard. Ladle the hot vinegar into each jar until it is full to the brim. Seal the lid and then invert the jar so that the 'air gap' is sterilised by the hot vinegar. Store in a cool, dry place.

CYRUS TODIWALA'S 'COUNTRY CAPTAIN PIE' WITH MUTTON AND SPINACH

I first ate this on the set of *Market Kitchen*, a food programme that I co-present. It was the first item of the day and I was suffering from an excess of booze the night before. At first, the idea of a mutton-based, Indian-tinged shepherd's pie seemed too much, with too many flavours bashing about, but, as is usual with Cyrus, the end result was superb. Try to find the best mutton, preferably about 2–3 years old, not some raddled old beast full of grease.

Originally, this dish was said to have been made with chicken, chilli and turmeric. 'The Raj's most celebrated chicken dish is country captain,' writes David Burton in *The Raj at Table*, 'but its origins are not entirely clear.' Apparently the term 'country' used to mean anything Indian rather than British in origin and the 'captain' refers to the boss of a boat. Cyrus's version was also served during the Raj years, at gymkhanas and polo games.

This is Indian shepherd's pie: fusion food for the homesick administrators of empire. Serve with hot naan bread or steamed rice.

Serves 6

Masala paste
1 tsp cumin seeds
1 tbsp coriander seeds

50 g (1¾ oz) ginger
50 g (1¾ oz) garlic cloves

Filling

2–3 tbsp sunflower oil
1–1.25 kg (2 lb 4 oz – 2 lb 12 oz) cleaned shoulder of
    mutton, trimmed and cut into large chunks
2 x 2½ cm (1 in) pieces cinnamon stick or cassia bark
1 whole green cardamom
2–3 cloves
3–4 peppercorns
2–3 large dried chillies, chopped
3 onions, peeled and chopped
200 g (7 oz) tomatoes, chopped
1 tsp salt
1 heaped tbsp fresh coriander, chopped

Topping

1 tbsp butter
½ tsp cumin seeds
3–4 large baking potatoes, peeled and cut into chunks
2–3 garlic cloves, peeled and chopped
1 dried chilli, snipped into small pieces
250 g (9 oz) spinach, washed and coarsely shredded
2–3 eggs, beaten

First make the masala paste. Preheat the oven to 140°C/
120°C fan/gas mark 1.

Toast the cumin and coriander in the oven until they

change colour, checking them regularly to ensure they don't overcook. Remove from the oven and allow to cool (but leave the oven on).

In a blender or food processor, grind together the ginger, garlic, roasted cumin and coriander to a fine paste with a little water. This is your masala.

Next, make the filling. Add the oil to a large casserole and heat until a light haze forms on the surface. Reduce the heat a little and add the pieces of mutton. Brown on all sides until the meat is well sealed.

Remove the mutton from the casserole and set aside. Add the whole spices and the red chillies to the pan and fry lightly for about 1 minute on a medium heat until the cloves swell slightly. Deglaze the casserole by adding a little water. Use a wooden spatula to scrape up all the flavour-rich bits from the bottom of the pan.

Add the chopped onions to the liquor and fry lightly until soft. Continue to cook until the liquid evaporates and you are left with a sauce.

Add the masala paste and stir to combine. If necessary, add a little more water to loosen. Continue cooking for 5–6 minutes.

Return the mutton to the casserole, stirring well to coat with the masala. Check the seasoning.

Lower the heat and cover the pan tightly with a lid. Cook for 35 minutes, turning the meat after 15 minutes.

Add the chopped tomatoes and some water if the pan is dry, cover and continue cooking for another 10–15 minutes or until the meat feels soft and the juices run clear.

Using a slotted spoon, remove the meat on to a tray and leave to cool. Remove all the whole spices carefully from the sauce and discard.

Once the meat is cool enough to handle, remove from the bone, shred and return to the casserole with the masala sauce. Return to the heat and cook very slowly until the meat and sauce reduce and become thick. Add the fresh chopped coriander and check the seasoning.

Transfer to a new, clean casserole dish, leaving approximately 3 cm (1¼ in) head room.

Finally, make the topping. In a medium frying pan, heat the butter, add the cumin seeds and let them colour gently but do not allow the butter to burn. When coloured, remove using a slotted spoon to a large bowl but do not wash out the pan.

Boil the potatoes until soft (about 15–20 minutes). Drain and pass them through a potato ricer. Add to the bowl with the cumin seeds and set aside. Retain the pan used for the cumin.

Add the garlic and chilli to the pan of butter in which the cumin was cooked and fry lightly for 1–2 minutes. When the garlic is pale golden, add the spinach leaves, toss for 1 minute until soft, then season. Spread the spinach and garlic mix evenly over the lamb in the casserole.

Blend the beaten eggs into the potato, and beat until soft and smooth. Spread the potato over the spinach evenly, roughen the surface a little with a fork, and bake in the hot oven for 10–12 minutes or until golden. To get a nice colour on top, after 3–4 minutes increase the oven temperature.

REAL PORK SCRATCHINGS

Served hot and sprinkled with salt, these make for a classic English snack or aperitif, best eaten with a glass of cider or strong ale to cut through the richness. Use the best rind you can find, preferably from an English pig. The Lop makes a superb version.

pork rind, sliced into strips 2½ cm (1 in) wide (as much as you think you can eat)
sea salt, for sprinkling
vegetable oil, for deep frying

Preheat the oven to its highest temperature.

Lay the strips on a rack placed over a roasting tray full of water (to stop the oven filling with smoke).

Sprinkle the sea salt over the rinds, then roast in the preheated oven for 10–15 minutes, or until the rind is bubbling and turning golden.

Remove the rind and cut into 4 cm (1½ in) pieces.

Half-fill a deep, heavy-based pan with vegetable oil and heat until a piece of bread turns golden brown in about 20 or 30 seconds. Remove bread, drop in rind and fry for 2–3 minutes, until puffy and golden. Remove with a slotted spoon and drain on kitchen paper.

Sprinkle over a little extra salt and eat immediately.

BALTI CHICKEN AND MUSHROOM

Despite its hailing from Birmingham, rather than the mountains of Baltistan, a good balti is still a wonderful thing, fresh, vibrant and packed with flavour. Sadly, I couldn't get hold of the recipe from the brilliant Al Frash, but this one, from Pat Chapman's *The New Curry Bible*, is a good 'un too. It does contain some ingredients that might seem less than Indian (basil and chillies) but, as I've said, this is not a real Indian dish but a modern mêlée of all sorts of influences. Adjust the number of chillies if you want more (or less) heat. Remember, it should be eaten with naan, not forks and spoons.

The basic recipe for the masala mix, given at the end of the main recipe, makes 200 g (7 oz), enough for 8–10 balti recipes, and it will keep for months in an airtight, screw-top jar.

Serves 4

2–3 tbsp butter or ghee
1 tsp white cumin seeds
½ tsp lovage seeds
3–6 garlic cloves, peeled and finely chopped
3–4 tbsp balti masala mix (see below)
200 ml (7 fl oz) chicken stock
500 g (1 lb 2 oz) skinned chicken breast fillets, cut into
*   3 cm (1¼ in) cubes*
225 g (8 oz) spring onions, leaves and bulbs, chopped
1–2 green chillies, chopped
350 g (12 oz) button mushrooms, cleaned and sliced

1 tsp garam masala
2–3 tbsp finely chopped fresh coriander leaves
1–2 tbsp finely chopped basil leaves
salt, to taste

Heat the butter or ghee in a karai or wok on a high heat and stir-fry the seeds for 10–15 seconds. Add the garlic and stir-fry for a further 30 seconds.

Add the balti masala mix with just enough stock to make a paste, and continue to stir-fry for 1 further minute.

Add the chicken and stir-fry at the sizzle for 8–10 minutes, drizzling in more stock, little by little, so that the sauce thickens but never overwhelms the dish.

Add the spring onions, chillies and mushrooms with any remaining stock, and simmer for about another 5 minutes.

Test that the chicken is cooked right through by removing a piece and cutting it in two. If there are any traces of pink, return the pieces to the pan and continue cooking. Keep testing until the chicken is fully cooked, then add the remaining ingredients and salt to taste. Simmer for another 1–2 minutes, then serve immediately.

Balti masala mix
10 g (¼ oz) aniseed
10 g (¼ oz) fennel seeds
10 g (¼ oz) allspice
70 g (2½ oz) garam masala
60 g (2¼ oz) curry masala
20 g (¾ oz) garlic powder

10 g (¼ oz) ground ginger
10 g (¼ oz) chilli powder

Roast and grind the aniseed, fennel seeds and allspice. Allow to cool, mix with the other ingredients and store in an airtight jar.

4

The East

Visit Kent, they say, and come to where the fun farming is. Not the boring stuff, the beets and the brassicas of Lincolnshire and East Anglia, but the sweet cherries and bitter hops, the cobnuts, plums and apples. This is Pop Larkin country, a place of foaming ales and groaning tables, doors left unlocked and buxom gals.

The reality is rather less bucolic. The stinking yellow of oilseed rape has overtaken the fragrant apple and cherry blossoms, and uniform blankets of barley and wheat have long since overgrown the hops. Of course, you can still find the odd independent hop farm or cherry orchard, but these are the exceptions rather than the rule. To see the true breadth of our national fruit collection, then the mighty Brogdale Horticultural Trust, near Faversham, is a revelation, with nearly 2,000 varieties of apple, 306 kinds of cherry, 305 types of plum and 70 strains of redcurrant. And that's just the start.

For centuries now, the country has been known for two famed breeds of sheep: the sturdy Romney Marsh graze on the eponymous salt marsh, big beasts with deeply flavoured flesh; and the Southdown, 'the best lamb in England', according to Dorothy Hartley, feed on the turf of the chalk downs. Because they are lowland sheep, their tails are docked (unlike their mountain cousins, which keep theirs intact), cooked and enjoyed as a spring treat, in a pie, with green peas and hard-boiled eggs. From the north coast come the best Whitstable oysters, and fat cockles too. It is here, a mile or so east of Whitstable, that I am headed, to see a chef whose passion for local ingredients is matched only by his fascination with the history of the region.

Stephen Harris is the owner and head chef of The Sportsman at Seasalter. The story of his life, and his findings about the area in which he works, are among the most fascinating and inspirational of my whole journey. His entire approach to the food he sources, cures and eats is intrinsically bound up in the history of the place, and what he is doing at The Sportsman is so localised and unique that I doubt it could succeed anywhere else.

However, if there's a more grimy, frustrating and downright gloomy road than that of London to north Kent, I'd be amazed. This is a route that makes the drive from Heathrow into the capital look like the Yellow Brick Road. It's like one never-ending concrete puke, from the excruciating crawl down the Embankment, all fumes and furious faces, to the dreary squeeze through the Blackwall Tunnel. Once you're out and on the other side, there's still more relentless urban sprawl. If

Kent is the 'Garden of England', then the A2 is its pock-marked, tarmac path, complete with rusting beer cans, empty fag packets and dirty, prefab sheds.

Yet Kent is a county often at odds with its traditional image. For those who like their Michelin-starred restaurants to be gleaming and picture-perfect, The Sportsman might initially disappoint. It sits with its back to the sea, which is a mere cobnut's throw away behind a bank constructed by fourteenth-century monks to keep the sea at bay. The restaurant is a slightly sprawling amalgam of seventeenth-century shooting lodge, late-Victorian main structure and Edwardian extension. A rather dilapidated caravan park spills across the back garden, just beyond the neat vegetable patches throwing up their first spring shoots. 'It's a very difficult building,' Harris admits with a rueful smile.

He's in early middle age, bearded and relaxed. 'Lots of people think I named this place to show I had Sky Sports, or something along those lines. Actually, this was once a great hunting area, hence The Sportsman.'

It's just after midday and the first guests are trickling in, a quartet of pensioners, regulars and locals, who mill about the bar, sipping Shepherd Neame beer. His route to Michelin glory, though, was hardly conventional. No sweaty stages in Parisian hell-houses or ritual, sadistic humiliation for over-cooking the cutlets. Harris has the easy air of a chef who's trodden his own path. Born in Whitstable, he didn't train as a chef but read History at King's in London.

'As a boy, on my way to school, I used to wonder what those mounds over there were.' He points out the window to what look like random lumps of earth. 'Then, I assumed they were Anglo-Saxon burial mounds but now I know that they're salt pans. I mean, with a name like Seasalter, you'd certainly expect some salt production.'

He taught history and geography in a London school for three years. An unusual start, I remark, for a Michelin-starred chef.

'I was always interested in food, and even when I was seventeen, back in 1977, I was constantly cooking up dinner parties, plaice stuffed with prawn mousse with tarragon beurre blanc, real fancy stuff. Oh, and I was a guitarist in a punk band too. To be honest, I don't think I was quite sure where my head was.'

By now, the car park is filling up, fat, smug Bentleys next to battered Fiats, growling, two-seater Mercedes crouching alongside family vans and motorbikes.

The seeds were sown early, after Stephen left university. He worked for a while in France, putting up campsites with ten other blokes. They pooled their money each week and Stephen took over the cooking. 'So I ended up spending ten months driving around each region, shopping in markets, boning chickens, making stocks, that sort of thing. While everyone else was sweating away, I got to swan about, sitting in cafés for most of the morning, then rushing around the market to get the food.'

Back in London, working in education, his interest turned into a fixation. 'I'd bomb down to Harrods or Harvey Nichols and spend all day preparing dinner. I was utterly obsessed but on a teacher's salary I couldn't afford to eat in any of the best restaurants.' His move into the City world of high finance meant more cash and his Damascene conversion occurred in the temple of Nico Ladenis.

'In 1992, I went to Chez Nico, my first Michelin place.' He stops, and his eyes glaze over. 'It was just, oh God,' he says, grinning at the memory. 'I just couldn't believe the attention to detail, the clarity of the flavours. It was stiff, formal, unashamedly grand, but I'll never forget it. Then I got to thinking, why couldn't you replicate the food in a more relaxed setting, so you could enjoy it even more?' He went back to eat there, again and again, 'Ten times, at least. Christ, even three times in one week. They probably thought I was a Michelin inspector.'

He glances up at the diners flooding in. He had told me that today should be quiet, a Tuesday with drizzle. He is wrong. The restaurant is near full and still they flood through the doors. He returns to London haute cuisine.

'Anyway, I went to all the best places, Marco Pierre White at the Hyde Park Hotel, Le Gavroche, La Tante Claire, The Waterside Inn. I wanted to be a chef and I was really doing all this because I don't believe you'll ever be a great chef without eating the very finest food. Now, let me show you outside.'

We climb the bank and face the sea. A small fishing boat lies stranded in the grass, about ten metres in front of us; behind it is a tractor, wrapped in green tarpaulin. There's not a soul in sight, just boarded-up beach huts and the relentless grey of the Thames Estuary. We stand in silence, a chill wind needling us with salty sleet, then turn, looking beyond the restaurant, to gaze at the marshes that stretch away from us, where sheep graze like dirty balls of cotton wool. Rain-blurred hills skirt the horizon.

'Now, I don't want to sound pretentious,' says Stephen, with a hint of embarrassment, 'but in great art there's always a story, the narrative that enhances the object's beauty. And it's the same with food.' He pauses, not for dramatic effect, but to allow my scratching pen to catch up. 'As a historian, I started to look into the history of Seasalter, to see if this could inform the way I cook. As I started digging, things got more exciting. Now, look around.'

We turn back into the wind and I squint against the onslaught.

'The sea provided cod, turbot, sole and the rest, and the bay is, of course, famed for the quality of its oysters and shellfish.' He turns again. 'Then we have the salt marsh, where the sheep would graze. Well, still do. And all manner of game in the land to our right, with pigs kept up on the hills. So it had everything you needed.' A lone seagull wheels high above our heads, its raucous squawk lost in the gusts. 'But here's the thing.'

He goes on to explain that Seasalter is one of only seven boroughs in the whole of Kent. These boroughs, back in the Middle Ages, had elevated status and special privileges not enjoyed by other, more lowly areas. There was no question why the other six gained this accolade: Canterbury and Rochester were chosen for their religious significance, while Sandwich, Hyde, Romney and Fordwich were important ports. But Seasalter was neither of these things.

'So why did this little patch of land get such exalted status?' His eyes gleam with excitement.

A few years back, entirely by coincidence, Stephen bumped into an old archaeologist mate, Tim Allen, in a café in Whitstable. And he, by a strange quirk of fate, had just written a paper, 'Swine, Salt and Seasalter'. In it, he had discovered that Seasalter's status came from the fact it was owned by monks and supplied the kitchen of the Archbishop of Canterbury. Back then, this was the equivalent of having a royal warrant plus a contract to supply every Gordon Ramsay restaurant, the Wembley Arena and The Fat Duck to boot.

The kitchens of the most important man in the Church, bar the king, were lavishly appointed and the feasts prepared there were every bit as grand and decadent as those of the royals. The lavishness of the archbishop's kitchen knew no bounds, getting through tonnes of dizzyingly expensive spice per year. Here you'd find the English haute cuisine of the time.

Stephen goes on: 'This was a genuine ancient *terroir*. The game, the fish, shellfish, lamb and pigs. And, most important of all, the salt from the marshes to preserve it all through the winter. It was like some eureka moment. I felt that my coming here – and I knew virtually nothing of the history – bumping into Tim and starting to produce my own food, was somehow fated, serendipitous. I mean, I'd been buying my meat from Monkshill Farm for years, over there, on the hill,' he points to a small cluster of buildings in the distance, 'and I never thought as to the origin of its name. I'd been banging on and on about the concept of *terroir*, without realising I was sitting right on top of one of my own.'

At the moment, he uses Large White pigs ('His firm bone stands up to his heavy weight,' writes Dorothy Hartley approvingly), Old Spots ('The low belly particularly full and thick to afford streaky bacon,' she coos) and the Oxford Sandy Black ('God, the fat on those pigs … just stunning,' Stephen sighs). As for sheep, he favours a Norfolk-Charolais cross, but he's also looking at the indigenous animals, Romney Marsh sheep. 'I work closely with Monkshill, experimenting with different feeds and mixes to find the perfect breed for this area.'

We stare through the driving drizzle, imagining the scene a century back. Little would have changed, save for the great ugly pylons, which bestride the view like mighty steel louts. 'Look at those bloody things.' He shakes his head, less angry than frustrated. 'This has been, and still is, a cheap holiday destination for the London working class. Close enough for an easy journey, offering sea, sand and the rest. And that's what gives Whitstable its character. But seeing as there's not much money here, no powerful rural voice, the powers-that-be couldn't care less and have absolutely no respect for the place. Typical. People often say, why don't we get rid of the caravans in the back garden and replace them with modern rooms, spas and all that? The caravans are quite ugly, but good people have been coming on holiday here, in these caravans, for many years. They're cheap and accessible and I don't want to be some bastard, kicking them out. So they'll stay put.'

We wander back into the restaurant, which hums content-edly, and go through into the kitchen. The atmosphere is one of quiet, unassuming focus, silent save for the bubble of a stock, the sizzle of steak meeting pan. What I find so fascinat-ing is how the history of the region – or, to be more specific, the history of the few hundred square yards of land surrounding us – fits so neatly with his philosophy of food.

'But I never want this to turn into some sort of culinary theme park, a stop on the map to tick off. I want to use this history in the way an artist would, as a means of inspiration.' He pauses, then grins. 'I'm sounding pretentious again, aren't I? We make all of our own salt from the sea and, apparently, we're the only restaurant in the world doing so.' He shrugs. 'It's hardly difficult, and the end product is great. So why not?'

As we walk through the small, slightly cramped kitchen, he introduces me to Dan, calm and bearded, forcing paprika-spiked pork into a slippery case.

'He's my number two, and brilliant at making sausages and chorizo. We also churn our own butter, from the local milk.'

We walk through into the beer store, where half a dozen barrels of Shepherd Neame beer lie on their sides, with tubes snaking through into the pub. Hanging from the ceiling, from a wooden clothes dryer, are about twenty hams, salamis and chorizo, all in different stages of ageing.

'Environmental Health hell,' he admits. 'But we work together. And our officer is brilliant.' However, like every other chef and producer, he's not a huge fan of the general idea of Environmental Health inspectors. 'Half of them wouldn't know how to fry an egg, let alone make a ham. And it seems some go out of their way to make life difficult. Still, at least ours is good. Now, look at this.'

He unhooks a withered piece of pig and puts it to my nose. It smells of must and old salt. 'This is over a year old and we make it in the style of the Spanish Jabugo. The pig leg is deboned – we don't have enough space, sadly, to keep the bone in – then salt is rubbed in and left for twelve days. We age it in here for up to eighteen months. I also do lardo,' he points to an off-white block of cured back fat, 'and can't wait to do more. At the moment, the rest of the stuff is hanging in Janet Street-Porter's cellar. She has a house around the corner and is a regular. So she's helping me out.'

I look at the cheeses, sitting in the corner. They're mainly French. 'Surely,' I ask, 'someone so particular about the food of the *terroir* would go for English cheese?' I'm wrong.

'You forget how close to Normandy we are here. Instead of getting some huge lorry thundering down the M1 with Mrs Kirkham's Lancashire, or decent Cheddar from Somerset, the Norman cheeses are actually much closer and more part of the *terroir* than many far-off English ones. People have to stop being so myopic with local food, open up a bit more and look at history. France is much closer than Manchester. That said, the Ashmore cheese is a good one, and made near by. But rather than eat it slightly aged, I think it has potential to improve with a far longer maturation.'

Traditionally, Kentish cheeses were rare, as little of the land was used for dairy herds. And Stephen's right. In many ways, this part of Kent is as much French as it is English anyway.

'So that's what I'm doing here. Experimenting, trying out new things. That's what I care about.'

Behind the kind, hirsute face, I sense, is a will of steel, a man who refuses to put anything into trite categories, or toe the well-worn line. He employs Spanish and French charcuterie techniques on English beasts, and uses the local seaweed, collected from the beach, in an oriental fashion. 'I make it into a seaweed butter and serve it with the scallops. You wait, it could be the star of a Japanese menu. Yet there's nothing more English, more of the area, than fresh scallops, with home-made butter and freshly gathered seaweed. It's all about what you do with these ingredients.' Admittedly, the Asians don't share our love for dairy products but it's Stephen's thinking that is so different.

'Without wanting to sound rude, when I first arrived, in November 1999, people wanted what they were used to, an incinerated steak, side portions of vegetables, everything piping hot. When I refused, they left. Funnily enough, though, after we got the Michelin star, they started to creep back. I want food and flavours and ingredients that no one else can do, staying loyal to local produce and to the *terroir*, but constantly moving forward. This is a work in progress and I feel that we've barely scratched the surface.'

The last time I heard about culinary works in progress was interviewing Ferran Adrià, the genius behind El Bulli on the Costa Brava, often cited as the Best Restaurant in the World. Adrià's food is complex and highly technical, both whimsical and deadly serious, treading a thin line between brilliant and bonkers. Yet despite the obvious differences – for all Harris's passion and ingenuity, he is not yet transforming his native oysters into glimmering, agar pearls – they share a similar philosophy and their food is a constantly evolving entity that cannot be pinned down with one iron-clad description. Harris is as much a visionary as Adrià, albeit on a different path.

'Alan Passard, the chef, said that nowadays great restaurants are about what goes on in the field. And I agree. English food can be so exciting. I mean, why can't we look at it the way the Thais do, as in a balance of sweet and sour, salty and hot? We have native products in all of those categories. I'm not trying to be clever, just thinking about English food in a different way. We have nearly a thousand years of food history in Seasalter, and I want to continue that line. And it would only work here.'

Far from being conceited and dismissive, he's low-key and modest, pragmatic rather than dogmatic, ambitious rather than avaricious. And he is as important a figure in the new English food pantheon as Heston Blumenthal, Mark Hix or Fergus Henderson.

Sitting down to lunch, I'm not sure what to expect. 'This isn't like a London gastropub,' he had explained earlier. 'They're supposed to be good neighbourhood places, offering solid food. We're a destination restaurant in the classic French style, a reflection of the area we're in. But if being part of the so-called gastropub movement helps – we are in a pub, after all – then so much the better.'

A tiny chunk of the sweetest, home-cured herring arrives first, plump and moreish. Then scraps of pork scratchings, still warm from the oil, with the sort of flavour and texture only the finest pigs can produce. They manage to both melt on the tongue and provide that delectable, all-important crunch, the sort that will jar fillings from deep in your jaw. 'Our pigs are fed on trimmings from the kitchen. Not, as someone reported, leftovers,' Stephen says as he plonks them before me. He's now in his chef's whites, back at the helm of his kitchen. 'That got us in the real shit with the Environmental Health.'

Alongside the deep-fried pigskin is a pile of his salt, clean and pure, and three kinds of home-made bread; a proper, chewy sourdough, a seriously lactic soda bread, in the best possible way, and a billowy foccaccia, studded with caramelised onion and rosemary. Usually, my disdain for flavoured breads knows no bounds. Why in God's name do I want walnuts chucked in my bread or, worse still, sun-dried tomatoes? What's wrong with an old-fashioned, honest-to-God, brown or white loaf? This, though, makes every ingredient fight for its place. For once, and once only, the flavoured bread gets a fulsome thumbs up.

The butter, too, is no mere gimmick, but impossibly creamy, possessed of that farmhouse acidity and charm so lacking in our commercial brands. Spread it on to the soda bread and you have double-cream action, dairy-on-dairy debauchery that titillates the palate and sends the mouth into spasms of joy.

Just as I'm recovering from bread hysteria (and that hasn't happened for a long while), a Whitstable rock oyster arrives, snugly wrapped in Stephen's home-cured ham, then quickly fried. Sea and field come together in joyous union. It's a one-chew treat and barely has it dropped into my stomach than a plate of the ham, thinly sliced but otherwise naked, arrives. The texture is initially dry but once the fat melts, with all the depth of a nutty Jabugo, it lavishes each and every taste bud with indecent attention. Seriously, and I speak as a ham freak, this would stand shoulder to shoulder with anything from Bromham to Parma.

At the table opposite me, a young couple discuss each mouthful in hushed tones. To my right, a middle-aged couple, serious and sensible, ooh and aah. 'The best soup I've had in a long while,' the slightly florid-faced man muses of the mussel and bacon chowder. 'Truly excellent.' He's spot on. Silken and creamy, it's studded with home-made bacon, not aggressively salty yet still tasting of pig. The mussels are fat and sweet, adding a burst of marine delight. As far as taste and texture goes, it is flawless.

I tune out of that conversation and on to the plate before me, faced with a piece of brill so pearlescent and perfect that I briefly consider slipping it into my pocket. 'Fresh from the boat today,' says Stephen, and it shows, with the seaweed butter giving a wonderful umami back-note. I see Stephen's point. Seaweed is integral to Japanese cooking, and this dish, despite the butter, has a definite Japanese twist. Brilliant ingredients, perfectly cooked. I haven't eaten a better piece of fish all year.

Then a taste of the Elizabeth David classic, lamb breast St Ménéhould, otherwise known as Park Rails. It uses breast of lamb, slowly braised, then slathered in mustard, covered in breadcrumbs and fried. Get it wrong and you're left with a fatty, inedible mess. Here, as you might have guessed, it is beautiful, served with a fresh mint dipping sauce. 'See, as English as could be, well, French really, but you know what I mean, just changed by the presentation,' he says as he puts it down. The lamb is rich and tender, the mustard suitably pungent and the mint sauce cuts an easy swathe through any fat. Wonderful, as is the roast rump of lamb, perfectly cooked and packed with flavour. The lunch lives up to every expectation, a modern taste of an ancient Kentish borough.

Just before I go, belly sagging and feet dragging, Stephen recommends a trip to visit Richard Green, the man who runs the Whitstable Oyster Fishery Company. To visit Whitstable and not take in some natives seems plain rude but I am out of time.

Later in the year, I return and wiggle down the coastal road, Stephen's map in hand. I pass The Blue Anchor, The Jolly Sailor, The Rose and Bloom, The Two Brewers and The Duke of Cumberland before spotting the main harbour and turning left into the East Quay.

Richard Green, tall, broad, with the sort of rugged good looks you'd expect from a seafaring man, is already waiting. After crushing my hand in welcome, he's keen to get me into the holding shed so we tramp down the pebble shingle, past beach huts and old oyster sheds, until we reach a nondescript door. Stepping inside, I'm greeted by eight tanks filled with water and oysters. The air is bracing, heavy with seawater and minerals, both invigorating and slightly overwhelming. The only noise is that of rushing water, flowing over the hundreds of oysters, ceaselessly through both day and night.

'In order to farm oysters,' he says, grabbing a dull-brown, flat native from the underwater pile before him, 'you need some stake in the future. We're not fishermen as such. Most of them think in the short term: what will we catch today? No, this company has always had to think three or four years ahead, as oyster growing, especially for the natives, is a long-term game.' He pulls a plastic pint glass from his bag, filled with lemon wedges, Tabasco and pepper. I relax. We're going to eat as well as talk.

Because no matter how much you've consumed there's always room for a dozen natives. He shucks the oyster with the ease of a man who's done this a million times before. 'Dentists make the best openers. All that controlled strength they have. Just look at that, isn't it beautiful?'

To the oyster virgin, there's little ostensible allure. A gnarled, coarse and dowdy shell is closed tightly to all but the most tenacious of suitors. And even when the hinge has been forced open, the quivering mass inside is not exactly pulchritudinous, being off-white and viscous, more monster of the deep than fruit of the sea. 'He was a bold man that first ate an oyster,' noted the great Jonathan Swift (although this is one of those quotations that is ascribed to everyone from Pliny to Churchill), yet once you are under its spell, this wobbling pile of snot is transformed into voluptuous, trembling folds, all a-quiver on a mother-of-pearl bed. It would take a man made of sterner stuff than me to resist their siren call.

'This is the best time of the year, I reckon,' Richard says, making quick work of another oyster. 'They're fat, sweet and properly saline in March. By the end of the season, in April, they can get a little milky.' And it is a perfect size too, neither grossly fat nor stingily lean.

A dribble of lemon juice and a drop of Tabasco (one drop, though; any more and you're obliterating all those slinky, seaside nudges and whispers) is the only dressing needed, before the shell is raised to my lips and the contents tipped down my neck. The first taste is of seawater, which is hardly surprising since the oyster has been plucked straight from the tank. This quickly fades and the more subtle nuances are released as you crush the bivalve between your molars. There's a rounded sweetness that works wonderfully with the yielding texture, followed by a brief embarrassed flush, as if it's not quite proper to be eating these in company. The experience is just the right side of obscene, erotic rather than pornographic, a silk slip rather than nylon crotchless panties.

I always save the liquor until last. Once the shellfish has been devoured, then it's time for the very essence of native oyster, that preciously delicate clear juice. Any more than a quick shot would be too much. A half-shell is the perfect natural measure. As world-class liquids go, it ranks alongside Chateau Léoville-Barton '82, Somerset cider brandy and Doctor Pepper. In Australia, they shuck oysters, then irradiate them, before putting them back in the shell. The liquid is poured away. Heresy. The treated oyster sits on its shiny perch, emasculated and embarrassed, its heart cruelly torn out.

Size is important too. For me, the perfect size is number 2. Just as a proper Martini should be downed in three sips so that the liquid stays ice cold as intended, an oyster should take no more than two chews between lips and throat. I've eaten monsters the size of dinner plates in New Zealand, so vast you need a knife and fork. The whole point of decent oysters lies in being able to fit the whole thing in your mouth at once.

As to the other so-called 'contenders' to the oyster throne, nothing comes close to a Whitstable or Colchester native. Nothing. In Louisiana, and New Orleans in particular, much is made of their blue oyster, shucked by the thousand on battered tin plates, yet the balmy waters of the Gulf of Mexico are no match for the icy grey of the Thames Estuary. Blue oysters are small and bland, calling out for litres of Tabasco to give them any hope of flavour. The best seafood, be it crab or cod, comes from cold, clean waters. The flesh is firmer, the taste as deep as some ancient, oceanic trench.

To cook natives would be sacrilegious (although the cheaper, less subtle and far more numerous rock oysters are far better suited to the flame). 'Rocks are a hundred times more prolific than the natives,' says Richard as he hands me yet another freshly shucked stunner. As John Bayes, the bearded genius behind the Reculver oyster hatchery, a few miles up the coast, is apparently fond of saying, 'The trouble with the native oyster is that it seems to be born with a death wish.' Although the natives have been here as long as there's been seawater, it was only thanks to the likes of Bayes and the Green family that they still exist at all.

Richard continues: 'When we started thirty years back, when my dad, Barrie, came in, the whole native oyster business was in tatters, in total rack and ruin. The so-called Whitstables were nothing of the sort, coming from all over the country to be merely cleaned and stored here. Now,' he points around the room, as proud as any father, 'things seem to be just about all right.' The story of the resurgence of this blessed bivalve is a tale of perseverance and inspiration, of passion and triumph over adversity. And a sobering reminder of the fragility of not just a revered shellfish, but of artisan food production everywhere.

'The poor Britons,' observed the historian Sallust sometime around Caesar's invasion of Britain, 'there is some good in them after all. They produce an oyster.' A fine historian, when not brown-nosing Caesar, he did have a point. The Romans, with their central heating, bijou villas and flushing loos, were not much enamoured of England. Too cold, too grey and as for the food ... well, at least there were oysters. Of course, the Romans were not the first to discover their joys; our ancestors, primitive hunter-gatherers, were thought to have been smoking and eating oysters 8,000 years ago. But the Roman invaders, no slouches when it came to all things edible, found the Kentish oysters as sweet as any they had ever tasted.

Gnaeus Julius Agricola, Governor of Britain between AD 78 and 85, was so impressed by the oysters' flavour that he decided his friends must taste them. Back in Rome. Slaves were sent out to the natural beds near Reculver, next door to Whitstable, to collect them by the thousand. They were then packed in snow and sent off west. Archaeologists have even found shells in special oyster fridges, built into the cellars of Roman villas. Yet the appetite for natives seemed to disappear along with the Romans, and little is heard of them until the fag end of the fifteenth century. Even in 1490, there was a dispute between the Lordships of Whitstable and Milton over 'ye dredging of oysters', something, according to Michael Cable in *Whitstable Natives*, that showed 'an early indication of the sort of turf wars that were still causing problems as recently as 1998'. The good news was that the Privy Council, which had jurisdiction in these sorts of matters, declared that young oysters should be left to grow, and that there was a closed season from 1 May to 1 August.

From that point on, Whitstable became known as an oyster town, and the oyster fisheries grew steadily throughout the eighteenth and nineteenth centuries until there were over seventy smacks, wide-sailed oyster boats, working the bay. The beds, out at sea, were the property of Viscount Lord Boling-broke, but he got into debt and sold them to a local landowner who, in turn, flogged them to the Company of Free Fishers and Dredgers. During the next century a small trade blew up into a massive industry.

'A hundred years ago,' says Richard, wiggling his knife into the hole at the base of the oyster's hinge, 'they were exporting 3 or 4 million natives from the bay per year. That's a lot of fucking oysters. Then man did what man always does, and got greedy, didn't think about the future.' He shakes his head. Between 1850 and 1865, the Company grew bigger still, with around 300 dredger men (the oysters were dredged from the seabed) running 100 smacks. At its peak, up to 80 million oysters were being sent to Billingsgate each year, making the Company rich, with an annual income of around £90,000. With a glut of oysters the price fell and they became the food of the poor, sold from barrels on every London street corner. 'It's a wery remarkable circumstance, sir,' says Sam Weller to Mr Pickwick in the well-known passage from *The Pickwick Papers*, 'that poverty and oysters always seem to go together.'

Business was booming in Whitstable. In 1896, the Company of Free Fishers and Dredgers became the Whitstable Oyster Fishery Company. It went public, issuing 25,000 shares of £10 each, and every member of the Company of Free Fish-ers and Dredgers was allotted twenty shares. This marked the beginning of the end. As Cable points out, 'The new set-up had been necessitated by a series of misfortunes that left the original company £50,000 in debt. Going public was a necessary evil, rather than a decision prompted by profit.

'One theory as to why the English fell out of love with oysters was that during the two world wars we lost our taste for fresh food, as we became so conditioned to living on tinned food,' says Richard. 'But there were other factors too.'

In 1894, the public were frightened off oysters by a health scare and, as a result, the company's income fell by around 70 per cent. Two particularly harsh winters, in 1890 and 1895, were ruinous too, 'extreme cold being one of the native oyster's greatest enemies', explains Cable. There was a decent harvest in 1901 but with rampant overfishing, and the English about to lose their taste for the oyster (mainly thanks to the increase in price), the future was increasingly bleak. Smoked salmon and prawn cocktail usurped the oyster's natural place as a starter, and with the fall in demand the oyster gatherers folded, one by one. The great fleets of smacks were a thing of the past, and the sons of the dredger men, after the Second World War, lost interest and went off in search of better-paid jobs.

There followed the cruel winter of 1947, at a time when England was on her knees, in which the sea froze right across to the Isle of Sheppey. This was the third of the century's killer cold spells, along with those of 1929 and 1940. The beds, already in a parlous state from having been neglected during the war, were further ravaged by the harsh conditions. Then there was the great flood of 1953, which inundated most of Whitstable and decimated the oyster beds, sending the clutch – the crushed shell to which the young oyster brood attaches itself – down the coast into Seasalter, a few yards from The Sportsman. Matters were made worse by pollution, partly caused by the anti-fouling solution slathered on the bottom of boats, and partly by paper fibre from the paper mills at Sittingbourne and Kemsley, which clogged the beds at Faversham. The situation became so dire that the Seasalter and Ham Company had to restock their beds with French oysters. By the mid-Sixties, the Whitstable native oyster business was all but finished, with stocks at an all-time low and the beds unkempt. The Whitstable Oyster Fishery Company was surviving, but only just.

In 1976, the Company was bought by Barrie Green, Richard's father, and John Knight. It seemed like a crazy purchase, as there was no value in the business, and the company was saddled with £40,000 of debt. Their only aim, they told friends, was to keep the business ticking over. After making his fortune in DIY shops, Green decided to settle in Whitstable. A lifelong seafood aficionado (his Weymouth childhood made him a keen shrimper and sailor), he was appalled by the prevailing state of affairs. 'The oysters being sold from here as Whitstable natives are all taken from beds hundreds of miles away in Devon and Cornwall,' he told the *Daily Express* in 1973. 'None have been bred here on the Whitstable beds since 1963. They are merely purified and distributed here.'

For a few years yet, this practice at least brought in cash, so they carried on, buying in natives from across the country, purifying them in the water-filled basement of the Royal Native Oyster Stores (it's still there, and as wet as ever), and selling them on. They also painted the beach huts and started to hire them out.

Barrie was determined that the natives should return to Whitstable and, with them, the fortunes of the town. It was only as recently as 2002 that he, along with sons Richard and James (the latter runs the restaurant side of the business), let down the dredge from their small blue-and-white fishing boat and, for the first time in decades, brought up Whitstable native oysters. The Whitstable Oyster Fishery Company was back in business, farming and harvesting natives and rocks alike. The rebirth of the company provided the impetus needed for the regeneration of the town, with seafood as an economic and social defibrillator, jump-starting its dicky heart. Suddenly the critics flocked in, raving about the oysters and the area's old-world charm. The beach huts became prime property; the tourists arrived in their droves. Whitstable was once more on the map, all thanks to the native.

'We have a half-share in a fisherman's boat,' explains Richard. By now, there's a pile of empty shells ('We never throw them away, because they're crushed and used for the clutch') on the side of the tank. 'We buy all of his stock as I'd rather give a local fisherman money than someone else. Our oysters, whether rock or native, have a lot of space, around three to four square metres each. If we go out for seven hours, we'll probably gather about 200 natives. That's not bad, but it's not brilliant either, just average. The rocks are far more numerous and much easier to gather. All this is thanks to John Bayes. He spent a fortune getting the natives going again, putting the seedlings back into the estuary.' Sadly, I never get the chance to meet the man himself, but all speak of him in hushed tones.

During the early Sixties, Bayes, a zoologist by trade, was employed to set up a hatchery for Seasalter and Ham, and immediately had huge success breeding the Pacific oyster, better known as the rock. This species is far more hardy than the native, faster growing too, reaching maturity in three years rather than five. The chances of a native egg making it right through to maturity is, according to Bayes, a million to one. The vast majority are either eaten by fish before they can reach a rock or shell on which to attach themselves, or are killed by the cold water.

At the moment, the native count is relatively low. Despite the best efforts of Bayes, they still cannot be farmed on a commercial scale. Rocks, on the other hand, make up 80 per cent of the English oyster market. Their shells are bigger and more rounded, but the flesh lacks the subtle charms of the native. They're grown to three millimetres in the hatchery, then put into open tanks, then into the inshore banks in mesh bags, safe from predators. Yet this is an entirely green enterprise. 'What we are doing is sound, sustainable and environmentally friendly,' Bayes has said. 'Shellfish actually help clean the sea.'

Richard agrees. 'There's no carbon footprint, no damage to the ecosystem. We use bio-diesel for our boats. The oyster gets everything it needs from the sea. All we do is purify them. The oysters get a rinse at sea, which is some of the cleanest water in the country, then are put into the tanks with some UV light to destroy microbes.

'But I do feel that the hoops that Environmental Health' – yup, it's our old friend the EHO again – 'makes us jump through are a disincentive to good healthy food. They make life for the small producer so bloody difficult. Look, over the road, that national chain of ersatz Italian food have boxed Thai chicken fillets delivered every day, cheap but unsustainable. There's absolutely no control as to how the chickens are kept, fed, raised and killed, as it all takes place out of the reach of our national jurisdiction. God only knows what goes on. Yet at our restaurant, the Whitstable Oyster Fishery Company, just down the beach, we cook everything from scratch from the best ingredients we can find, but the systems put in place seem determined to not help, rather to make life more difficult. The Environmental Health lot would far prefer some homogenised, industrialised and centralised food system, as it's far easier to control. They should be supporting us, not making life harder.'

This is a commonly echoed complaint and one I hear again and again, from chicken farmer to Cheddar-maker. Surely, it's time for government to take a proper look at the often ridiculous and expensive procedures that irk producers so. In 95 per cent of cases, the farmers and fishermen have forgotten more about their art than the EHO could ever learn. Part of the problem with English food is that we're so in thrall to the endless regulations that are conjured up in some Brussels meeting room with little thought as to the practical consequences.

The Greens also run a brewery, producing a beautiful oyster stout. Rich and malty, it's best served ice cold with a dozen of their natives.

Barrie, Richard and James Green; Stephen Harris; John Bayes: modest heroes all, fighting for what they believe tastes best and benefits the community too. Not for financial gain or personal glory, just a belief in good food. They would balk at being called heroes. They just feel lucky to be doing what they adore. For the rest of us, gratitude is due and a promise to support them in any way we can. In a world where the bland and industrialised are becoming ever more powerful, and thickets of red tape strangle any initiative, these are not just food heroes. They are keepers of a torch lit many centuries earlier, of an English eating tradition. They believe the Whitstable native is worth fighting for. And they're right.

Driving back to London, away from native oysters and home-cured ham, I begin to think about the unsung heroes – and heroines – of English food. Mrs Beeton is so often dubbed a talisman, and the hundreds of thousands of her books sold are cited as evidence of her everlasting appeal, but the main drift of her *Book of Household Management* is given away in the title. Published in 1861, this was a guide for ladies on how to run a household, rather than a cookbook per se. We tend to see her as the Delia of her day rather than as an amalgam of accountant and physician, counsellor, event organiser and cook. Her vegetables are boiled to mush and her recipes rarely enlighten. One heroine who's frequently overlooked is Florence White, one of the great campaigning figures of English food. She sits alongside Glasse and Acton, Hartley and Grigson, Patten and Fitzgibbon, as one of the great collectors of English recipes. She believed that unless our regional recipes were recorded for posterity, they'd die out altogether.

White, the founder of the English Folk Cookery Association, was an unlikely saviour of English food. A lifelong spinster who lost the sight in one eye as a small child, Flossie (her nickname) was constantly broke and moved from post to post: from governess to teacher to journalist to English food evangelist. She was born in Peckham in 1863 and her mother died when she was only just of school age. Her father, Richard White, a lace-buyer turned headmaster, married again, choosing a woman who made Flossie's life unbearable. So started Flossie's rather sorry, sad life. She moved all over the country, writing books on dressmaking, working as a cook and housekeeper, even travelling to Burma. Eventually she began writing cookery pieces (and she was one of the first freelance cookery writers) for the likes of *The Times*, *Spectator*, *Daily Mail*, *Glasgow Herald*, *New York Tribune*, *Daily Express* and *Daily Telegraph*. There seem very few publications that she didn't contribute to, although she admits to being useless with money.

You'd imagine the author of the wonderful *Good Things in England* to be chin deep in Kentish huffkins and jugged pigeons, almond puffs and beefsteak pudding. Nothing could be further from the truth. Dinner was largely bread and milk, breakfast a boiled egg 'or a bit of cooked ham'. She confessed that 'My greatest extravagance was a cup of tea.' It's a fascinating, grim tale, shot through with a very Victorian stoicism. 'My life has been one succession of loss, sorrow, and difficulty,' she writes in her autobiography, *A Fire in the Kitchen*, published in 1938, 'ever since my mother died when I was not quite six. It began with her loss, followed by the loss of my right eye. After that, sorrows came not as single spies but in battalions … Yet I can honestly say that no girl or woman I have ever known has had a richer or fuller life. I envy no man …' All this tragedy and desolation is vindicated by her tireless work on behalf of her beloved food. 'We had the finest cookery in the world but it had nearly been lost by neglect; a whole lifetime would not be sufficient for one person to rediscover it.'

While she is certainly overstating her case a little, she was entirely unmotivated by flag-waving patriotism and easy jingoism. 'There is no reason why the famous French cuisine and our fine, traditional English cookery should be bitter rivals. Both are absolutely distinctive, but equally good in their different ways.'

Florence White was not alone in her thinking. Almost 200 years earlier, Hannah Glasse was stouter still in her defence of English food, railing endlessly about the French and their cooking and berating them for their high-handed ways: 'So much is the blind Folly of this Age, that they would rather be imposed on by a French Booby, than give encouragement to a good English Cook!' She was writing in 1747, at a time when French, rather than English, cookery was the chosen cuisine of the rich and aristocratic. Her first chapter, 'Of roasting, Boiling etc', is classically British. Chapter 2, however, is stuffed full with fricassees, ragouts and daubes, and nearly half the recipes are either French or foreign, the choicest ones being stolen from the likes of chefs La Chapelle and Massialot. Why? Because they're 'very good'. She constantly contradicts herself, and her relationship with French food ricochets between disgust and admiration. Chapter 3 is headed 'Read this Chapter, and you will find how expensive a French Cook's Sauce is'. She'll include a long and elaborate recipe for 'The French way of Dressing Partridges', with bacon, truffles, garlic and the like, yet end with the statement, 'This dish I do not recommend; for I think it an odd Jumble of Trash.' And her 'sauce for a Brace of Partridges, Pheasants, or any Thing you please' concludes with her claim that this 'is equal with boiling a Leg of Mutton in Champaign'. Some claim her anti-French feeling had its roots in jealousy, because she was unable to afford her own French chef, a breed more expensive than their home-grown counterparts.

A century later, the snobbery attached to French food and French chefs was equally rife. The French influence was found everywhere in polite society; the great chef Ude worked for the Earl of Sefton and at Crockford's. Carême cooked, unhappily, they say, for the hugely bloated Prince Regent in 1816 and 1817. Alexis Soyer was chef at the Reform Club in the 1830s and 1840s, while Francatelli, an Englishman who studied French cooking under Carême, was in service to Queen Victoria in the 1850s. As the upper classes and the wealthy adopted French dishes, traditional English ones suffered as a consequence.

Spurred on by abuse of English food in the press, Florence White started to travel the land in the late 1920s, following the trail of Stilton in Leicestershire or tracking down Sally Lunns (a light, semi-sweet bread) in Bath. Much to her frustration, her published pieces were then lifted by other writers without giving her any accreditation. National interest in English food at the time was pitiful.

In *A Fire in the Kitchen* White says: 'In 1926 no one had any idea that England possessed any national cookery beyond roast beef, Yorkshire pudding, and Christmas plum pudding. It was perfectly sickening to hear nothing but these dishes mentioned as England's cookery. It had been the same at one time with clothes and music ... Such fools are English men and women where their country's interests are concerned. And many of our fellow-countrymen were starving.' Her views are echoed in later years by the likes of Rupert Croft-Cooke, David and Richard Mabey and Arabella Boxer, yet White was a true pioneer, bound on her mission not for money or glory but from a deep-held belief that our national food deserved celebration.

'Every place I visited I found had, or used to have, some local delicacy, and I began making a gastronomic map of England. Then I submitted it to a popular newspaper in 1927, but it was turned down.' The newspaper was more than happy to publish French gastronomical maps, but anything English was seen as a joke. Taking the view that good food made life more bearable, she believed that 'many unhappy marriages are due to bad cooking and bad management on behalf of the wife.'

In 1928 she started the English Folk Cookery Association. It was meant to coexist with the more popular English Folk Lore Society, a place where old recipes could be collected and kept for posterity. Although there was some interest, the society acquired few members, reflecting the bleak view taken of English food: 'when I started the English Folk Cookery Association it would have been impossible to get subscribers. English cookery was under so much of a cloud that people might have paid a subscription to keep out of it!' This was not a society aimed at the poor, who hadn't the luxury of either choice or nostalgia, nor the rich, who were revelling in their own, modern English food. It was aimed squarely at the middle classes, who were virtually indifferent. She was soon at work on a cookbook intended to change all that.

Good Things in England, 'Containing Traditional and Regional Recipes suited to Modern Tastes contributed by English Men and Women between 1399 and 1932', was published on 23 May 1932 and was immediately lauded as a classic by a leader in *The Times*. 'There isn't another book like it, but I never considered it mine. It is England's.' Even after this accolade, she was dogged by poverty, having to sell her cookery library to a friend, who allowed her to borrow it back.

'It was quite time, in 1926,' she writes towards the end of her autobiography, 'that something was done to put English cookery on the map. May it never again be obscured. In 1937 it is fashionable and popular.' Then came the wars and, with them, rationing. England's food would take many years to recover once more.

Good Things in England, and its sequel, *Good English Food*, endure to this day. They are invaluable culinary documents, attempting to 'capture the charm of England's cookery before it is completely crushed out of existence'. Florence White can overromanticise the past, and there's little mention of the daily drudgery of the poor – she focuses very much on the food of farmers, squires and the like – yet this was the first time that a single book had gathered together in one place recipes for

Coventry Godcakes, Staffordshire frumenty, Snowdon pudding, Ifield Vicarage hog's pudding, Chesterfield soup, Oxford brawn sauce and a thousand other long-lost regional gems. 'No nation's cookery is so peculiarly its own; and one of our aims should be to preserve its individuality and not allow our proximity to the Continent to destroy its traditional distinction and difference,' she wrote.

Florence White is also scathing of those English who praise foreign food while giving scant regard to their own. She sees our national food as every bit as integral to our history and society as politics, economics, playwriting or popular songs.

> Many of those who are enthusiastic about foreign cookery have not the remotest idea what real English cookery is like. From childhood they have been accustomed to food badly cooked, either at home, at school or some cheap restaurant; then they suddenly make a first trip to the Continent, and are of course enchanted with the unaccustomed well-cooked food … and returning home abuse their home cookery, giving themselves the airs of the monkey who has seen the world, or the fox without a tail.

Again and again, we see echoes of the past in our attitude to food in the present. Over the past hundred years, the voices might have grown more numerous, and louder too, but the song remains the same. 'Flavour and variety seem to be two of the greatest losses we have suffered through neglecting the cookery precepts our forbears knew so well that they never thought of mentioning them. They only knew when a thing was right and when it wasn't.'

If only Florence was alive today, Stephen Harris would make her proud.

STEPHEN HARRIS'S ANGELS ON HORSEBACK

Stephen says, 'This recipe is my own adaptation for angels on horseback – claimed by many in Whitstable to be a local invention.

'It was originally made by wrapping an oyster in bacon and frying in a pan. I changed it because every so often we get a particularly fat pig from Monkshill Farm, which means it's time to make my own lardo. This is like supercharged bacon and has the benefit of being pure fat so it crisps up even better than bacon. It also reflects a recurring theme in style at The Sportsman, which is to use techniques from other food cultures and apply them to our local products – thus we cure hams in the Jabugo style, dry seaweed in the Japanese way and, here, cure our own lardo as they do in Italy.'

If you don't have the time to make your own lardo, buy it from your local Italian deli.

Makes 1

Open a large native oyster and wrap around it a thin slice of lardo (see below). Secure with 2 cocktail sticks.

Deep-fry for just 1 minute, drain on kitchen paper and remove one of the cocktail sticks. Eat immediately.

Lardo

Take a layer of skin and fat (around 5 cm or 2 in thick) from the end of the pork loin. Bury it in good-quality sea salt for around 5 days.

Wash off the salt with cider vinegar. Hang in a cool, dry place for at least 1 month. Then slice it thinly with a knife.

LINCOLN'S INN CHERRIES

This recipe comes from *The Gentle Art of Cookery* by Mrs C.F. Leyel and Miss Olga Hartley. It's a fragrant and fascinating collection of recipes, with a real scent of the Middle East, much admired by Elizabeth David, who commented: 'I wonder if I would ever have learnt to cook at all had I been given a routine Mrs Beeton to learn from instead of the romantic Mrs Leyel, and her rather wild and imagination-catching recipes.'

Cherry orchards were once a common sight all over Kent, great tall trees towering over the landscape. In spring, their blossom was a sight to gladden the heaviest of hearts. Now, English cherries are a rarity. Thanks, though, to Henrietta Green and her CherryAid, they are making a comeback. Hallelujah to that.

Serves 4

450 g (1 lb) sweet black cherries
stock syrup (see recipe below)
2 tbsp Kirsch or maraschino
150 ml (5 fl oz) cream
4 macaroons
handful pistachio nuts

Stone the cherries and tip into a pan. Cover with the stock syrup and stew gently for about 10 minutes, or until tender.

You want to keep the cherries in one piece. Remove from the heat and allow to cool. When cool, add the Kirsch or maraschino and stir to combine.

Take 4 champagne glasses, put a macaroon in the bottom of each and nearly fill the glasses with the cherry compote.

Whip the cream until stiff and divide between the glasses. Decorate with pistachio nuts. Serve immediately.

Stock syrup
1 kg (2 lb 4 oz) white sugar
1 litre (1¾ pints) water

Stir the sugar in the water over a gentle heat until all the sugar is dissolved.

DRESSED CRAB

This is taken from Dorothy Hartley's *Food in England*, one of the great books of English food. Comprehensive and opinionated, it is also knowledgeable and erudite. It's one of my favourite cookbooks of all time. This recipe for dressed crab is a classic, although I would tend to leave out the breadcrumbs but add a few dashes of Tabasco sauce plus the juice of half a lemon.

I like serving dressed crab with crusty bread, home-made mayonnaise (just a little) and a glass of crisp white wine.

The Kentish crabs are excellent, by the way, but use any brown crab. Buy alive and put in the freezer for 2–3 hours, then plunge into boiling water, salted with about 175 g (6 oz) salt per 5 litres (8¾ pints). Rick Stein, the god of all things piscine, suggests 15 minutes from coming to the boil for crabs weighing up to 600 g (1 lb 5 oz); 20 minutes for crabs weighing up to 900 g (2 lb); 25 minutes for crabs up to 1.6 kg (3½ lb); and 30 minutes for anything larger.

'Remove the big claws and legs whole, crack and pick the meat out of the small claws, and put it in a basin. Now take away the whole front fringe part, and cut around the crab on the white side, so as to take away the whole of the white under-shell (there is a natural crack between the shells that is easy to follow). Remove the head and green intestinal part, and then scoop all the brown crab meat into a basin.

'The "dressing" of the crab meat is a matter of taste – do not deluge it with mayonnaise, as most men prefer it plain seasoned. If you have never dressed a crab before, try this simple dressing the first time and afterwards adapt it to suit your own taste.

'For one sizeable crab [about 1.25 kg or 2.5 lb], take 1 heaped teaspoon of fresh breadcrumbs, 1 small saltspoonful of salt, and 1 large saltspoonful of black pepper, 1 large dessertspoon of oil, and 1 small dessertspoonful of vinegar mixed with a little made mustard. Put all in a basin with the brown crab meat, and leg scraps, mix lightly and pile back into the deep-red back shell; a teaspoon of finely chopped parsley dusted over the top improves the dish. The big claws should be laid on either side – and picks provided.

'Brown bread and butter go with this dish, which most working men like very much for their late teas. Crab is a much more flavoursome fish than lobster, and should never be iced.'

KENTISH HUFFKINS

Once hugely popular in Kent, at a time when cherries were plentiful, these flat, oval cakes are known by a variety of names across the country, from 'Cornish splits' to 'Hawkshead wigs'. The Kentish ones had a hole in the middle that could be filled with hot, stoned cherries and eaten as a pudding.

This recipe comes from Florence White's *Good English Food*, the follow-up to *Good Things in England*, and was, she says, 'kindly given to us by Dr. Lillian Wemyss Grant'. It works just as well with stewed cherries, apples, pears, or a compote of these fruits.

Makes 10 huffkins weighing 70 g (2½ oz) each

450 g (1 lb) flour
25 g (1 oz) yeast
1 tsp sugar
1 tsp salt
rather more than 300 ml (10 fl oz or ½ pint)
    lukewarm water

Preheat the oven to 180°C/160°C fan/gas mark 6.

Combine all the ingredients and make into a soft dough as for bread. Shape into 10 round cakes, press a hole in the centre of each with a finger, and put down to rise in a warm place. Bake for 10 to 20 minutes in the preheated oven, or until golden.

Eat hot or cold the same day as they are baked.

5

London

'If you want to provoke an argument between a South and an East Londoner,' says Terry Ball, one eye fixed on me in the rear-view mirror, the other on the road, 'ask 'em which pie and mash shop is the best. Then get the bloody hell out of the way.'

He laughs, then waves a fellow cabbie past. 'I'm a cockney and while everyone has their preferences, I've never had a bad 'un at Cooke's on Broadway Market. The best pies are always handmade, with good mince, proper pastry and doused with chilli vinegar for that extra kick.'

He pauses for a moment, silent, his mouth filled with imaginary pie.

'I live out of the East End now. I mean, the original East Ender has moved on and the place is a lot more ethnic now. Actually, it was an ethnic place when I grew up, fifty years back. I went to school with two boys from Lahore. Their dads used to sell Indian, well, Pakistani, food from their front door.'

London has long been a great ethnic and cultural stew, and has been cosmopolitan ever since the Romans liked the look of a ford on the River Thames (it was the lowest point they could build a bridge), back in AD 50, and decided to set up shop. Although no one is entirely sure whether the first buildings were military or mercantile, the small town was named Londinium. Its defending troops were drawn from across the empire – Italians and Syrians, Spanish, even Germans – enslaved and forced to work as mercenaries for their masters. The French, or Normans to be more precise, moved in next, in 1066, bringing with them the noble art of the sauté and the fricassee, alongside rich, heavy sauces and all manner of heavy spicing. London quickly became a trade centre, with merchants flogging everything from pasta and turmeric to tea and hot chocolate. There were opium dens and chophouses, pie stalls and the grandest gentleman's club, coffee and chocolate houses, muffin men, cookshops and taverns. Today, no city in the world offers such a diversity of restaurants, races and cultures.

As a conduit and centre of our own empire, London gathered its booty from across the globe: Indian tea, Caribbean sugar and Australian beef. The second Italian invasion, sometime in the mid-eighteenth century, brought teashops and provision stores, new restaurants and confectioners. Then came the Jews and the Chinese, Malays and Turks, Africans and Arabians, Indians and Bangladeshis, Australians and Eastern Europeans. London is defined by the sprawling mass of different cultures, and the cooking spices, methods and techniques they brought with them.

Imagine a London without the hookah smoke and shawarmas of Edgware Road; or minus crisp, lacquered duck, winking from the windows of Queensway and Chinatown; a place bereft of Polish stores in Shepherd's Bush, with their pickles and fat links of kielbasa; a city lacking the spice bazaars and tandoori lamb chops of Southall and Wembley. Imagine a dearth of steaming bowls of pho, fragrant and filling, in Kingsland Road; no Lina Stores in Soho, its air thick with Parmesan and Italian promise, no snooty, shabby South Kensington bistros. No jerk chicken or saltfish and ackee on Harrow Road, no baccalà or couscous on Golborne Road, no Turkish grills in Stoke Newington.

Diversity makes London great, makes London what it is, looking out and gathering in. To talk about London food is to talk about food of the international diaspora, yet there are dishes as unique to London as dim sum is to Canton and Hong Kong. And nothing encapsulates this more than eels, pie and mash.

'Although I no longer live around here,' Terry carries on, 'I'll still drive a sixty-eight-mile round trip from home for pie and mash. That's how much I love the stuff.' He drives on for a few hundred metres, then stops. 'Well, here you are. G. Kelly. Not bad. But nothing's a patch on Cookie's. What did you say you did?'

I tell him I'm spending a few days in search of pie and mash shops.

'Bloody hell, tough life. Anyway, good luck.' He grins and drives off.

I'm left staring at a wooden door, flanked on either side by large, rectangular windows. Inside is a clean, workmanlike café, all gleaming tiles and potato-scented fug. I was born in London, and have lived here for more than twenty years, but my experience of what could be described as the city's most famous dish is embarrassingly minimal.

'Today only a fraction of the original eels, pie and mash houses remain, and the majority are now situated in London's East End,' writes Paolo Hewitt in his introduction to *Eels, Pie and Mash*. 'In consequence, many people associate the dish with its geography, believing that it is a purely East End tradition. This is not so,' he goes on. 'Eels, pie and mash is particular to *London*.'

Too often now, we see the traditional eel, pie and mash shop as some anachronistic part of a cockney heritage, a brace-twanging relic of the past, places where Alfred P. Doolittle would moan about the trouble and strife while goosing the Pearly Queen. We treat these shops, many of them art deco classics, resplendently clad in marble and tile, as quaint idiosyncrasies, places to admire but avoid. 'Oooh, they do look nice. But we get our pies from Greggs these days.'

And it's true that they can, unwittingly, be a touch daunting. As in any old English institution, there's an unwritten code of conduct within its doors, the sense of not belonging if you don't know the code. Despite my being a professional eater and a long-time resident of London, I had eaten in a pie and mash shop only once, at Manze's just twenty-four hours before my cab ride. Shameful, I know. I'm happy to tramp across town to try a new Sichuan joint, or voyage to the very boundaries of the M25 for perfect sashimi. Somehow, London pies and eels seemed to have slipped under the radar, as I'm both rabid pie eater and eel adorer. I'm certain this wasn't gastro-snobbishness, as McDonald's cheeseburgers and Cherry Coke hold the same appeal for me as any ris d'agneau aux écrevisses. Perhaps I thought there were better things with which to expand my gut: pork pies, Ma Po's bean curd or skirt steak taco. As I stand outside gazing in, I feel I am about to enter a lost world of London life, a place untouched by the modern age.

M. Manze, on Tower Bridge Road, Bermondsey, is the oldest operating pie and mash shop in England. It opened in 1892 and is as imposing and attractive a shopfront now as it ever was. The seating is communal, in wooden pews, stretching down the left and overflowing at the back. The diners sit, hunched over their pies and eels, as if in prayer. Conversation is soft and to the point – 'Ethel's a bit poorly,' 'Came in at fucking twenty to one, the old nag,' and 'Pie good today' – a nod or shake of the head being sufficient response. The walls are tiled green and white, while huge mirrors add depth to the room as well as a sense of the theatrical. The tables, in between the pews, are made from thin slabs of marble, cool and unyielding. It's a magnificent room, far removed from the spluttering buses and spitting children outside. Yet all that marble, all those tiles, were installed for practical rather than aesthetic reasons. They're far easier to wipe clean, an important consideration in an ever-bustling restaurant.

The counter on the right is manned by a good-looking, middle-aged lady. She sits behind a couple of vats of steaming mash, and another of gloppy, green, viscous stuff, the infamous liquor. Say what you like about this food, it's not exactly a visual treat. The stewed eels sit in their own area, just below the front window. Every few minutes, a new tray of fresh burnished pies is brought up from downstairs. It's just after twelve noon, and the place is steadily filling with local builders and families; an elderly black man, tall and immaculately dressed, studies the form as he chews slowly on his pie. A couple of bemused Japanese tourists giggle in the corner, as if not convinced the whole place isn't some sort of immaculately reconstructed theme park, Crafty Cockney Time Warp World. They nibble daintily at their pie, pushing the mash from one side of the plate to the other. The eels, though, hold no fear for citizens of a country that worships this wriggling beast.

I wander up to the counter, determined to look every inch the seasoned pro. 'Pie and mash, please.'

'One and one?' comes the response. 'Or two and two?'

Shit. I have no idea what she means. It's like staring, dumbfounded, at the empty betting slip in the bookie's, without the faintest clue as to where to begin. Or calling when you should have stuck at the blackjack table. Not just a trifle embarrassing but deeply humiliating. It's about wanting to fit in, to seem part of the crowd. Does she mean the pies, or the eels piled on the same plate, or some other arcane piece of long-lost terminology? Christ knows.

'Two and two, please.' That should do it.

She nods her agreement and throws two pies on the plate, along with two scoops of mashed potato. Has she noticed my ignorance? Her face remains impassive.

'Oh, and some stewed eels too.' If that doesn't buy me respect, nothing will. Then I realise that ordering eels in an eel shop is hardly the stuff of legendary derring-do. I loiter in silence, not entirely sure what to do next. Will this be delivered to my table, or do I grab it now? I don't want to seem either pushy or aloof.

She pushes the plate of pies towards me. 'We're just waiting for the next batch of eel to come up. Give us a minute and I'll bring 'em over.'

I slink over to an empty space in a nearby booth and slide in.

The Roman contribution to our national food, which could be relentlessly dreary, managed to be both transitory and hugely important. A minor player was garum, a sauce made from fermented anchovy guts and pepper, used in dishes both sweet and savoury. In this form, it hardly permeated our cuisine, although the anchovy sauce that we still use today is a close relative. They made a real impact, however, in the area of game. Without Caesar and his legions, there would today be no pheasant, geese, guinea fowl or fallow deer. They also introduced the ridiculous peacock, for which we should be less than grateful. The Romans were great farmers too, creating a brickwork system of agriculture where lots of small, enclosed plots fanned out from a central farmhouse. Orchards and vines were walled in, a practice that continues to this day. But it was what escaped from those walls that really mattered: dill, fennel, garlic and mint, sage, savoury, rosemary and thyme. Then they gave us mulberries, damsons, peaches, plums and cherries, and all those vegetables that seem so immutably British, asparagus and globe artichokes, parsnips and carrots, onions and cucumbers.

Strangely enough, despite having the seeds and the capacity to grow these vegetables, we made very little use of any of them for the next few centuries, save onions, cabbage (usually in soup), garlic and the occasional leek. And when we did finally embrace the vegetable, it was usually boiled to within an inch of its life, more noxious liquid than crisp legume.

Eel had entered the national cuisine by medieval and Tudor times, although only the big houses had adequate space and fuel to roast their own meat. The rest of the townspeople would use the ovens of the local baker or cookshop. One such establishment sat on the bank of the Thames.

> There daily, according to the season, you may find viands, dishes roast, fried and boiled, fish great and small, the coarser flesh for the poor, the more delicate for the rich, such as venison, and birds both big and little … Those who desire to fare delicately, need not to search to find sturgeon or 'Guinea-fowl' or 'Ionian francolin,' since all the dainties that are found there are set before their eyes. Now this is a public cookshop, appropriate to a city and pertaining to the art of civic life.

However, eel was not on its menu. For Londoners who wanted eel, it was back to the street, for a pie, from the pieman. The eel, pie and mash shops were still some way off.

Modern times have treated the eel with disdain. Once a much loved London staple, the eel's stock has not so much dipped as plummeted into a bottomless abyss. Ask the average

Londoner their view of this oft-maligned creature and the reaction is one of disgust. The eel is seen as little more than a writhing, aquatic snake, dark, slippery and sinister – the sort of malevolent beast that squirms in the black depths of your nightmares, all sinuous curves and penetrating stare. Some people are even convinced that eels have a taste for human flesh, able to strip the flesh from your bones before slipping through your empty eye socket to suck out your brain. With a reputation like this, it's little wonder we've lost our taste for their meat. Little matter, too, that smoked eel is superior even to smoked salmon, its fat as sweet as a mountain stream. Or that the Chinese have a thousand ways with eels, each as exquisite as the last. No, the eel looks dodgy, so therefore it must taste rank.

I have to admit a slight obsession with the eel. Ever since I went elver fishing, a few years back, on the banks of the River Severn (an elver is a baby eel), they've managed to wriggle their way into my heart. Their life cycle, for a start, is incredible, a voyage so epic it makes that of Odysseus look like a paddle round the bath. It all starts, and ends, in the Sargasso Sea, a place I'd long imagined as sultry and torrid, where dusky maidens wear little more than bougainvillea, and languid poets scratch limpid odes in the shade of the jacaranda tree. The truth is rather more mundane.

The Sargasso Sea is made up of 2 million square miles of warm, clear water, somewhere between Bermuda and the Azores in the Atlantic Ocean. It's not fixed, but rather floats about like some discombobulated spectre, covered with a thick thatch of sargassum seaweed. 'It is one of the emptiest, least known areas in the world,' writes Richard Schweid in *Consider the Eel*, 'and it is vast.'

The sea is also at the heart of the Bermuda Triangle, where planes vanish off the radar and ships go down without a trace. The perfect place, then, for the ever-enigmatic eel. Allegedly. Because no adult eel has ever been seen swimming in the area, let alone mating or dying. We've put man on the moon, created the computer and the internal combustion engine, beaten typhoid and cholera. And we've put cheese in an aerosol can. When it comes to a sinuous fish, though, we really don't have a clue.

They spring from the dark, silent depths and it is only when they become *leptocephali*, a transparent, leaf-like mass, that scientists can pick up their trail. Eels spend the next three years drifting across the Atlantic, at the mercy of birds from above and fish from below. As they approach shore, and brackish water, they become elvers, tiny, transparent matchsticks. Although they have already travelled for thousands of miles without the slightest protection, the next stage that faces them is harsher still. Because in addition to their natural predators, the voles and water rats, the pike and tench, they now have to avoid man's nets too.

The males tend to loiter in the brackish water, while the females hunt upriver for a muddy corner to call home. Nothing as ineffectual as a wall or a weir is sufficient to stem their flow, as they crawl across fields and up salmon ladders, as relentless as any gun-toting Terminator. Once they are suitably ensconced, their summer nights are spent hunting crayfish, insect larvae and small fish (they prefer fresh to rotten, despite what popular opinion might suggest) and their winter is passed sleeping, buried deep in the mud. They might follow this pattern for twenty years before some primeval gong summons them back home. They gorge, building up fat for the journey ahead, turning from a greenish muddy yellow (yellow eels) to a darker, white-bellied magnificence (the silver eel, and the best for eating). Off they trot, downriver and back out into the Atlantic, where the female produces eggs for the male to fertilise and the whole cycle starts once more. Next time you grimace at the thought or sight of an eel, remember what they've battled through to arrive at your disgust. A little respect is the least they deserve.

Even in Shakespeare's time, the eel and the cockney were entwined in the popular imagination. 'Cry to it, nuncle,' jibbers the Fool at Lear, 'as the cockney did to the eels when she put them in the paste alive.' Back in the nineteenth century, the Thames was teeming with eels, although the majority eaten in London were, ironically, Dutch. 'The eels are all purchased at Billingsgate early in the morning,' writes Henry Mayhew in the mid-nineteenth century in *London Labour and the London Poor*. 'The parties themselves, or their sons and daughters, go to Billingsgate, and the watermen row them to the Dutch eel vessels moored off the market. The fare paid to the watermen is 1d for every 10lbs purchased and brought back in the boat, the passenger being gratis.'

Eel Pie Island, near Richmond-upon-Thames, was a popular picnic spot, named after this classic London dish. 'These pies would be made,' writes Mark Hix in *British Regional Food*, 'with eels, butter, sherry, parsley and lemon, and covered in puff pastry.' The pies were also sold in the street, alongside pea soup or parsley sauce, with chillies and vinegar for added kick, although Mayhew describes how the costermongers – or sellers of all manner of food – avoided them. ' "We never eat eel-pies," said one man to me, "because we know they're often made of large dead eels. We, of all people, are not to be had that way. But the haristocrats eats 'em and never know the difference." '

Robert May, in his 1685 cookbook, *The Accomplisht Cook*, lists nine ways with eels, from boiled to stewed via hashed and roasted, including jellied, while Eliza Acton, in her 1845 classic *Modern Cookery for Private Families*, offers three ways. 'London … steams and teems with eels alive and stewed,' says the Reverend David Badham in *Ancient and Modern Fish Tattle* of 1854, talking of the second classic eel recipe. 'For one halfpenny a man of the million may fill his stomach with six or seven long pieces and wash them down with a sip of the glutinous liquid they are stewed in.' But it's the third, after pie and stewed, London way with eels, cold and set in jelly, that is perhaps the most infamous, a dish still capable of inducing nausea by its very mention. Only tripe comes close in any list of hated English foods, both being shunned as much for their texture as their taste.

As quintessential a London dish as you'll ever find, jellied eels now exists as some sort of edible freak show, a concoction mocked and pointed at, every bit as bizarre as the bearded lady or Jo-Jo the Dog-Faced Boy. The savoury jelly is bad enough, they say, fishy and wobbly, but studded with chunks of eel it becomes a culinary Black Museum, a depraved slice of London history. I'm fairly ambivalent, preferring my eels hot or smoked. Mark Hix is a huge fan, raving about 'that lovely texture, the sweet nuggets of flesh', as is Matthew Fort. 'Oh, God, yes, give me jellied eels,' he exclaims. 'One of the best dishes I ever had was Paul Heathcote's jellied eel terrine. I think he only ever sold two portions, both of them to me.'

The eel is not only unpopular, as another generation grows up feeling nothing but loathing for these marvellous fish, but endangered too. Thanks to pollution, overfishing of elvers and loss of natural habitat, eel stocks are in freefall. And since no person has ever managed to farm them from scratch, the English eel could soon become a taste of the past.

The mash at Manze's is distinctly institutional, lumpy, slightly dry with barely a hint of dairy. Try as I might to adore it, I can't muster a smile. I ate better at my prep school, which managed to debase and demean any raw material that came into its compass. Yet this is the traditional method and much loved. By people other than me.

The pies are small, the pastry crisp and slightly flaky on the outside, the underside lusciously chewy. The filling itself is finely ground mince, with a hint of pepper. Compared to the more traditional, country, chunky pies, they seem lacking a little heft. Actually, I'm distinctly underwhelmed, as the meat has small chunks of gristle and oozes menacingly all over the plate. But as I move on to the second, I start to see the point. Well, almost. Baked fresh every day, the pastry is handmade and rolled, then filled with fresh beef and a dash of gravy before being baked on trays in a stone oven. It's not at all what I expected, but it does, I suppose, have a peculiar charm.

A cheap, OK pie is a rarity these days. You either have the posh versions from the likes of the Square Pie Company, or Pieminster, superior creations with a price to match, or the greasy, limply flavoured specimens from Greggs or Ginsters, that slick the tongue in cheap fat, offering little that is memorable on their journey across the taste buds. This pie sits somewhere in between, but nearer to the latter than the former.

'A local taste,' was the best Matthew Fort could offer on the subject of these pies, 'like Icelandic rotten shark.'

Then there's the liquor. Matthew had long warned me of this 'nefarious brew'. 'Ugh' was all he could say. 'It takes real skill and ingenuity to come up with something as disgusting as that.' Fergus Henderson, the man behind St John Restaurant, agrees. 'Gristle and bad gravy,' he says with a shudder. 'I mean, many of the shops are really beautiful and the notion of fresh pies, wahoo. But those pies are not for me. As for the liquor, yuck. But they are what they are, I suppose.'

Before a massed army of cockneys approaches Casas Fort and Henderson with burning effigies and a dunking barrel of searing liquor, I should point out these two men are entirely without culinary airs and graces. Their only concern is whether or not the finished products taste any good. Still, it would be a brave man who stood on Bethnal Green Road and screamed abuse at pie and mash. Even Hix was unusually ambivalent. 'It's all right, I suppose,' he shrugged. 'Wouldn't cross the street for it.'

My feelings on liquor were less passionate but, as acquired tastes go, it was up there with incest and Quorn. The texture is viscous but the flavour, in this particular example, had long since left the building. The sauce seems like the first, unfinished stage of some Heston Blumenthal experiment, tried, then thrown away. Quite why liquor, rather than the Northern gravy, prevailed, I don't know. I suppose that minced-meat pies are less likely to create their own gravy, and any that does make an appearance is kept in the mix. I really do think you have to be brought up suckling this stuff from your mother's breast to truly appreciate it, because even after ten pints of Stella, I'd still be pushed to force a smile as it slithered down my throat.

I asked around as to the origins of liquor and the usual answer was tradition. Tradition? That all-purpose unguent used to cover the fact that you don't have a clue. Traditional it might be, but then so was bear-baiting, Morris dancing and witch dunking. Does that make them any more palatable? Why waste perfectly good butter, flour and parsley on this mess?

Admittedly, this was my first taste, with many more to come, so as I was a newcomer to the whole scene, perhaps I should keep my opinions to myself. That said, I couldn't help seeing the liquor as a virus, infecting pastry and meat with a callous disregard. All the same, many aficionados argue that this is the best bit, the glue that holds the whole thing together.

The stewed eels, on the other hand, are a different prospect altogether, sweet and falling off the bone. A few years back, the bones are simply spat out on the floor, with sawdust spread to make cleaning up all the easier. Sadly, things are a little more proper these days. However, the eels in their wobbly broth (not far removed from liquor, but infused with eel and therefore far more palatable), spiked with vinegar and dusty white pepper, are a London dish to praise and be proud of. Rich, filling and unexpectedly subtle, it is a worthy end for a wonderful beast.

Walking out, I can't help feeling a niggle of disappointment. The food is cheap and edible, the eel actually memorable. Perhaps I had expected too much from this unpretentious, working-class classic, building it up into some sumptuous feast instead of good-value, freshly made stodge. Still, in comparison to Wimpy, even the liquor tastes like angels weeping on my tongue.

Traditionally, there were three families that dominated the eel and pie trade: the Manzes, as seen above, along with the Cookes and the Kellys. 'Theirs is an empire,' continues Paolo Hewitt, 'a "Cockney Nostra," whose roots and history have become so entangled over the past 130 years that it is difficult to piece together their story.' We know that the street piemen of London provided cheap, filling sustenance for the London poor and the city was famed for its markets, especially those held on Saturday night – smoky and crowded, with hundreds of stalls greedily anticipating the newly gained wages of the working man.

It was the light that impressed Henry Mayhew most, the stalls of the Saturday street market 'either … illuminated by the intense white light of the new self-generating gas-lamp, or else it is brightened up by the red smoky flame of the old-fashioned grease lamp. One man shows off his yellow haddock with a candle stuck in a bundle of firewood; his neighbour makes a candlestick of a huge turnip, and the tallow gutters over its sides.' It was a place where everything had a price, from parsley to penny prints to opium and haggard old whores.

Little boys, holding three or four onions in their hand, creep between the people, wriggling their way through every interstice, and asking for custom in whining tones, as if seeking charity. Then the tumult to the thousand different cries of the eager dealers, all shouting at the top of their voices, at one and the same time, is almost bewildering. 'So-old again,' roars one. 'Chestnuts all 'ot, a penny a score,' bawls another ... 'Twopence a pound grapes.' 'Three a penny Yarmouth bloaters.' ... 'Now's your time! Beautiful whelks, a penny a lot.' 'Here's ha'p'orths,' shouts the perambulating confectioner. 'Come and look at 'em! here's toasters!' bellows one with a Yarmouth bloater stuck on a toasting-fork. 'Penny a lot, fine russets,' calls the apple woman: and so the Babel goes on.

Covent Garden fruit and vegetable market is equally spectacular:

As you glance down any one of the neighbouring streets, the long rows of carts and donkey barrows seem interminable in the distance. They are of all kinds, from the greengrocer's taxed cart to the coster's barrow – from the showy excursion-van to the rude square donkey-cart and bricklayer's truck ... Along each approach to the market, too, nothing is to be seen, on all sides, but vegetables; the pavement is covered with heaps of them waiting to be carted; the flag-stones are stained green with the leaves trodden under foot; sieves and sacks full of apples and potatoes, and bundles of brocoli and rhubarb, are left unwatched upon almost every doorstep ... At every turn there is a fresh odour to sniff at; either the bitter aromatic perfume of the herbalists' shops breaks upon you, or the scent of oranges, then of apples, and then of onions ... brocoli tied up in square packets ... the sieves of crimson love-apples, polished like china, – the bundles of white glossy leeks, their roots dangling like fringe ... the dark purple pickling-cabbages – the scarlet carrots – the white knobs of turnips – the bright yellow balls of oranges, and the rich brown coats of the chestnuts – attract the eye on every side. Then there are the apple-merchants, with their fruit of all colours, from the pale yellow green to the bright crimson.

But although the piemen were as popular as they were populous, they were mobile salesmen rather than shopkeepers. The first to sell direct from his house was said to have been John Antink, a Dutch eel trader who sold his wares to the piemen. Sometime in the middle of the nineteenth century, he turned the bottom floor of his house into a shop. As ever, there is scant evidence to back this up. Yet there is evidence of an eel and pie shop owned by Henry Blanchard in 1844, where all manner of pie, from fruit to meat and eel, were flogged. It was hugely popular, though less so among the mobile piemen.

'The penny pie shops, the street men say, have done their trade a great deal of harm,' noted Mayhew. 'These shops have now got mostly all the custom, as they make the pies much larger for the money than those sold in the street.'

By 1874, Kelly's Trade Directory listed thirty-three eel and pie shops. A few years later, in 1889, Robert Cooke decided to open up his own shop in Baker's Row, EC1, buoyed up, no doubt, by the success of other pie emporiums. The shop was smart and clean, the staff uniformed and polite – a haven of civility, if not tranquillity, in a filthy world. Situated close to the market, the shop received a never-ending stream of ravenous customers. Such was his success that his wife, Martha, also opened up another near by.

Back in 1878, Michele Manze walked from Ravello to Naples to set sail for England and a new life. After dabbling in the ice business, he became friends with Robert Cooke, married his daughter, Ada, and opened up the first Manze shop in Bermondsey.

The last member of the trio was Samuel Robert Kelly, an Irish immigrant who opened a shop in 1915 in Bethnal Green Road. Thirty years later, he had four further shops. Business thrived and actually survived through wartime rationing (the shops escaped closure because they offered cheap, rib-sticking food, although eels were scarce) and boomed in the aftermath, thanks to returning soldiers desperate for a taste of their youth. Things began to sour in the late Fifties and Sixties when the price of London property and rents became so high that many factories were pushed into the suburbs and, with them, the eel-loving workers. The glory days were over, never to return.

'I've had some pretty bad imitations, mind you, both pies and jellied eels,' eel lover and cabbie Terry Ball had told me on the way to G. Kelly in the Roman Road, Hackney. 'Second-rate eels and pies filled with cheap mince. These are simple dishes, but they have to be done well. With pies, the crust is everything, especially that soft, doughy interior. A proper East Ender has their pie crust down, belly up.'

G. Kelly is a little more utilitarian than the fancy splendours of Manze – the tiles are white and the tables covered in Formica rather than hewn from marble.

No longer a virgin, I order with confidence. 'One and one please …' I stop myself adding 'love'. A pie eater I may be, but a cockney, sadly not.

The pie here is superior to the Manze's version, with a slightly bigger grind of mince and good chewy pastry, and it is well seasoned. Not a classic pie, by any means, but a decent minced-meat pie all the same. The mash was as institutional as ever and, as for the liquor, I just looked in the other direction.

Last on my list was F. Cooke's in Broadway Market. 'He's a right character, is Cookie,' warned Terry the taxi driver, usually a not-so-subtle euphemism for off his bloody rocker. But that was not the case.

Bob is the grandson of Frederick Cooke, who opened the shop in 1900, and great-grandson to Robert Cooke. Small but well built, with spiky hair and glasses, he's pragmatic about the future of the shop, a skill learnt, no doubt, from years of following Tottenham.

'We're not as busy as we once were,' he says, sitting down below an old Spurs line-up. 'Especially the eels. We do stewed and jellied but it's mainly the older lot who buy them.' The pies, though, seem as popular as ever. 'I've got the market outside on Saturdays, with 2,000 people passing by on a good day. They're a different type of Londoner now, not real East Enders. They've all buggered off to Harlow and the like. Still, it's nice to see the place busy. There's been a pie shop on this spot for four generations. We used to have half a tonne of live eels downstairs and, at our Dalston place, eight tonnes. We used to supply Billingsgate, not the other way around. Still, eels are not that popular any more. A shame.'

He's talkative and open, illustrating every point with his hands, but he has no time for idiotic questions.

'It's a secret,' he snaps when I ask for his recipe, because his pies, as Terry had said, were the best of the lot. The mash is superior, too, still lumpy but a little less Spartan than the others. Even the liquor is decent, tinted green with an excess of fresh parsley. I say decent as in edible, but an improvement nonetheless. The chilli vinegar has a mild kick, despite a label warning 'Caution! Hot!'

What does he look for in the perfect pie? He shrugs. 'I couldn't really say. It varies from shop to shop. But we always bake on the premises.'

'Bob,' cries a voice from below. 'Can you come down?' He shrugs an apology and disappears into the depths.

Without getting too misty-eyed, the pie and mash shop is a great London institution. It might lack the popular appeal of the fish and chip shop (chips are portable and digitally edible, unlike mash) but why shouldn't we embrace fresh-cooked food, made with pride? Pies and mash, even liquor, are still far superior to the most upmarket of ready meals and come in at half the price.

Many of this generation of shop owners feel that they'll be the last. Yet even the most eel-and-pie averse could not argue as to the beauty of the classic façades, the expanses of marble and the often ornate tiles. The finest of all is F. Cooke, the second shop of Frederick Cooke, opened in 1910. Now closed down and housing a Chinese restaurant, the exterior and interior are still protected by English Heritage. The wide tables are marble and light floods in from four glass domes in the roof. Eels are carved, squirming, into the mirrors' wooden frames, and appear, entwined, at the top of some of the pale-green, blue-and-white tiles. The floor is intricately covered in mosaic tiling, an East End work of beauty to rival any jumped-up Chelsea salon. It's all very well the buildings being saved, but what of the original occupiers? For the time being, their future looks safe, the pies selling like proverbial hot cakes. As for the eel, who knows?

'The food is, in general, bad,' wrote Freidrich Engels in *The Condition of the Working Class in England*, published in 1844, 'often almost unfit for use, and in many cases, at least at times, insufficient in quantity, so that, in extreme cases, death by starvation results.' In 1892, a survey found that the indigent children of Bethnal Green subsisted almost entirely on bread, 83 per cent having no other solid food for seventeen out of twenty-one meals in the week. Engels paints a harrowing, sordid picture of how the poor lived in London.

Every great city has one or more slums, where the working class is crowded together … the worst houses in the worst quarters of the towns; usually one or two-storied cottages in long rows, perhaps with cellars used as dwellings, almost always irregularly built ... The streets are generally unpaved, rough, dirty, filled with animal and vegetable refuse, without sewers or gutters, but supplied with foul, stagnant pools instead ... the atmosphere that prevails in these working men's quarters may be readily imagined.

Little wonder that the pies, cheap and filling, were in such huge demand. He goes on:

On Monday, 15 January 1844, two boys were brought before the police magistrate because, being in starving condition, they had stolen and immediately devoured a half-cooked calf's foot from a shop ... The mother of the two boys was the widow of an ex-soldier, afterwards policeman, and had had a very hard time since the death of her husband, to provide for her nine children. She lived at No. 2 Pool's Place, Quaker Court, Spitalfields, in the utmost poverty. When the policeman came to her, he found her with six of her children literally huddled together in a little back room, with no furniture but two old rush-bottomed chairs with the seats gone, a small table with two legs broken, a broken cup, and a small dish. On the hearth was scarcely a spark of fire, and in one corner lay as many old rags as would fill a woman's apron, which served the whole family as a bed. For bed clothing they had only their scanty day clothing. The poor woman told him she had been forced to sell her bedstead the year before to buy food. Her bedding she had pawned with the victualler for food. In short, everything had gone for food.

While the new middle class obsessed with wearing the right clothes and serving fashionable dishes, the poor survived on scraps from their tables. 'As with clothing, so with food,' notes Engels. 'The workers get what is too bad for the property-holding class.'

James Greenwood, a journalist writing for the *Englishwoman's Domestic Magazine* in 1866, stumbled across a makeshift shop on the edge of a Westminster slum.

It was as though the fragments of a hundred feasts were here gathered – pecks and bushels of bread-crumbs, and meat-crumbs, and the crumbs of game, and poultry, and jellified soups, and all manner of rich puddings ... where did it all come from? Clearly the meat was of the best, and it was wonderfully cheap ... The shopkeeper was also a pig-keeper, and in his second guise collected the kitchen rubbish from the clubs and local lunatic asylums.

A mile or so across town, Fortnum & Mason were selling the finest foie gras, truffled pheasant, 'real West Indian turtle', vintage wine, choice tea and sumptuous hampers. 'Never, to be sure, were there so many carriages ...' writes Charles

Dickens about Derby Day in *Household Words*. '... so many fine ladies in so many broughams, so many of Fortnum & Mason's hampers, so much ice and champagne! If I were on the turf, and had a horse, and had to enter for the Derby, I would call that horse Fortnum & Mason, convinced that with that name he would beat the field.'

As Dickens knew so well, the food of the London rich was an entirely different proposition. Towards the end of the nineteenth century, gluttony and overeating was rife, especially among the prosperous. On experiencing his first Lord Mayor's banquet in 1883, Frank Harris was appalled: 'The first thing that struck me was the extraordinary gluttony displayed by seven out of ten of the city magnates.' His gargantuan neighbour managed three helpings of turtle soup, followed by great chunks of Southdown mutton, 'fit for a prince to eat', splutters the glutton; 'fair melts in your mouth, it does.' The excess of cooked flesh is a common theme in the literature of the time: 'there are few things more unwholesome or disgusting than lumps of one sort of meat, such as we find served up in dear old England,' declares the eponymous organ in Sydney Whiting's *Memoirs of a Stomach* published in 1853.

Nowadays, dazzled by choice and cheapness, we take food – and an excess of food – for granted. We are seldom far from a supermarket packed full with pert, perfectly round and blemish-free apples, bottled pesto, freshly made chorizo and pre-prepared curries. And hard as we might try, it's near impossible to envisage an England where the rich gorged while the poor starved, despite the stories of childhood poverty in Blackpool and elsewhere.

As society began to relax its strictures in the nineteenth century and industrial money flooded in, so the rise of the middle classes began. We always want to better ourselves, to eat finer, whiter bread, more meat, better milk. As food adulteration became endemic, in towns at least, during the eighteenth and nineteenth centuries, the British never stopped to ask why food was so cheap. They just wanted to keep up with the Joneses, and seem able to afford more meat than their neighbours. At the top end of society, English food began to disappear altogether in a riot of omelettes and tartines, while the new middle classes, for the most part, looked up to them in awe.

'This dinner at General Dickson's taught me that good eating was more studied in London than anywhere else in the world ...' wrote Harris. 'But it is only among the better classes that one dines to perfection in London. The best restaurants are no better than the best in Paris or Vienna or Moscow and the English middle class dine worse than the French middle class because they know nothing of cooking as an art and the poor live worse and fare harder than any class in Christendom.'

This was an era of seismic social and economic shifts, when the English moved from the agrarian to the industrial, the soot and smut of the factory stacks replacing the turned earth and bunched stooks of the rural world. Someone born towards the end of Victoria's reign would hardly recognise the England of 100 years earlier. The modern age was upon Britain and, with it, increased prosperity, although this came in partnership with a gradual slide in not just the quality of our food, but our attitudes towards it.

English fare was seen as heavy and unsophisticated, more ruddy-cheeked simpleton than elegant aesthete. The loftier echelons of society should have been protecting our national food, rather than fixating on the next trend. It was their obsession with French food that was as responsible for the decline in our national cuisine as were enclosures and industrialisation. The rich English kitchens regressed to medieval times, with highly ornate, sumptuous dishes, carved and moulded, worked and turned to within an inch of their lives. Out went the pies, stews and pottages, to be replaced by timbales and vol-au-vents, quenelles, soufflés and civets. The middle classes too, concerned with keeping abreast of the latest fashions, aspired to this elaborate French cuisine. Although the diet of the majority of the population grew steadily simpler – fewer sauces, garnishes and flavourings – the food for those at the top became more intricate and complicated.

Another problem was that, towards the end of the century, food, or the enjoyment of it, was seen as an improper subject of conversation. Puritanism was back once more, hiding under a quivering stiff upper lip. The institutional food of the ruling classes was unspeakably poor, on the basis that a little hunger, hardship and greasy mutton gruel was important in the development of one's character. The empire wasn't built on hot chocolate and cream buns, rather on scraps of wretched meat, soggy vegetables and turgid sponge pudding. Because of these ridiculous and hypocritical notions, an entire generation grew up with palates dulled and the notion that food was merely functional. This laid the foundations in later years for a nation uninterested in its national food.

*

Mark Hix and Fergus Henderson are unlikely heroes in the battle against these attitudes. Both are highly respected chefs, specialising in, I suppose, modern British food. Both would balk at that description, as neither likes to be pigeonholed by constrictive labels. They have a love of good food, decent ingredients, cooked well. Hix, originally from Dorset, is a British regional-food fiend. Crumple-faced, modest and as convivial a man as you'll ever meet, he's as far as you can get from the stereotypical, gurning, screaming chef. In the dozen or so years I've known him, I've never heard him so much as raise his voice. The morning after the night before might find his chat a little more subdued, and his hair rather more dishevelled. But having travelled around Dorset, Louisiana, Jalisco and Soho with him, fuelled by the occasional drink, I've learnt there's very little he doesn't know about food, English or otherwise. Anything new is taken in and filed away in his head.

I'll suddenly get a call, sometime in the early evening, telling me to get over there now, as he has a new smoker and has come up with a Hix cure for his salmon. He makes his own celery salt and crackling, has a vast, home-built pizza and bread oven in his back garden (still sitting forlornly, thanks to some tiny flaw yet to be fixed), has created a Hix oyster stout at a local brewery and can talk food for ever. He's initially quite shy and restrained, but after a few drinks you'll find a strong arm curled around your neck, and in your ear the exhortation, 'Eel, I need eel,' as you stumble through Soho in the early hours, trying to remember the Chinese place that stews it so well.

It's his restaurant, the Hix Oyster and Chop House in Clerkenwell, that for me not only sums up Hix's style of cooking, but is also the very essence of London and English food. I wander in on a Thursday afternoon and it's already packed. The place is modern and airy, filled with City escapees and scruffy artists alike. A Tracy Emin neon hangs on the wall and, downstairs, there are blurred photos by the loo of Tim Noble and Sue Webster's artworks. Look closer and you'll find an extreme close-up of a puckered arsehole. 'Most people don't have a clue what they are,' he laughs as we sip his beer, malty and ice cold, from battered silver tankards. As he talks, he smiles at regulars, whispers to staff and types, incessantly and unceasingly, as he does at every hour of the day across the world, on his BlackBerry. With most other people this would be irritating but with Mark it hardly grates at all. The silences are just as comfortable as the talk, making him the most civilised of travelling companions.

So why open a chophouse, I ask, as we demolish a plate of sweet crackling, fresh from the fryer.

'Chophouses and taverns were the London eating houses of the 1800s. Taverns would be simple eating places and the chophouses would be a bit more sophisticated where you could buy big cuts of meat and there were hooks to hang your hat.' At the former, you'd find solid, comfort grub, such as cheese on toast, oysters and soup, while the chophouses were a little more grand, offering steaks and mutton chops cut as thick as a bible, and stews and hotpots too. While the poor relied on the costermongers for street food, and the rich wallowed in the nursery food of their clubs, it was the eating houses that formed the middle ground. Many of the dishes served in them, from boiled beef and carrots through to steak and kidney pudding (Kate and Sydney in cockney), went on to become English classics.

The menu at Hix's is a celebration of good food: native oysters from Colchester and Helford; Cornish crab soup with Julian Temperley's brandy. (Hix is a one-man marketing miracle for Temperley's spirits, using dozens of bottles of the stuff every week. I asked Temperley who looked after his marketing and PR. Mark Hix, he replied with a grin.) You know there's trouble ahead when Mark plonks a bottle of Alchemy on the table, sometime around midnight, and says no one's leaving until it's empty. He stays true to his roots, with Dorset crab on toast and the sweetest prawns from fisherman Billy Winter, but there's also wild rabbit with Peter Gott's black pudding, devilled Herdwick mutton kidneys, roast wood pigeon and ham hock with pease pudding. Steaks are cooked on the bone: Dexter rump for two, Aberdeen Angus porterhouse, shorthorn rib. Simple, English food. Nothing rammed down your neck, no finger wagging or pretentious guff about air miles and the like. Good ingredients, cooked well. This is his mantra. 'I've always loved the idea of the chophouse, with great cuts of really good meat, cooked on the bone. They're part of London's heritage, and in its blood. Now, stop writing and have a bloody drink.'

I meet Fergus Henderson downstairs at St John, the Smithfield restaurant he opened with Trevor Gulliver in 1994. For all the wanton adoration the place inspires, you'd expect Henderson to be some sort of spokesman for English food, a flag-waving advocate for his home country. Henderson and his restaurant staff have trained and inspired a whole new generation of chefs in pursuit of pared-down English food, the likes of Tom Pemberton at Hereford Road (formerly head chef at St John Bread and Wine), Tom Norrington Davies at Great Queen Street, and Jonathan Jones (another protégé) at The Anchor and Hope. All share a love of fine, seasonal ingredients, simply cooked, and the style in which their menus are written – brisk, no-nonsense prose, terse even – owes everything to Henderson: 'Beetroot, boiled egg and anchovy', 'Terrine' or 'Faggot and Mash'. The stars of the dish are the ingredients themselves. In early summer, 'fresh peas in the pod' are just that, freshly picked and impossibly sweet.

As Jay Rayner, restaurant critic of the *Observer*, points out, 'Fifteen years ago, when St John first opened, his menu was regarded more as a curio, designed for the metropolitan, modern-art crowd who liked to hunker down in this bit of London, than something for the masses. If he listed a starter as peas in the pod, that's what you got: the freshest, brightest green peapods. And nothing else. It was seen as a provocation rather than what it was: the celebration of a great ingredient. He cooked with the animal parts others left behind. Today, at last, the gospel according to Henderson is fully understood. Britain is littered with gastropubs and restaurants doing a roaring trade in pig's head galettes and glistening jewels of bone marrow in pigs' trotters, and roast beef served cold and pink on bread fried off in dripping.'

Originally trained as an architect, Henderson is self-taught with close-cropped brown hair and twinkling eyes magnified behind round, tortoiseshell glasses. A few years back, he was diagnosed with Parkinson's disease and in 2005 had electrodes implanted in his brain, a radical new form of treatment that has severely curtailed the spasms he used to suffer. Typically, he brushes off concerns for his health. Just half an hour spent with him somehow improves one's mood and restores faith in humanity. He gesticulates wildly as he talks, as if plucking the suitable word from the air around him. At times, he sounds poetical.

'I enjoy the limitations of the seasons. My food is just plain common sense.' You could fire questions at him for hours, attempting to wear him down by the sheer pomposity of your approach, and he'd never break, nor take credit for what he has done. 'My mum was a great cook, hence St John. And my father, well, he was a great eater. Our aim here is to provide a good lunch or dinner. If that's the case, then I'm happy. I don't mind being seen as English as long as we're not bracketed into some English-themed box. I like the way we've become part of the city's make-up. But it's always good food first. I eschewed, purposefully, the usual English marble and brass, low-voltage lighting and all that.'

He is baffled by the florid, verbose style of many modern menus, 'the ones that have to list every farm, every breed, every bloody name'. He shakes his head. It's eleven in the morning and we both take a sip of Fernet Branca, a viscous brown medicinal draft that he drinks at this time each and every day (either that or Madeira), one small glass, accompanied by a short espresso and slice of seed cake. 'It gets everything going,' he says with a smile. The taste is hardly alluring, but the effect is magical. Suddenly, the sun streaming through the glass doors seems brighter and the white walls glow with bonhomie.

'It's like, hang on, are the customers stupid? Or are they just justifying the extra price? Sometimes we might mention the breed but never go over the top. It seems to me that by going into such detail, you're assuming the customer doesn't trust you. If I have chicken, or lamb, or whatever on the menu, I hope our customers trust us enough to know it will be of good quality.'

Despite St John being held up as the godfather of the new English cookery (a term which, like any other blanket description, he hates), he has little time for fervent culinary patriotism either. 'I'm not jingoistic about food. That's just not good. And it seems foolish in this day and age. I am proud to use olive oil with my skate, or lemons. This is not some sort of themed English restaurant. We didn't set it up with that in mind at all. I'm English, cooking mainly English ingredients in England. So I want our role to be a permanent one, serving food cooked well.'

Around us, waiters bustle about, readying themselves for service. The air is thick with the smell of fresh baking bread and Eccles cakes, sourdough and rye. Fergus has no ego and everyone, from porter to maître d', calls him by his first name. He's also scrupulously polite, in a way that is natural rather than mannered. In a notoriously bitchy world, I've never heard so much as a negative whisper about him. And he's modest too.

A few months back, I had sat on the panel of the *Observer Food Monthly* Awards and, after a very short debate, we had decided to give him the 'Outstanding Achievement Award'. Tonight, he is due to pick it up. Most people would be delighted but Fergus seems surprised, shocked even. Not that he would ever refuse – that would be most impolite – but his cocked eyebrow and slightly embarrassed grin, upon hearing the news, gives the impression he thinks we're all mad for giving it to him. 'I just cook,' I can hear him saying. 'I'm not the man behind any great resurgence in English food. Don't be so silly, dear boy.' Despite this genuine modesty, he is just such a man.

As Jay Rayner, a fellow judge, says, 'Through his restaurant and his books, but mostly through the cheerful, life-affirmingly enthusiastic business of being Fergus Henderson, he has fostered a style of cookery that is uniquely our own; which draws on our traditions without being in hock either to the past or the heavy-handed dominance of French or Italian methods. Because of Fergus Henderson, we finally have a style of food we can call British.'

The dining room itself is as clean and Spartan as the menu's prose, a blank canvas on to which you can project whatever you want. For me, its simplicity is part of its elegance. There are no paintings to distract the eye, no ornate sculptures or second-rate installations to take your mind off the company of friends and the food placed before you. St John is as discreet and modest as its creator, and quintessentially English too. 'The eaters are the decoration here. There are hooks for the coats, and thick tablecloths. You come here to sit down, eat, drink and enjoy.' The fact that the restaurant suffers from a grisly reputation, as a place where only the offally minded will survive, annoys Henderson. 'You get City boys coming in and asking for what they see as the scariest thing on the menu, tripe or chitterlings. That's not the point. People continually want to see this as some concept or thought process. We're just here to provide decent food.'

Before I go, I ask him to name his biggest influence. Grigson? Hartley? Glasse? 'Marcella Hazan [a great Italian cook],' he answers. 'Her recipes are straightforward and they work.' This isn't quite as controversial as it sounds, as he is the first to admit to the Italian and French influences on his menu. English food has always been influenced from abroad. 'Throughout history, the rich ate French, the poor ate shite. That's just the way it was. Even now, though, it amazes me when I hear people complaining they have no time to cook. Putting a rabbit in the oven to braise for two hours actually *gives* you time, for a bath, or a Martini – a good time. It amazes me too when people say, ooh, aren't you clever with your tripe dishes, perfect for the credit crunch. Tripe is always good, recession or not. Perhaps we should think about that more. I mean, look how we embraced chicken Kiev. No bones, lots of breadcrumbs. Very worrying.'

Later that night, at the awards ceremony, a film appears, lionising Henderson and explaining exactly why he won the award, as well as his ongoing influence and inspiration. Other recipients have been known to give Oscar-worthy speeches, thanking everyone from their primary-school teachers to their colonic practitioner. Fergus walks on, accepts the award, smiles briefly and lifts it up an inch, before walking off the stage and disappearing into the crowd. He's off to dinner at

Royal China, just down the road, and doesn't want to miss a mouthful.

Fergus's comment about our readiness to accept foreign food as superior to our own is important. By midway through the nineteenth century, there was a view among the educated that French food was everything that British was not. To quote again from the fictional *Memoirs of a Stomach*: 'I observe, with some degree of surprise, that although Mr John Bull has a reputation for being a great glutton, the French freely pay a much larger sum for their dinner than we do. People whom one could easily imagine not able to afford so many sous, invest from five to twenty francs for their grand meal as a matter of course.' The British are unthinking, all-troughing pigs, while the French are held up as bastions of refinement and elegance. 'But then the Gallic gourmet is an artist,' the stomach goes on.

> Every dish has a chromatic relation with its antecedent. Every condiment has a studied specific purpose; and every bottle of wine is either harmonic, or a proper discord with, the particular entremets over which it is destined to commingle. The English system of cookery it would be impertinent to describe; but when I think of that huge round of par-boiled ox flesh, with sodden dumplings, floating in a saline, greasy mixture, surrounded by carrots looking red with disgust, and turnips pale with dismay, I cannot help a sort of inward shudder, and making comparisons unfavourable to English gastronomy ... Some of these days the gentle

Londoners will, I hope, make it worth while for clubs and taverns to establish a table d'hote, where variety and conversation are both attainable at a reasonable charge.

English food was bland, eaten with patriotic pride. There was no tradition of haute cuisine in England and seemingly no inclination to invent one. Matters were not helped by the fact that cooking was seen, by anyone with money, as something rather base and best left to servants.

The first breath of fresh air came with Eliza Acton's *Modern Cookery for Private Families*, first published in 1845 and described by Elizabeth David as 'the final expression, the crystallisation, of pre-industrial England's taste in food and attitude to cookery'. It remains a first-class cookery book, squarely aimed at the well-to-do middle classes. 'Why should not all classes participate in the benefit to be derived from nourishment calculated to sustain healthfully the powers of life?' she asks in her Preface.

And why should the English, as a people, remain more ignorant than their continental neighbours of so simple a matter of preparing it for themselves? Without adopting blindly foreign modes in anything merely because they are foreign, surely we should be wise to learn from other nations, who excel us in aught good or useful, all that we can which may tend to remedy [our] own defects ... Something definite, practical, easy of application must open the way to our general improvement.

The book is filled with traditional English recipes, as well as a smattering of others from across the world. Sensible, intelligent and easy to use, it's for me one of the very best English cookbooks, a distillation of everything that should be celebrated about our food.

We tend to romanticise the past, imagining the eighteenth and nineteenth centuries as a time when food was fresh, clean and untouched by chemicals, all city streets were infused with the scent of gently roasting chicken and the soft, rounded waft of chestnuts warming on an open fire. The smell of cooking food, while ever present, would have to compete with the stench of open drains and sewage, animal shit and decay.

Conditions were still desperately unhygienic, with market gardens using raw sewage as fertiliser. The Reverend Dr Trusler warns, in *The London Adviser and Guide*, published in 1786, that 'persons used to the country ... will not relish the vegetables and fruit sold in London,' which he attributed to rather too much use of 'night soil'. Pierre Jean Grossley, in *A Tour to London* (1772), is equally scathing of the capital's vegetables. 'All that grow in the country around London, cabbage, radishes, and spinnage, being impregnated with the smoke of sea-coal, which fills the atmosphere of that town, have a very disagreeable taste ... I ate nothing good of this sort in London, but some asparagus.'

As London appetites grew with increased wealth and an expanding population, so did the role of the tricksters and shysters, the scammers and con artists. During the reign of George III, the main roads were improving although many were still in an advanced state of disrepair. Fish often arrived at market stinking and rotten, their gills painted red in sham freshness; meat crawled with maggots, and vendors would often do everything in their power to pass it off as fresh. 'I believe my innocent attendants imagined they were giving me ground corn,' exclaimed the eponymous hero of *Memoirs of a Stomach: Written by Himself, That All Who Eat May Read*. 'Corn indeed! ... when, I say, I came to test it by a strong acid, I found that there was not more than twenty percent of flour in the whole composition, the remainder being made of a common sort of starch, alum, ground bones, potato flour, and often plaster of Paris!' Throughout the previous 400 years, the richer you were, the lighter and more refined the bread you ate. The above allusion to the use of bones, suggesting that graveyards were plundered by dishonest bakers, is mere urban myth, but it was nonetheless taken as truth and perpetuated throughout the period.

It took a German scientist, Friedrich Christian Accum, to expose true culinary sleights of hand in his immensely important *Treatise on Adulterations of Food, and Culinary Poisons* in 1820. In it, he laid bare the hideous truth that wormwood was employed to improve the bitterness in beer and green vitriol to produce a better head, or that poisonous copper was used to make pickles appear more verdant (although this was common practice in the kitchen, born of ignorance, not profiteering), or, worse still, red lead and copper went into children's sweets, to make them appear more garish and attractive. All of these claims were backed up with serious chemical analysis.

Bee Wilson, in *Swindled*, her definitive work on the subject, discusses Smollett's accounts of London life in

Georgian times and argues that 'no one reading Smollett at the time would have believed that London food was really so bad. He exaggerates for the sake of comedy. What is so startling for Accum's earliest readers was the discovery that so many of the adulterations which people had assumed to be comic distortions were actually true.'

Accum did admit that he had had 'abundant reason to be convinced that a vast number of dealers, of the highest respectability, have vended to their customers articles absolutely poisonous, which they themselves considered as harmless, and which they would not have offered for sale, had they been apprised of the spurious and pernicious nature of the compounds'.

When the book was published, it sold over a thousand in a single month and was reprinted many times. Sadly, there was no change in the law as a result. Accum was accused of tearing leaves and plates from books in the reading room of the Royal Institution, and was finally caught red-handed (via a secret peephole) ripping pages from the *Journal of Natural Philosophy, Chemistry and the Arts*, commonly known as *Nicholson's Journal*. He was arrested and charged with robbery. As to why, no one is entirely sure. Although he was not convicted, the Royal Institution prosecuted him separately and his publishers dropped him. Instead of attending the hearing in April 1821, he jumped bail and went back to Germany, humiliated and broken, never to return. Many claimed that he was the victim of a conspiracy, that his naming and shaming of all the adulterators and scammers had provoked their revenge.

'Accum was subjected to a violent and bitter campaign of abuse on the part of those he had so ruthlessly exposed,' write Drummond and Wilbraham. 'It seems likely that Accum was guilty [more than likely], but that does not absolve those who were instrumental in bringing the case from a charge of vindictive persecution.'

Yet Bee Wilson is rather more clear-headed in her summing up. 'Even though he had powerful enemies, they were merchants and not scientists; the humble assistant librarian of the Royal Institution seems to have had no motive for lying about what he saw through the peephole.'

Although Accum disappeared in a cloud of scandal, his legacy ensured that the likes of Dr Hassell wrote powerfully on the subject of the adulteration of coffee in *The Lancet* in 1851, also naming and shaming the guilty. There were other, similar exposures over the next four years, with the eventual result that a Select Parliamentary Commission was set up in 1855 to look into food adulteration. By 1860, the first Food and Drugs Act was passed, although it was fairly impotent until 1872, when the Act was amended to stipulate that the police had to employ analysts. By 1875, it had grown teeth, and fines for manufacturers convicted of adulteration were actually quite severe.

Accum's views on British food were as valid as his experiments on adulterations. He venerated the raw materials but deplored what was done to them while despairing that the British were more obsessed with appearance than actual taste. In a time of intense change and social mobility, everyone wanted to sip the finest teas, or bite into the whitest, most refined bread, yet they never wondered why the products were sold so cheaply. As long as the item *appeared* like the real thing, the detail was irrelevant. This unfortunate legacy continued for the next 200 years.

Now, things are rather different. Provided you know where to look, away from the Leicester Square cack vendors and tartan steakhouse, London is one of, if not *the* greatest eating city on earth, unlike Paris, where it's virtually impossible to find any decent food other than French, or Milan, where it's actually impossible. London has an entire international spread of foreign restaurants. And English food, in particular, has boomed. At the start of the twenty-first century, we've finally come full circle, through the horrors of food adulteration and the strictures of rationing, to a true appreciation of English food once more.

ROAST BONE MARROW
AND PARSLEY SALAD

This is a modern English classic, and one of the most popular dishes at Fergus Henderson's restaurant, St John. The combination of wobbly marrow, crunchy salt and crisp, sourdough toast is one of the best in the world. Add a sparky, verdant parsley salad, studded with capers, and you have London perfection.

As to the marrowbones, you'll need to order them from your butcher and you'll need long, sundae-like spoons to scrape out every last morsel. The recipe, as you'll see, is testament to Ferguson's laconic, elegant style.

Serves 4

12 x 7–8 cm pieces of middle veal marrowbone
healthy bunch flat-leaved parsley, picked from its stems
2 shallots, peeled and very thinly sliced
modest handful capers (extra-fine if possible)

Dressing
juice of 1 lemon
extra-virgin olive oil
pinch sea salt and freshly ground black pepper
good supply sourdough toast
coarse sea salt

Do you recall eating Sultana Bran for breakfast? The sultana to bran-flake ratio was always a huge anxiety, to a point, sometimes, that one was tempted to add extra sultanas, which invariably resulted in too many sultanas, and one lost that pleasure of discovering the occasional sweet chewiness in contrast to the branny crunch. With administering such things as capers it is very good to remember Sultana Bran.

Put the bone marrow in an ovenproof frying pan and place in a hot oven. The roasting process should take about 20 minutes depending on the thickness of the bone. You are looking for the marrow to be loose and giving, but not melted away, which it will do if left too long (traditionally the ends would be covered to prevent any seepage, but I like the colouring and crispness at the end).

Meanwhile lightly chop your parsley, just enough to discipline it, mix it with the shallots and capers, and at the last moment, dress.

Here is a dish that should not be completely seasoned before leaving the kitchen, rendering a last-minute seasoning unnecessary by the actual eater; this, especially in the case of coarse sea salt, gives texture and uplift at the moment of eating. My approach is to scrape the marrow from the bone onto the toast and season with coarse sea salt. Then add a pinch of parsley salad on top of this and eat. Of course, once you have your pile of bones, salad, toast, and salt it is 'liberty hall'.

DEVILLED BONES

One variation on the theme of marrowbones is the clubland classic, Devilled Bones. This recipe comes from Florence White's *Good Things in England* and was found at Boodle's Club, in St James.

Serves 4

115 g (4 oz) butter, at room temperature
1 tsp dry English mustard
1 tsp freshly ground black pepper
1 tsp salt
1 tsp curry powder
½ tsp cayenne pepper
1 tbsp Worcestershire sauce
4 veal bones with a little meat on

Preheat the oven to 220°C/200°C fan/gas mark 7. Work together the butter, mustard, pepper, salt, curry powder, cayenne pepper and Worcestershire sauce. Chill in the fridge.

First score the meat, then roast the bones for 20 minutes in the preheated oven.

Coat the bones with the devilled butter and put under a preheated grill for 2–3 minutes and serve immediately.

DEEP-FRIED WHITEBAIT

The annual whitebait season used to be a greedily anticipated affair, when these little fish were caught in huge shoals around July by vessels anchored just off Blackwall in the Thames tideway. The collective term for the fry of herring and sprat, they were so delicate that they had to be fried up the moment they left the water, hence the crowds converging on taverns around Blackwall and Greenwich.

But it wasn't just the average Londoner who had a taste for whitebait. MPs, too, would feast on them at the end of a parliamentary session. Ministers dined on them at the Trafalgar Tavern, while to ensure the peace was kept the opposition indulged at the nearby Old Ship Tavern. There was also a tradition of starting these dinners with 'watersouchy', a seventeenth-century English fish soup that used up any unwanted stragglers in the whitebait nets.

This recipe comes from Mark Hix's *British Regional Food*. Whitebait are rarely found fresh any more, but I did happen across some at a local fishmonger recently and I took the whole lot.

Serves 4

vegetable oil, for deep frying
100 g (3½ oz) flour
pinch sea salt
good pinch cayenne pepper

400 g (14 oz) frozen whitebait, defrosted
100 ml (3½ fl oz) milk
lemon wedges, to serve
tartare sauce, to serve

Preheat about 8 cm (3 in) oil to 160–180°C in a large, heavy-based saucepan or electric deep-fat fryer.

Mix the flour with a pinch of sea salt and the cayenne pepper. Dust the whitebait in the flour, shake off the excess and dip briefly in the milk, then back again in the flour. Ensure they are well coated and shake off excess flour again.

Fry the fish in 2 or 3 batches, depending on how many you're cooking, for 3–4 minutes each batch, until crisp. Drain on kitchen paper and season again with sea salt.

Serve immediately with lemon wedges and tartare sauce.

STEAK, KIDNEY AND OYSTER PUDDING

OK, so steak, kidney and oyster pudding might not be a quint-essential London dish but it's one I always associate with good pubs in the city. The Cheshire Cheese pub was renowned for its huge steak and kidney pudding, weighing up to 36 kg (80 lb) and taking 20 hours to boil. It's proper pub grub, rich and hearty, using local oysters, and beef from across the country.

Although we assume it's as ancient as cold water, the first time this dish is recorded is in Eliza Acton's *Modern Cookery for Private Families*, without the kidney, listed under 'John Bull's Pudding'. Mrs Beeton added the first kidney to the recipe in 1859. Her recipe came from Sussex, a county famed for its puddings, but I still see it as a Londoner. This comes from Jane Grigson's classic, *English Food*.

Serves 6

Filling
1 kg (2 lb) rump steak
500 g (1 lb) veal or ox kidney
2 tbsp seasoned plain flour
1 large onion, peeled and chopped
90 g (3 oz) butter
600 ml (1 pt) beef stock, or half each of stock and red wine
250 g (8 oz) mushrooms, sliced
1 bouquet garni
18 rock oysters

Suet crust
300 g (10 oz) self-raising flour
1 level tsp baking powder
¼ tsp salt
freshly ground white pepper
¼ tsp fresh thyme, chopped
150 g (5 oz) chopped suet
cold water

Preheat the oven to 140–150°C/120–130°C fan/gas mark 1–2. To make the filling, cut the steak into neat 2 cm (¾ in) pieces and slice the kidney. Discard the fat and skin from both meats. Sprinkle them with seasoned flour. Cook the onion until lightly browned in two-thirds of the butter. Remove from the pan with a slotted spoon and set aside. Add the meat to the pan, to colour rapidly. Transfer the meat, as it is browned, to an ovenproof casserole.

Pour the stock, or stock and wine, into the frying pan and allow it to boil hard for a few moments, while you scrape in all the nice brown bits and pieces. Pour this over the meat. Fry the mushrooms in the remaining butter and add them with the bouquet garni to the casserole. Cover with lid and simmer in the preheated oven, until the steak and kidney is almost cooked – about 1½ hours.

Leave the casserole to cool. If the liquid part of the filling is on the copious and watery side, strain it off and boil it down. Then open the oysters and add them, liquor and all. Taste and season.

To make the crust, mix all the dry ingredients in a large

bowl, so that the suet is evenly distributed. Stir in enough cold water with a wooden spoon to make a firm dough. Roll out on a floured surface into a large circle, cut away a quarter and put to one side for the lid. Butter a 1½ litre (2¾ pint) pudding basin generously, and press the three-quarter circle of pastry into it to fit, allowing 2½ cm (1 in) to overhang the rim. Put the filling in the basin: it should not come higher than 2½ cm (1 in) below the rim. Roll out the remaining crust and cut a circle to make the lid. Press the edges together to make a firm seal.

Cut some foil to make a circle 5 cm (2 in) larger all round than the top of the pudding basin. Fix it in place with your fingers so that it balloons above the pudding, leaving it room to rise. Tie a string handle round the rim of the basin, for easy lifting.

When the water is boiling in the lower part of the steamer, put the pudding in and leave for 1½–2 hours. Keep an eye on the water level and top up with more boiling water if necessary.

If you do not have a steamer, put a trivet on the base of a large saucepan and add about 10 cm (4 in) water. Bring to the boil. When boiling steadily, lower the basin into it. The water should come about two-thirds of the way up the sides. Put the lid on the large saucepan and leave it to boil for 1½–2 hours.

Once cooked, serve immediately.

EEL PIE

Here's another London classic from Florence White. 'Mr
Aeneas Dallas of *The Times* (during the 1860s and 1870s) says:
"This used to be a famous pie, but we hear little of it now."'
At the start of the twenty-first century, it's all but extinct. This
comes from Mr Dallas, and is a Richmond recipe from 1873.
My additions are in square brackets.

Serves 4

2 Thames eels [or any others]
2 shallots
15 g (½ oz) butter
small faggot fresh parsley, chopped
freshly grated nutmeg [a good pinch]
freshly ground black pepper
salt
2 glasses sherry [Fino or Manzanillo]
55 g (2 oz) butter
55 g (2 oz) flour [plain]
juice of 1 lemon
hard-boiled eggs [3 or 4]
puff pastry

Skin, cleanse and bone the Thames eels. Cut these into pieces.
Chop the shallots; pass them in butter for 5 or 6 minutes
[soften them over a low heat] then add parsley, nutmeg,
pepper, salt, and the 2 glasses of sherry.

In the midst of this place the eels, add enough water to cover them, and set them on the fire to boil. When they have boiled up, take out the pieces of eel and keep them hot. Strain the stock in which they were cooked.

Melt the butter and add the flour in the usual way for a foundation sauce [that is, make a white roux]. Add the strained stock, beat quite smooth, boil up and finish with the lemon juice.

Arrange the pieces of eel, and quarters of hard-boiled eggs in a pie dish. Pour the sauce over it, and when cold, roof the pie with the puff pastry.

Bake in a hot oven at first [about 200°C/180° fan/gas mark 6 for 20 minutes, or until risen and golden], to raise the pastry and then in a cooler one [170°C/150°C fan/gas mark 3 for 30 minutes), 1 hour all told.

Mr Dallas concludes, 'and lo! A pie worthy of Eel-Pie Island. It is a great question debated for ages on Richmond Hill whether this pie is best hot or cold. It is perfect either way.'

6

Full English

'No one who can get good porridge,' grumbled P. Morton Shand in one of his more restrained moments, 'would ever want to eat those nauseating proprietary cereals.' The cereals in question, in 1927, were American arrivistes, conveniently packaged bags of dried wheat and oats to be served with milk as a lighter start to the day. Healthy, rather than heavy, and more pious than indulgent, they were seen as a fresh-faced, gleaming-toothed alternative to the pot-bellied, constipated and sallow English breakfast.

'Throughout the 1920s, the growing taste for all things modern and American made The English Breakfast seem very old fashioned,' writes Kaori O'Connor in *The English Breakfast*, 'although to its partisans that was its very appeal.'

Who, in their right mind, would prefer soggy flakes of corn to plump, peppery sausages or half a dozen rashers of good smoked streaky? It's not just a question of taste, but attitude.

Cereal is food as fuel, to be spooned into the mouth while digesting the sport and gossip. Can there be more wretched a sight than the office worker, late for work and sprinting up the escalators at Piccadilly Circus, shovelling what looks like sodden cardboard from a plastic tray into his mouth, his tie splashed with milk and his eyes still bleary with sleep? It represents all that is wrong with cereal. A once-noble feast demeaned and truncated, neatly boxed and packaged into yet another fast food.

I realise that most people have neither the time, nor the inclination, to wake up at six and cook themselves a gut-straining breakfast before shuffling off to work. The majority of us no longer need the extra calories to carry us through a long day of hard manual labour. Nor do we have a glut of idle mornings to fill with platefuls of devilled bones and snipe on toast. All the same, eating cereal is a miserable way to start the day.

'Our peculiar and substantial breakfast,' continues Shand, 'daunts a great many of those brought up in the bacon odour of its sanctity. While anything but an ideal repast for the average intellectual worker, it is far from inspiring dismay among the numerically preponderant sportsmen, for whom it has a serious advantage in our climate when considered in relation to a light lunch.'

The English breakfast reached its apotheosis in Victorian and Edwardian days, in particular among the landed gentry. The cold grouse and hot, buttered eggs, the plover's eggs and pigeon pie, the ox tongue and rissoles of hare, were as much an edible display of power and Englishness (despite the numerous French recipes), of control over one's estate, as they were the first meal of the day.

> My bread is sweet and nourishing, [writes Matthew Bramble to Dr Lewis in Smollett's *The Expedition of Humphrey Clinker* (1770)] made from my own wheat, ground in my own mill and baked in my own oven; my table is, in a great measure, furnished from my own ground; my five-year-old mutton, fed on the fragrant herbage of the mountains, that might vie with venison in juice and flavour; my delicious veal, fattened with nothing but the mother's milk, that fills the dish with gravy; my poultry from the barn door, that never knew confinement but when they were at roost; my rabbits panting from the warren; my game fresh from the moors; my trout and salmon struggling from the streams; oysters from their native banks; and herrings, with other sea-fish, I can eat in four hours after they are taken.

This is the popular vision of bucolic splendour and self-sufficiency, and although the above is fictional it could easily be applied to a hundred such estates. These vast breakfasts didn't represent just the local, but the national too. The Edwardian breakfast was Rule Britannia on a plate, the ballast that made England great. How was a man supposed to set off for a decent day's empire building on the slender offerings of a continental breakfast?

Now, of course, breakfast has taken on a new importance, as the meal no sensible person dare miss. We're endlessly harried and lectured as to its nutritional importance by a thousand earnest little men with neatly trimmed nails. Skip this meal, they warn, and you'll suffer a cruel and untimely death. One mention of the Full English, though, and peppermint-scented outrage spews forth from thin, bloodless lips. Phrases like 'saturated fat', 'hardened arteries' and 'death wish' are bandied about, with little thought for the true significance of the Full English. It's one of our great contributions to world food, a paean to the pig and the egg. As Heston Blumenthal points out, 'The Full English is unique and a brilliant way to showcase produce.'

Times have moved on a little since Somerset Maugham remarked, somewhat uncharitably, that 'To eat well in England you should have breakfast three times a day.' Contrary to popular legend, the Celts weren't scrambling eggs as the Romans arrived in AD 43, nor were the Anglo-Saxons dipping their sausages in beans when William of Normandy dropped by in 1066. Despite seeming as traditionally English as Miss Marple playing old maid with Vera Lynn at a Ditchling tea dance, the Full English is a relatively modern invention.

You're never far from a Full English. Whether it's Italians cooking up eggs in East End art deco palaces, Poles shovelling beans or caff workers filling your plate with chips, it's a universal institution. From the thick-carpeted hush of the grander hotels, all cloches and tailcoats, to the early-morning babble of the local caff, the key ingredients remain the same. Eggs, bacon, grilled tomato and sausage are the regulars, flanked by any combination of mushrooms, black pudding, bubble and squeak, baked beans, chips, kidneys and even steak. This is a construction that stands and falls by the quality of its ingredients but is the thirty-quid breakfast really ten times superior to the £3 blow-out?

I decide to start local, and Zippy's on the Goldhawk Road has come recommended. Well, recommended in a particularly English way. 'At least it's clean,' said the veg man at the nearby market. Only in England could the hygienic standard of a restaurant be reason enough to visit. Still, it looks the part, with red-and-white, faux-leather banquettes and wood-effect tables. On one side, mirrors cover the wall, while any other available space is plastered in those cheap, generic, Seventies photographs of 'Cheeseburger, Yum' or 'Enjoy Our Mixed Grill' with various pieces of neatly symmetrical meat lined up for the camera. The menu is classic caff, taking in everything from spaghetti bolognese and lasagne to liver and bacon and curried chicken. The room is full, mainly with builders fuelling up for the day ahead, and the odd older lady, chewing slowly on an egg sandwich while glued to the *Express*.

I sit down and order the Big Breakfast: 'two eggs, two rashers, fried slice, tomatoes, mushrooms, one sausage, tea and toast.' The simplicity of the prose comes as an unexpected relief. No 'pan-fried' bacon, or 'vine-ripened' tomato (as if a tomato could ripen anywhere else but on its vine), 'hand-picked' mushrooms or 'rare-breed' sausages. Granted, I am pretty certain the bacon will be Dutch, the tomatoes wan and insipid and the sausage filled with meat of indeterminate quality, but as English breakfasts go, this is the average, the mean against which all others are measured.

The tea is dark and tannic, the perfect accompaniment to this feast of grease. The eggs are perfectly runny, the bacon well cooked (if bland and oversalty) and the fried slice? It is a piece of cheap white bread, marinated in hot grease, just as it should be, and utterly delectable. The sausage is a touch unnerving, very much of the old school (that is, 'slurry-filled condoms', in the immortal words of Jonathan Meades), though far from grotesque. The tomatoes have barely been introduced to the grill, while the mushrooms ooze oil and lack any flavour whatsoever. As for the bubble and squeak, the portion is generous but the edges sadly uncrisped.

There are no baked beans, because I feel they sully a decent breakfast, creeping insidiously across the plate and tainting everything with their sweet tomato tang. On toast, great, even eaten cold from the can, but for breakfast they're extraneous and plain wrong. All this, though, plus endless toast and tea, for £4.50. A hell of a deal and a perfectly respectable breakfast. Not a prizewinner, nor a dunce either. Solid and workmanlike. Oh, and the restaurant is spotless, just as the veg man had said.

The Romans saw breakfast as the least important meal of the day, as did the Anglo-Saxons. The French were equally unimpressed by the concept, making do with a piece of bread and the odd sip of wine. As for the clergy, they ate just twice per day, once at noon and once at dusk. Anyway, in an age when the Church still ruled supreme, it wasn't particularly good form to be seen feasting before morning prayers. Skipping breakfast was also closely connected to snobbery. The more prosperous you were, the later you ate your first meal. While the peasants rose with the sun to tend to their fields and flocks, the rich had no need.

However, after William and his Norman conquest, the food of England took two rather different paths, in a pattern that would be endlessly repeated throughout the centuries. All classes ate bread and drank ale, yet the peasant subsisted on maslin, a rough loaf of wheat and rye, while the wealthy enjoyed pandemain, a thrice-sifted loaf. Thanks, though, to the medieval system of agriculture, which offered benefits alongside disadvantages, the lot of the peasant wasn't entirely wretched. The lords of the manors were all-powerful and owned huge fields, worked by manor employees with help from the villagers. In what certainly wasn't a voluntary arrangement, they owed their lord a set number of days' work, which could also be discharged in cash or kind. Yet once they had done m'lud's ploughing and planting, they were free to farm their own patch of ground. These shared fields were divided into long strips of about an acre and each family held between four and six. In the spirit of fair play, these were evenly divided out so that no one family got the prime plot. Evidence exists of some villagers working up to thirty acres of land, but this was rare. Although this system offered some freedom, the lord came first, so at busy times such as ploughing and harvesting, everyone mucked in together.

As to the standard of life of the average peasant, it wasn't all bad. If the harvest went well, and the winter wasn't too harsh, all the basics would be in decent supply. 'In the good years they were well nourished, probably considerably better than the poor country people in the rest of Europe,' according to Drummond and Wilbraham in *The Englishman's Food*. The villein could grow barley or rye for coarse bread, and his little plot would support a few legumes and beans. When the harvest was poor, he would resort to bread made from beans, peas, even acorns. There was common land where he could graze his cow, sheep or goat, and a few chickens that foraged, pecked and scratched. The cow would provide essential 'white meats', curds and whey, buttermilk, salty butter and cheese. This, along with the ever-present bread, was a winter staple.

Bacon was also popular, although meat was very much a luxury, eaten rarely and sparingly. 'And yet I seye, by my soule!/I have no salt bacon,/Ne no cokeney [egg] by Crist!' bewailed Piers Plowman. While bacon was not eaten for breakfast, this is the first mention we have of the famous pairing, bacon and eggs. The pig was the ideal beast, foraging for food so as to need little attention. As winter drew on, it would be slaughtered and cured. In the Middle Ages, pigs were more similar to wild boars than the swine we know today, with long snouts and a shock of coarse hair along the spine.

Pottages were eaten by all classes and were often much loved. 'Potage is not so moch vsed in al Crystendom as it is vsed in Englande,' wrote Andrew Boorde in his *Compendyous Regyment, or a Dyetary of Helth* of 1542. But the less money one had, the more dull your pottage would become. The peasants made do with a basic pease pottage, while the rich would mix stock with meat, herbs, cereals or pulses. These soups were generally thick and hearty, sometimes so dense you could slice them with a knife.

Oysters were cheap for those who lived by the east coast, and whelks too. Otherwise, the nearest the inland peasant would get to fish would be a scrap of rigid salt cod. After the

Norman conquest, all game was deemed the personal property of the king and his lords, and poaching was often punishable by death. While this did not deter the starving, it still made for a particularly risky meal. The food of the poor was basic and hardly exciting, but it was nutritious and it laid the basis of the English diet for years to come. Breakfast, as we know it today, would be the invention of a wealthier class.

> By the thirteenth century there was a social hierarchy with the king at the top, [writes Kaori O'Connor] followed by the nobility or magnates and then the knights ... The word 'knight' comes from a Saxon root, showing that many Saxons had attained knightly rank. Yet even though some Saxons had prospered and the Normans now spoke English, there were still two cultures, the 'old' England of the Saxons and the 'new' England of the Normans ... It was from among the knightly families that a new social group emerged who would be closely linked to the English breakfast. These were the squires.

English, rather than French, in their outlook, they celebrated their Anglo-Saxon roots, lauding the traditional and the English, whether in hunting, eating or writing. While the midday meal was still the main one, if earlier business needed the squire's attention then cold meat, eggs and cheeses would be made available.

However, it was the arrival of that rare and expensive delicacy tea, in the middle of the seventeenth century, that turned breakfast into a proper meal. Such was the popularity of this hot drink that fashionable types began throwing breakfast parties, with toast, hot chocolate and coffee. Breakfast rooms came next, followed by a never-ending arsenal of teapots and toast racks, cups and saucers, braising dishes and tea strainers. It was a revolution that took place at the top of society, so to sample an equivalent these days, I'd have to find a suitably grand and old-school establishment. What I didn't expect was a dress code.

'Gentlemen should be appropriately attired,' said the voice on the end of the telephone.

'Appropriately attired for what?' I wanted to scream. Fishing? Battle? Exploration of the Amazon?

When pressed further, she admitted that this meant 'smart casual', two words that fill me with hate. Smart is easy enough, a suit and all that. If the dress code says tie, then you know where you stand. And casual is, well, whatever you want. But a mixture of the two is a loathsome hybrid, a code understood only by chino-clad merchant bankers and regional BBC presenters.

What about jeans, I ask? 'If they're smart,' she replies. And trainers? 'Ditto.'

Now Simpson's-in-the-Strand is a London institution, a temple to vast ribs of beef, expertly sliced at the table. It first opened in 1828 as a chess club and coffee house, called The Grand Cigar Divan, and was celebrated as 'the home of chess'. The legend goes that the large joints of meat were originally placed on silver-domed trolleys so that they could be silently wheeled in without disturbing the players, a tradition that continues to this day. It's a nice story, but why not just carve the meat in the kitchen and bring it out? Or carry in the joints and set them down, quietly? And in any case, surely the eating of a full roast would naturally disturb the flow of play? That aside, Simpson's is certainly an institution, if the calibre of its clientele is anything to go by – Dickens, Disraeli, Gladstone and Van Gogh to name but a few. These days, the main room smells of faded grandeur. The carpets are thick and soft, but worn and frayed at the edges. The room is staid, wood-panelled and only a third full. Its customers are a curious mixture of tourists, earnest businessmen discussing sales targets between bites of kipper, and clubbable types, transfixed by their *Daily Telegraph*. The waiters are clad in tails. The walls are clad in wood. And I'm clad in a collared shirt, my only concession to the ghastly smart casual.

The breakfast menu contains the usual greatest hits of kippers, eggs and bacon and the rest, but calling itself the 'Ten Deadly Sins' grabs my attention, for all the wrong reasons. It's a Great English Breakfast (eggs, bacon, black pudding, toma-toes, mushrooms and Cumberland sausage) with the addition of lamb's kidney, fried bread, bubble and squeak and baked beans. A mighty plateful, sure, but why the stupid name? It reduces an august cast of ingredients (baked beans excepted) to some end-of-pier novelty, like calling a frozen, processed pudding 'Death by Chocolate'. Am I supposed to feel oh-so-indulgent and wicked for ordering a big breakfast? Is gluttony represented by the sausage or the fried bread? Which sin is the tomato? Lust? Envy? This is not the sort of debate needed at eight o'clock on a Friday morning. I just want a damned fry-up.

The orange juice is, at least, freshly squeezed, and the twenty-five minutes it takes to cook my breakfast give me ample time to study the orchid flower, incongruous among all the pomp and dark wood, floating on a glass of water on my table. The toast is brought, made from cheap, sliced bread. If anyone could stretch to decent bread, you might have thought it was Simpson's, but there's a moribund air to the whole place, as if the Savoy Group (the owners) are letting the place die of natural causes before burying the body and starting anew.

When the hot food eventually arrives, the plate seems more sinned against than sinning. Parsimony is the first word that springs to mind – a lonely fried egg squatting next to a slender slice of black pudding, a blob of bubble and squeak, a couple of undercooked tomatoes, some gloomy-looking bacon and a minuscule kidney. The sausage, though, is a magnificent specimen, plump, porky and peppery. The bacon seems as if it has sat around for too long, perfectly OK but only a jot superior to the pork at Zippy's. What little there is of the kidney is a little overcooked but still pleasingly tender. The black pudding would have been chased out of Bury market for sheer mediocrity. Simpson's take on bubble and squeak is more herby croquette than crisp shards of potato and cabbage. It tastes fine, if overseasoned. As for the fried bread, you really have to try hard to bugger up bread cooked in fat, and one version differs little from the next.

The bill comes: £22.55 for a semi-comfortable seat and a superior sausage. Daylight bloody robbery. The service is polite and efficient, but no different, save the tails, from Zippy's, and I had to tackle the whole 'smart casual' crap too. Simpson's might once have produced a breakfast to beat them all but now the place seems to be resting on its laurels, hoping that an illustrious past will cover up the shortcomings of the present.

By Victorian times, lunch had become the least important meal of the day, and breakfast, for the middle and upper classes at least, was increasingly dominant. Breakfast was also the most informal of meals, with the servants very much behind the scenes. It was customary for guests to serve themselves and hot dishes were either cooked to order or kept warm under great silver cloches. The cold dishes, hams and game pies, perched on the sideboard. Ladies were free to take their breakfasts in bed while the men fuelled up for the day's shooting or hunting ahead. The choice was often staggering, in terms of variety and volume – devilled partridge and potted beef, omelettes and baked truffles, veal and ham pie, kidneys and crumpets, collared beef, pickled veal, brawn and boiled fish, pickled mackerel and oyster loaves, prawn pudding and kippered mackerel. There were stews and civets, raised pies and pressed caviar. In fact, there was very little that didn't appear at breakfast, save soup, hot roasts, green vegetables and steamed puddings.

Even twenty years ago, when I was shooting with my father, the country-house breakfast was still a magnificent affair. I'd pad downstairs, head a little fuzzy from the previous night's excess, to find multiple copies of every paper, pressed and neatly laid out on one side. Conversation was kept to the bare minimum, a smile and a nod being quite sufficient. P. Morton Shand was a great believer in silence as he ate his bacon and eggs: 'Breakfast, an essentially unsociable meal,' he wrote, 'is an appropriate time to choose for disinheriting one's natural heirs.' You suspect he was only half joking.

However, the contents of the silver chafing dishes that awaited me on these occasions were balm for even the most bloodshot of eyes. Armfuls of crisp, streaky bacon, home-made sausages, burnished and sticky. Eggs cooked however you pleased, fresh field mushrooms in the late autumn and tomatoes grilled to the point of collapse. This would serve as a preamble to a thick slice of York ham, pink and alluring, toast and home-made marmalade, even a brace of cold grouse or woodcock for the truly greedy. Sunday, once the shooting was over, meant kedgeree, studded with flakes of smoked haddock and just a hint of curry. Too much, and all is ruined, the spice stamping over any subtleties and dominating the entire dish.

The public schools, those staid institutions where sons of the middle and upper classes were taught that the world was theirs for the ruling, venerated breakfast. While every other meal might have consisted of unspeakable stodge, breakfast had the advantage of being eaten all day long, because it was cooked by junior fags. Even when I was at Eton, at the end of the Eighties when fagging and corporal punishment were on the way out, staple breakfast food, such as bacon, sausages, eggs, toast and cereal, could be devoured at any hour. Shand saw the public-school art of breakfast as justification for the entire system of education.

Our public school fags can make perfectly golden, perfectly crisp and yet perfectly spongy toast, for the simple reason that they are properly beaten should any one of the eight, pluperfect, decrusted triangles, which constitute a fag-master's traditional portion, evince the slightest sign of scraping, uneven cutting, excessive thickness or imperfect saturation with butter ... The public school system seems to me amply vindicated in that it teaches boys to make toast and ... to prepare such simple dishes as buttered eggs, or to fry bacon and kippers to perfection ... It may be an abominable action to beat a boy for a bad translation of Livy ... but it is certainly laudable to beat him for clumsily burning one's toast.

Successfully indoctrinated in the art of breakfast, the future masters of the universe could go forth, from Canada to Calcutta, and spread the good word.

But it was at the table of Edward VII, that monarch of mighty appetites, where breakfast reached a pinnacle of gluttonous excess. We tend to look back on the Edwardian era as some kind of golden age, 'constantly described as a long and sunlit afternoon' in the words of Roy Hattersley, before the wars came and changed the nation irrevocably, killing almost a whole generation of men and forever depriving us of our innocence.

'Ah! – those wonderful parties in town, Season after Season, when we danced until dawn – those long summer afternoons, when we sauntered through the gardens of the great houses that entertained us in those days, those afternoons that somehow shrivelled, faded, then vanished from the world! What days, what nights! What nostalgia, what regrets!' writes J.B. Priestley in *The Edwardians*, although as a self-proclaimed lower-middle-class Northerner he had little interest in the japes of the upper classes. 'But nobody must be deceived; I am merely being rhetorical. I never enjoyed such days, such nights, except in print ... Not only was I far removed from Edwardian high society but I never set eyes on a single member of it.' For those who occupied the most exalted echelons of Edwardian society, life was hardly arduous. The cost of living was still low, personal taxation fairly non-existent, and hordes of servants, hidden below stairs, kept the whole machine running smoothly. The King, dismissed by Hattersley as a man who 'personified benevolent self-indulgence', made the perfect leader for this gilded time.

'In the last years of her reign Queen Victoria had made few suggestions concerning the menus that were presented for her passing each day by the chef,' Gabriel Tschumi recalls in *Royal Chef*, 'but we found that King Edward and Queen Alexandra took a far more active part in making decisions about the meals served in their Household. They also had very definite likes and dislikes in food, and were quite firmly of the opinion that the meals served at Buckingham Palace should be the best in the world.' French haute cuisine, or the *cuisine classique*, was still very much the dominant force at formal state banquets. Edward, a man whose appetite was admirably matched by his girth, was well known for his adoration of foie gras and ortolans sautéed in brandy, but he was equally enamoured with good, plain English food. Beef stew and dumplings were held in the same high regard as the finely tuned fripperies of Chaufroix de Volaille à la Christiania. It's telling that Tschumi, who started as apprentice chef under

Victoria and ascended to royal chef to Queen Mary, writing in 1954, talks of Edward's love of 'plain food – what was called, in the days before the expression lost its original meaning and became tinged with a certain amount of scorn, "good English cooking"'.

His love of this good English food was such that he introduced the tradition of serving roast beef, Yorkshire pudding, roast potatoes and horseradish sauce every Sunday night at Buckingham Palace, replacing the usual cream-rich Gallic creations. It was a custom popular with the entire royal household. His shooting lunches were equally traditional, usually made up of rib-sticking comfort food, thick Scotch broths, mulligatawny soup, hashed venison, stewed mutton, game pies, Irish stew and plum pudding. Edward was more than happy to mix haute cuisine and English food, and certainly appreciated the more classical efforts of his kitchen. Tschumi talks, with breathless admiration, of a typical lunch at Royal Ascot in June 1908. It reads like the entire menu of some high-church French pleasure palace: consommé froid and mousse de crabe with sauce rémoulade, then filets de saumon à l'Isabelle, chaufroix de volaille à la Christiania, noisettes d'agneau nappées à la Valenciennes, jambonneaux à la Montranchez, cailles froides à la Bohémienne and asperges en branches froides. This was followed by a multitude of puddings: Eton mess aux cerises, gooseberry fool, pâtisseries à la Parisienne, biscuits glacé aux pêches and mignardises. For those poor, unfortunate souls who found this fare a little too delicate, there was always the essential fall-back of a vast cold buffet table, piled high with Derby beef, lamb and mint sauce, roast beef, pressed beef, veal galantine, York ham, jellied chicken, chicken pâté, Romaine salad, cakes and tarts. How anyone managed to crawl down the stairs after all this, I'll never know.

A night at the opera was equally lavish, with nine or ten courses, all cold, served from gold plates by six of Edward's footmen. Tschumi, in *Royal Chef*, remembers that 'these supper menus always began with cold consommé and ended with patisserie ... there would be lobster mayonnaise, cold trout, duck, lamb cutlets, plovers' eggs, chicken, tongue and ham jelly, mixed sandwiches, and a choice of three or four desserts.' For the gastronomically inclined toff or millionaire, it was a fine time to be alive. 'No doubt rich English landowners had always wanted to make sure their guests did not go hungry,' notes Priestley. 'There may have been equally large single meals at earlier times in history [far larger, actually], but people then ate little before or after them. In these Edwardian great houses, however, there were processions of food and drink from eight in the morning until late at night. Not since Imperial Rome can there have been so many signposts to gluttony.'

Edward VII is often cited as the quintessence of all this decadence, a man more in thrall to his belly than his country, but he was no fool: sharp, informed, quick-witted and dedicated to his duty. My great-grandmother, Sonia Keppel, was the daughter of Mrs Keppel, his mistress, who well remembers Kingy, as she called him, 'with his beard and his kind, deep voice and plump, beringed hands'. In her autobiography, *Edwardian Daughter*, she tells the story of a game they used to play.

With a fine disregard for the good condition of his trouser, he would lend me his leg, on which I used to start two bits of bread and butter (butter side down), side by side. Then, bets of a penny each were made (my bet provided by Mamma) and the winning piece of bread and butter depended, of course, on which was the more buttery. The excitement was intense while the contest was on. Sometimes he won, sometimes I did. Although the owner of a Derby winner, Kingy's enthusiasm seemed delightfully unaffected by the quality of his bets.

What Gaya (our nickname for her) never alludes to, of course, is the exact nature of the relationship between King and Keppel.

If the Victorian breakfast was lavish, the Edwardian version went further still. Ethel, Lady Raglan, describes such meals at Port Eliot, the home of her grandfather, the Earl of St Germans.

There would be a choice of fish, fried eggs and crisp bacon, a variety of egg dishes, omelettes and sizzling sausages. During the shooting parties, hot game and grilled pheasants always appeared on the breakfast menu ... On a side table was always to be found a choice of cold viands; delicious home-smoked hams, pressed meats, one of the large raised pies for which Mrs Vaughan (the cook) was justly famous, consisting of cold game and galantine, with aspic jelly.

By now, breakfast was a meal enjoyed by every class, although the eight-course Windsor Castle menu eaten by Edward VII, from petits soles frits and haddock à l'anglaise to bacon à l'anglais and poulets frilées à la diable, was out of the reach of all but the deepest pockets. Tschumi notes: 'The King's tastes were more hearty [Queen Alexandra ate only oeuf en cocotte and a little cold meat in jelly]. He liked to have haddock, poached eggs, chicken and woodcock before setting out on a day's shooting or racing.' Still, even a plateful of bacon and eggs, consumed just once per week, was an English treat to equal roast beef. Breakfast had also become the most democratic of meals, once it was shorn of its Edwardian excess. As the gap between rich and poor closed, albeit slowly and cautiously, in the Thirties and Forties breakfast turned into a universal symbol. The rich might have their buttered crab and potted pigeon but the poor could now afford a few eggs and pieces of bacon, a sausage and a couple of mushrooms too. At heart, the ingredients are simple and relatively cheap. And as long as you can operate a frying pan, the Full English is a uniting entity up there with tea.

'The English Breakfast is the national dish of a mythic and indivisible England,' sighs Kaori O'Connor in *The English Breakfast*, 'a repast that, despite differences in execution, binds its people together as one.' Wherever I travelled in the country, cooked breakfasts were on offer, but while it was one thing to sample sausages at Simpson's and chug tea at Zippy's, what of the nationwide chains, offering up oversized plates to the mobile masses? My experiences at places like Happy Eater had always been pleasurable. That said, I last managed an Olympic-sized breakfast aged about nine and I remember the free orange lollipop that came with it far more clearly than how the bacon was cooked.

The modern equivalent of the coaching inn is Little Chef. To call it a national institution would be a compliment too far, yet somehow this perma-cheery roadside chain, started in Reading in 1958, has managed to cling on, despite the generally wretched quality of the food. As I travelled the highways and byways of England, it was hard to miss that beaming chef, although no matter how fierce my hunger I could never quite convince myself to go in.

However, the morning comes when driving down the A303, the most glorious of England's A roads, I decide to stop for breakfast at Barton Stacey in Hampshire. The joint is all but deserted, save for a pair of bewildered American tourists and what seems to be a regular guest.

'No full Olympic today, John?' the cheery waiter-cum-manager-cum-short-order-chef asks.

'No, mate, just eggs and bacon. Had a rough one last night.' He then goes back to gloomily contemplating his coffee.

The menus are attractive enough, if cosmetically altered, overlit photographs of food are your thing. Of course, the reality bears no resemblance to the finished product but who cares when you can get an Olympic Breakfast, 'The biggest and still the best!' for a mere £7.25.

The dining room itself is tired and seedy, with all the cheer of an airport smoking lounge. The lighting is low in a dirty rather than a moody way and the only newspapers are the *Express* and the *Star*. So that's where they all go. It's estimated that the chain still serves more than 20 million customers per year, who sip 10 million cups of tea and chew through 12 million rashers of bacon and 13 million sausages and egg.

Despite the staff being both charming and enthusiastic, the breakfast itself is a turgid, charmless plate of barely edible despair. A disconsolate slice of industrial black pudding is dry and gritty, crumbling unpleasantly between the teeth. Come back, Simpson's black pudding, all is forgiven. The bacon is nearer to salt-lick than cured pig, and the sausage shows that 'outdoor reared' doesn't necessarily mean porcine perfection. It is dull and sludgy, with not even a whisper of pig. The orange juice comes in a bottle, the mushrooms are soaked in oil, like fungoid sponges, and mean in flavour too. Still, the free-range eggs are well fried and the toast is, well, toast.

Taken as a whole, breakfast here is a dispiriting affair, poor ingredients piled on a plate and sold as good value rather than good quality. Just like the sporraned Steak House and chain pubs, they offer an awful snapshot of our national food. Plus, after completing the Herculean task of devouring the whole lot, the last thing I want to do is drive. Sleep, perhaps, then run a half-marathon to clear the stodge that squats stubbornly in my stomach for days to come.

OK, so it's ridiculous to judge Little Chef as you would a proper restaurant. It was certainly preferable to a breakfast I'd forced down a few days earlier at a Moto service station. But then again, I'd rather eat my own face than once again endure the horror of that particular meal. Little Chef have never claimed to be aiming for Michelin, but doesn't the population of England deserve better? Done properly, Little Chef could revolutionise our eating habits, offering good, home-cooked and locally sourced food at attractive prices. Decent English food for the family, a place to stop, eat and enjoy, rather than just stop, refuel and forget. Good God, driving might even become a pleasure again. Enter Heston Blumenthal, one of the world's greatest chefs and a man known for his culinary magic, as an unlikely saviour of Little Chef.

In an inspired move by the management, they called in Heston to revamp their Popham services, just a few miles back along the A303. 'What chefs like me do is very selective, for a very small part of the population,' says Blumenthal on a damp weekday morning. Despite a body seemingly hewn from granite, industrial-steel glasses and a buzz cut more suited to Millwall than Michelin massive, he's one of the softest-spoken, kindest chefs of them all. 'I'm well aware that The Fat Duck is out of the reach of a good deal of the population. I had only been to Little Chef once before, in Norfolk when I was about twenty. I grew up in London and whenever we travelled, we took sandwiches from home. And the only other time we went out was to Windsor, for a picnic. And we'd go to the local shop to pick up chicken, bread and the rest. So I had no experience of the place, no nostalgic hook, although I was always very aware of the brand and food has moved on hugely in England over the last twenty years. Imagine if a family from France stopped at Little Chef, which is so out of kilter with a lot of what's happening over here in the food world. They'd probably come out thinking badly of all English food. Little Chef is classless; we all drive cars and get hungry. I was looking at providing something good for everyone.'

A television programme recorded the experiment and made gripping viewing. The characters seemed too good to be real: a dementedly bitchy manager, who spent most of the time hissing behind Heston's back, and a managing director who tossed about business-bullshit expressions like 'thinking outside of the box' and 'blue-sky thinking' with scant regard for common sense. Yet the Popham Little Chef offers a blue-print for what the chain could really become. As Fay Maschler, the celebrated restaurant critic, told him at the time, 'This could be the start of a revolution.' And she was spot on.

'I have to say that I was sceptical when I was first doing it. I mean, Little Chef spent £300,000 in all and got three, one-hour prime-time TV slots in return. They were basically using the programme as a marketing tool, for really cheap advertising. But, and this is a big but, the group was run by a collection of venture capitalists with no interest in changing the way we eat. They wanted to make money, because that's what they do. I agree that rolling out my new concept to every single site doesn't make sense. Roads have changed and some branches no longer have enough passing trade. All the same, I do think that what we've done at Popham could be repeated in certain sites.'

The decor at Popham is bright and diner-like, flooded with natural light and a feeling of space. At nine in the morning, the place is packed. Families, tourists, salesmen, couples – there is barely a spare seat to be found. The razzle-dazzle of celebrity and telly, admittedly, might have lured some star-struck punters, desperate for a glimpse of the great man himself. The car park, though, tells its own story. Audis and Mercedes, with jackets hung up neatly in the back, sit next to Skodas and cara-vans. BMWs and Lexi (to quote Alan Partridge) nestle up to Rover Metros and generic Japanese crap.

The orange juice is freshly squeezed and the Olympic Breakfast is actually 30p cheaper here, with finer ingredients (although one of the waitresses, typically charming, whispered that you do get a little less on the plate). The plate is certainly less crowded than at the old Little Chef, but there's an empha-sis on quality instead. The sausage recipe is Heston's own, sitting somewhere in between Zippy's and Simpson's, and the Wiltshire cured back bacon is the best of the lot, with good flavour, texture and fat. The black pudding, from bacon-curer Ramsay of Carluke, is a winner too, close textured with just the right hint of spice and fat. The roasted tomatoes have actu-ally been cooked for a decent length of time, concentrating the sweetness and offering a good foil for cutting through any excess piggy fat. The sprinkle of sea salt on top, while hardly revolutionary, is just one of the myriad small touches that elevate this breakfast way above the average. A single field mushroom is a fine specimen, mighty and meaty, and the eggs are beautifully cooked too.

With the most subtle of tweaks – the removal of the greasy potato croquette, the addition of fresh seasoning, more care with cooking and ingredients – Blumenthal has created a genuinely decent breakfast, far superior to those of most cafés. This is a model that should be pounced upon and celebrated, not scorned.

Some time later, I return for lunch. This is where Heston really went to work, with Scottish mussels and Kentish Bramley apple pie, braised ox cheeks – ox cheeks, for Christ's sake, in a Little Chef – and Hereford beef and Abbot Ale pie. All English classics, interspersed with the likes of coq au vin, macaroni cheese and chilli con carne. This is a sexed-up Little Chef, who has become a fat man in a bespoke suit, with an expense account and a splendidly expensive mistress. The mussels come in a cast-iron container, sweet and tender. Ox cheeks arrive in a sticky pile, surrounded by a generous moat of proper gloopy liquor. They fall apart at the touch of a fork, just as they should, and are packed with bovine heft. Fresh parsley – yes, a fresh herb at Little Chef, too, oh still my beating heart – is scattered on top, along with chanterelles buried in the wonderful meaty mess. The mash isn't perfect but who's complaining when the main attraction is this fine?

And it isn't just me tucking in. In the forty or so minutes I am in here, I see at least six different orders for ox cheeks flying out of the kitchen. You'd expect to see this sort of offal munching at St John, but at a Little Chef a few metres back from a main road? It's nothing short of miraculous. The whole place has a healthy, bistro sort of buzz and the diners actually look as if they are enjoying their food, instead of just bulking up on carbs and sugar to get them through the day.

'Did you enjoy your lunch?' a waitress asks one couple as they leave.

'Can't you see the satisfaction on our faces?' they beam, their cup brimming over with good cheer.

A section of the wall is given over to customers' rave reviews: 'Would be confident in stopping here again for any meal, knowing we'll get tasty, good-quality food. Hope you go ahead with the roll-out!' 'As a smallholder from a long line of farmers, I'm used to breakfast cooked by large buxom women ... the new Olympic was better than my grandmother's and you can't say better than that.' 'At last somewhere to eat on a journey that isn't McDonald's. Thank you.' 'Vast improvement! Bacon = yummy, sausage = tasty, eggs = perfectly done. Enjoyed the experience, England needs more of this – good food, good price.'

Little Chef now have the chance to change mass-market English food for the better, to purge their restaurants of the glum, institutional mediocrity of the past and become a bastion for good, cheap food for everyone. 'My feeling is that they might do another half a dozen, then flog the company.' Heston laughs. 'But what was so great about it – and I did question it, all the way through – was seeing the end result. I realised that there is a real hunger for good food. The great British public are a great deal more aware and more interested in where good food comes from, and how it is made. And many more people are more interested in quality than just quantity. For something like this to succeed, it means that the UK is a far better place, culinarily speaking, than ever before. And one of the main battles was to get people to cook whole dishes, such as breakfast, from scratch, rather than simply heating up pre-packed stuff. I would love to see Popham roll out, offering good roadside food for all.'

The past twenty years have seen English farming under attack. The government's reaction to BSE and Foot and Mouth was every bit as devastating as the diseases themselves but some good might have come from these twin blights. All of us are more focused on where our food comes from and although the days of the faceless industrial, food-processing system are certainly not over, the cracks are appearing. The renewed interest in English food is heartening too, as shown by the farmers' markets and food fairs, the Slow Food symposiums and the revival of rare breeds. While we still have many miles to travel, a few months spent eating my way around England has left me cautiously optimistic. The pioneers of good English food, from Robert May, Eliza Acton and Florence White right through to Fergus Henderson, Mark Hix and Heston Blumenthal, were and are instrumental in spreading the word. Yet the elite have only so much power. The rest is up to the English eaters. We may not be in the midst of a food revolution, but there's no doubt we're at its inception. For that, we should be thankful.

DEVILLED KIDNEYS

There's nothing evil about devilled kidneys, a classic Victorian and Edwardian breakfast dish, from a time where men were men and breakfasted on bounteous feasts of meat, fish, potatoes and eggs. No ghastly arriviste cereals here, thank you very much.

The word 'devilled' refers to the spicy kick of the dish, which was originally produced by cayenne pepper and mustard powder. I've added a few shakes of Tabasco, that most glorious of sauces. This dish can be breakfast, lunch, a snack, dinner or a savoury. You could substitute veal kidneys too.

Serves 4

3 tbsp plain flour
2 tsp cayenne pepper
12 tsp Colman's English mustard powder
salt and freshly ground black pepper
knob butter
10 lamb's kidneys, slit in half and cored
splash chicken stock
splash Tabasco
Worcestershire sauce, to taste
2 pieces toast
lemon juice
handful flat-leaved parsley, chopped

Mix together the flour, cayenne, mustard powder, salt and pepper. Then heat a pan until hot and throw in the butter. Toss the kidneys in the flour mixture and shake to remove excess. Cook for 2 minutes each side, adding the stock, Tabasco and Worcestershire sauce. Then remove the kidneys from the pan and place on the toast. Taste and reduce the sauce and pour over the kidneys. Squeeze over lemon juice and sprinkle with parsley. Devour with gusto.

KEDGEREE

Despite this being a great Anglo-Indian dish, I like mine without curry powder. Its origins are far removed from the breakfast classic we know today. Khichri, from where the name evolved, was a mixture of dhal and rice, boiled with the likes of coriander, ginger, chilli and cardamom. When the British arrived in India in the seventeenth century, they ate khichri for their breakfast, swapping fresh fish for the dhal. The spices were later thrown out, and hard-boiled eggs were added for that true, British nursery feel. Smoked haddock, for me the heart of the dish, was added later, back in the UK.

Serves 4 greedy people or 8 with more delicate appetites

800 g (1 lb 12 oz) good smoked haddock, undyed
enough milk to cover the fish
vegetable oil
2 large onions, peeled and finely chopped
350 g (12 oz) long-grained rice
500 ml (18 fl oz) water
300 ml (10 fl oz) cream
4 eggs, hard-boiled for about 10 minutes, then chopped
2 tbsp butter
big pinch cayenne pepper
salt and freshly ground black pepper
4 tbsp fresh parsley, chopped
2 lemons, quartered, to serve

Poach the haddock in very gently simmering milk until tender and falling apart in flakes, about 5 or 6 minutes. Drain and set the fish aside.

Heat oil in a heavy pan, add the onions and cook until soft, about 15 minutes. Add the rice and cook, stirring, until all the grains are coated and shiny with oil. Then add the water, cover and cook for about 20 minutes or until all liquid has been absorbed. Add the cream, stir and cook for 1 minute further.

Add the haddock, eggs, butter, cayenne pepper, salt and pepper, and stir. Transfer to a warm serving bowl or plate and scatter with parsley. Serve immediately.

FRIED PLAICE WITH SHRIMP BUTTER

This dish is seemingly substantial but not at all difficult. We might balk at eating fresh fish for breakfast, but kippers are a classic and rather more hearty than plaice.

This recipe comes from *Fifty Breakfasts* by the splendid Colonel Arthur Robert Kenney Herbert, a former military secretary to the Governor of Madras and a great expert on manly, colonial cookery. He stood for little nonsense and when he returned from India founded the School of Common Sense Cookery in London.

Serves 6

1 plaice
2 eggs, beaten
handful fresh breadcrumbs
1 lemon, cut into 6 slices, for garnish

Marinade
4 tbsp olive oil
1 tbsp vinegar
1 onion, peeled and sliced into rings
1 tbsp fresh parsley, chopped
1 tbsp mixed fresh green herbs, chopped
peel of half a lemon
1 tsp freshly ground black pepper and salt, mixed

Prawn butter
6 whole cooked prawns, in their shells
50 g (2 oz) butter
1 saltspoon salt, freshly ground white pepper and mace,
  blended

Skin and trim the plaice, dividing it into fillets 6 cm (2½ in) long and 4 cm (1½ in) wide. Combine the ingredients for the marinade. Add the plaice and marinate overnight in the fridge.

Make the prawn butter. Remove the shells from the prawns but do not discard. Pour a jug of cold water over both the shells and the meat also; when quite clean, pound the meat and shells together in a mortar and pestle using 25 g (1 oz) butter to assist the pounding. When thoroughly pounded, pass the paste through a fine-meshed sieve into a bowl of cold water. Skim it off the water, drain it and add another 25 g (1 oz) butter, seasoning it with the blend of salt, white pepper and mace. Chill.

Remove the plaice pieces from the marinade and wipe dry. Dip in the beaten egg, then in the breadcrumbs. Fry in very hot fat until golden brown and drain on kitchen paper. Serve on neat fish-paper, garnished with slices of lemon and accompanied by a little plate of the prawn butter.

SNIPE ON TOAST

The perfect start to a day's shooting, this game dish relies on a good supply of snipe. Included in Miss L. Allen's *Breakfast Dishes for Every Morning of the Month* (1884), it was a critical and commercial hit. The snipe is the smallest of our edible game and the season runs from 12 August until 31 January. As snipe are all wild, grab them whenever you can. Yorkshire Game (www.yorkshiregame.co.uk) is always a good bet.

If you don't possess an open fire and a bird-spit, brush the snipe with butter and roast in a hot oven (200°C/180°C fan/gas mark 7) for approximately 15 minutes, then lower the heat and cook for a further 10–15 minutes.

Serves 3

3 snipe, plucked
handful plain flour
salt and freshly ground black pepper
big knob butter, melted
3 thick rounds slightly toasted bread

Do not draw the snipe but wipe them with a soft cloth and truss them with the head under the wing. Suspend the birds with their feet downwards on a bird-spit, flour them well, season and baste with melted butter. Lay a thick round of slightly toasted bread, previously buttered on both sides, in the pan below the birds to absorb the juices. The birds will be done in 20 minutes. Lay the toasts in a very hot dish and dress the birds upon them.

Acknowledgements

With grateful thanks to the following:

Bloomsbury for kind permission to reproduce Fergus Henderson's recipe for Bone Marrow and Parsley Salad from his book, *Nose to Tail Eating*, published by Macmillan.

Quadrille for kind permission to reproduce Mark Hix's recipe for Deep-Fried Whitebait from his book, *British Regional Food*.

Persephone Books (at www.persephonebooks.co.uk) for kind permission to reproduce Florence White's recipes for Cheese Toast, Devilled Bones and Eel Pie from her book *Good Things in England*.

John Blake Publishing for kind permission to reproduce the recipe for Balti Chicken and Mushroom from Pat Chapman's *The New Curry Bible*.

Neil Richardson Publishing and Marjory Houlihan for kind permission to reproduce Majory Houlihan's recipe for Battered Tripe from her book, *A Most Excellent Dish: Tales of the Lancashire Tripe Trade*.

Anne Willan at Grub Street for kind permission to

reproduce Margaret Costa's recipe for Lancashire Hotpot from her book, *Four Seasons Cookery Book*.

Random House and Penguin for kind permission to reproduce Jane Grigson's recipe for Steak, Kidney and Oyster Pudding from her book, *English Food*.

Little Brown Book Group for kind permission to reproduce Dorothy Hartley's recipe for Dressed Crab from her book *Food in England*.

Every effort has been made to clear permissions. If permission has not been granted please contact the publisher who will include a credit in subsequent printings and editions.

This book would never have been written without the support and generosity of all those below. I'm deeply grateful for all of their help, advice and time.

Charles and Sylvia Campion
Terence and Vikki Conran
Gerard Greaves
Richard Green
Geordie Greig
Stephen Harris
Nigel Haworth
Chris Hay
Paul Heathcote
Fergus Henderson
Mark Hix
Simon Hopkinson

Kara Johnson
Reg Johnson
Roger and Rose Keen
Graham Kirkham
Bob Kitching
Atul Kochhar
Prue Leith
Celia Levett
Reza Mahammed
Jamie Montgomery
Marguerite Patten
Polly Russell
Winnie Swarbrick
Julian and Di Temperley
Cyrus Todiwala
The Reading Room Staff at The British Library, Imperial War Museum and London Library

Special thanks go to Grainne Fox and Rowan Yapp, for all their help, advice and inspiration and Ed Griffiths too. And to Matthew Fort and Bill Knott, who trawled through early drafts with endless patience. Last of all to Sara, for putting up with me.

Bibliography

Acton, Eliza, *Modern Cookery for Private Families*, first published 1845 (Southover Press, 2002)

Allen, Miss L., *Breakfast Dishes for Every Morning of the Month* (J.S. Virtue, 1892)

Arthur, Max, *Lost Voices of the Edwardians* (Harper Perennial, 2007)

Ayrton, Elizabeth, *The Cookery of England* (André Deutsch, 1974)

Badham, Revd David, *Prose Halieutics; or Ancient and Modern Fish Tattle* (J.W. Parker & Son, 1854)

Boorde, Andrew, *Compendyous Regiment, or a Dyetary of Health* (Robert Wyer, 1542)

Boswell, James, *Life of Johnson*, first published 1791 (Oxford, 1998)

Boxer, Arabella, *Arabella Boxer's Book of English Food* (Hodder & Stoughton, 1991)

Bruce, Mandy, *The Oyster Seekers* (Metro, 2003)

Burnett, David and Saberi, Helen, *The Road to Vindaloo* (Prospect Books, 2008)

Burnett, John, *Plenty and Want* (Routledge, 1989)

Burnett, John, *England Eats Out* (Pearson Longman, 2004)

Burton, David, *The Raj at Table* (Faber & Faber, 1993)

Cable, Michael, *Whitstable Natives* (Live Wire Books, 2003)

Campbell, Fred, *Oxen, Oat-Cake and Ale* (Neil Richardson, 1985)

Chapman, Pat, *The New Curry Bible* (Metro Publishing, 2004)

Clarkson, Leslie (ed.), *The Industrial Revolution: A Compendium* (Macmillan, 1990)

Clifford, Sue and King, Angela, *The Apple Source Book* (Hodder & Stoughton, 2007)

Cobbett, William, *Rural Rides* (William Cobbett, 1830)

Colquhoun, Kate, *Taste* (Bloomsbury, 2007)

Copas, Liz, *A Somerset Pomona* (The Dovecote Press, 2001)

Costa, Margaret, *Four Seasons Cookery Book* (Grub Street, 2008)

Country Recipes of Old England (Country Life Ltd, 1929)

Croft-Cooke, Rupert, *English Cooking: A New Approach* (W.H. Allen, 1960)

Crowden, James, *Ciderland* (Birlinn, 2008)

David, Elizabeth, *Spices, Salt and Aromatics in the English Kitchen* (Grub Street, 2000)

Davidson, Alan, *The Oxford Companion to Food* (Oxford, 1999)

Defoe, Daniel, *Tour Through the Whole Island of Great Britain* (G. Strahan, 1724–7)

Driver, Christopher, *The British at Table* (Chatto & Windus, 1983)

Drummond, J.C. and Wilbraham, Anne, *The Englishman's Food* (Jonathan Cape, 1939)

Ellis, Hattie, *Eating England* (Mitchell Beazley, 2001)

Engels, Friedrich, *The Condition of the Working Class in England*, first published 1844 (Penguin Classics, 2005)

Evelyn, John, *The Diary of John Evelyn*, first published 1818 (Everyman's Library, 2006)

Fitzgibbon, Theodora, *Traditional West Country Cookery* (Fontana Paperbacks, 1982)

Fitzgibbon, Theodora, *A Taste of England* (Pan, 1986)

Fort, Tom, *The Book of Eels* (HarperCollins, 2002)

Freeman, Sarah, *Mutton and Oysters* (Gollancz, 1989)

Freeman, Sarah, *The Real Cheese Companion* (TimeWarner, 2003)

Glasse, Hannah, *The Art of Cookery Made Plain and Easy*, first published 1747 (Prospect Books, 1995)

Grigson, Jane, *English Food* (Penguin, 1993)

Grossley, Pierre Jean, *A Tour to London* (J. Exshaw, 1772)

Harris, Frank, *My Life and Loves*, first published 1922 (The Obelisk Press, 1960)

Hartley, Dorothy, *Food in England*, first published 1954 (Little, Brown, 1999)

Hattersley, Roy, *The Edwardians* (Abacus, 2006)

Heath, Ambrose, *Open Sesame: The Way of a Cook with a Can* (Nicholson & Watson, 1939)

Henderson, Fergus, *Nose to Tail Eating* (Macmillan, 1999)

Herbert, Colonel A.R.K., *Fifty Breakfasts* (Edward Arnold, 1894)

Hewitt, Paolo and Clunn, Chris, *Eels, Pie and Mash* (Museum of London, 1995)

Hix, Mark, *British Regional Food* (Quadrille, 2006)

Houlihan, Marjory, *A Most Excellent Dish: Tales of the Lancashire Tripe Trade* (Neil Richardson, 1988)

Houston Bowden, Gregory, *British Gastronomy* (Chatto & Windus, 1975)

Jefferies, Richard, letters to *The Times* (1772)

Kay, J.P., *The Moral and Physical Conditions of the Working Classes* (1832)

Keppel, Sonia, *Edwardian Daughter* (Hamish Hamilton, 1958)

King, Gregory, *National and Political Observations and Conclusions upon the State and Condition of England in 1696* (John Hopkins Press, 1936)

Knight, Katherine, *Spuds, Spam and Eating for Victory* (The History Press, 2007)

Leyel, C.F. and Hartley, Olga, *The Gentle Art of Cookery* (Chatto & Windus, 1974)

Lodge, Thomas and Greene, Robert, *A Looking Glasse for London and England* (The Hunterian Club, 1881)

Lund Simmons, Peter, *The Curiosities of Food* (Ten Speed Press, 2001)

Mabey, David, *In Search of Food* (Book Club Associates, 1978)

Making a Meal of It (English Heritage, 2005)

Mason, Laura, *Food Culture in Great Britain* (Greenwood Press, 2004)

Mason, Laura with Brown, Catherine, *Traditional Foods of Britain* (Prospect Books, 1999)

May, Robert, *The Accomplisht Cook*, first published 1685 (Prospect Books, 2000)

Mayhew, Henry, *London Labour and the London Poor*, first published 1851 (Wordsworth Editions, 2008)

Mennell, Stephen, *All Manner of Food* (Blackwell, 1987)

Michelson, Patricia, *The Cheese Room* (Penguin, 2001)

Minns, Raynes, *Bombers and Mash* (Virago Press, 1999)

Misson, Henri, *Misson's Travels* (trans. Mr Ozell) (D. Browne, 1719)

Mrs Beeton's Book of Household Management (Ward, Lock & Tyler, 1869)

O'Connor, Kaori, *The English Breakfast* (Kegan Paul, 2006)

Orwell, George, *The Road to Wigan Pier*, first published 1937 (Penguin Classics, 2001)

Oyler, Philip, *The Generous Earth*, first published 1950 (Penguin, 1961)

Panayi, Panikos, *Spicing up Britain* (Reaktion Books, 2008)

Patten, Marguerite, *Marguerite Patten's Century of British Cooking* (Grub Street, 1999)

Patten, Marguerite, *Victory Cookbook* (Chancellor Press, 2006)

Priestley, J.B., *The Edwardians* (Heinemann, 1970)

Pullar, Philippa, *Consuming Passions* (Hamish Hamilton, 1970)

Rance, Patrick, *The Great British Cheese Book* (Macmillan, 1982)

Richardson, Paul, *Cornucopia* (Little, Brown, 2000)

Rogers, Ben, *Beef and Liberty* (Chatto & Windus, 2003)

Root, Waverley, *The Food of France* (Cassell & Co., 1958)

Seebohm Rowntree, B., *Poverty* (Macmillan, 1903)

Schweid, Richard, *Consider the Eel* (University of South Carolina Press, 2002)

Shand, P. Morton, *A Book of Food* (Jonathan Cape, 1927)

Shephard, Sue, *Pickled, Potted and Canned* (Headline, 2000)

Smollett, Tobias, *The Expedition of Humphrey Clinker* (W. Johnston, 1771)

Soyer, Alexis, *Shilling Cookery* (Routledge, 1855)

Soyer, Alexis, *The Modern Housewife* (Simpkin, Marshall & Co, 1849)

Spencer, Colin, *British Food* (Grub Street, 2002)

Spry, Constance and Hume, Rosemary, *The Constance Spry Cookery Book* (Grub Street, 2004)

Stein, Rick, *English Seafood Cookery* (Penguin, 1988)

The Food Lover's Introduction to Britain (Grub Street, 1992)

Tschumi, Gabriel, *Royal Chef* (William Kimber, 1954)

Tusser, Thomas, *Five Hundred Points of Good Husbandrie*, first published 1580 (Kessinger Publishing)

Walton, John K., *Fish and Chips and the British Working Class* (Leicester University Press, 1992)

White, Florence, *Good Things in England*, first published 1932 (Persephone Books, 1999)

White, Florence, *A Fire in the Kitchen* (Dent, 1938)

White, Florence, *Good English Food* (Jonathan Cape, 1952)

Whiting, Sydney, *Memoirs of a Stomach*, first published 1853 (Kessinger Publishing)

Wilson, Bee, *Swindled* (John Murray, 2008)

Wilson, C. Anne, *Food and Drink in Britain* (Penguin, 1984)

Wright, Joseph, *English Dialect Dictionary* (Henry Frowde, 1889–1905)

Young, Arthur, *Annals of Agriculture* (R. Phillips, 1784–1815)